D0040405

About Religion

Religion and Postmodernism *A series edited by Mark C. Taylor*

a b o u t

r | e | l | i | g | i | o | n

Economies of Faith in Virtual Culture

M a r k C . T a y l o r

The University of Chicago Press
Chicago & London

MARK C. TAYLOR is the Cluett Professor of Religion and Humanities and
Director of the Center for Technology in the Arts and Humanities at Wil-
liams College. His many books include *Erring: A Postmodern A/theology; De-
constructing in Context; Altarity; Nots; Disfiguring: Art, Architecture, Religion;
Hiding;* and *The Picture in Question.* He is the editor of *Critical Terms for
Religious Studies* and coauthor/producer with José Márquez of *The Réal—
Las Vegas, Nevada,* a CD-ROM published by the Massachusetts Museum of
Contemporary Art and the Williams College Museum of Art. Taylor is also
director of the Critical Issues Forum for the Guggenheim Museum.

The University of Chicago Press, Chicago 60637
The University of Chicago Press, Ltd., London
© 1999 by The University of Chicago
All rights reserved. Published 1999
08 07 06 05 04 03 02 01 00 99   1 2 3 4 5

ISBN: 0-226-79161-0 (cloth)
ISBN: 0-226-79162-9 (paper)

Library of Congress Cataloging-in-Publication Data

Taylor, Mark C., 1945–
    About religion : economies of faith in virtual culture / Mark C.
Taylor.
        p.   cm. — (Religion and postmodernism)
    Includes bibliographical references and index.
    ISBN 0-226-79161-0 (alk. paper). — ISBN 0-226-79162-9 (pbk. :
alk. paper)
    1. Religion—Philosophy.   2. Religion and culture—United States.
I. Title.   II. Series.
BL51.T394   1999
291.1′75 — dc21   98-40817
                                                                        CIP

♾ The paper used in this publication meets the minimum requirements of the
American National Standard for Information Sciences—Permanence of Paper
for Printed Library Materials, ANSI Z39.48-1992.

For
Margaret M. Weyers

Contents

About About

Religion is about a certain about. What religion is about, however, remains obscure for it is never quite there—nor is it exactly not there. Religion is about what is always slipping away. It is, therefore, impossible to grasp what religion is about—unless, perhaps, what we grasp is the impossibility of grasping. Even when we think we have it surrounded, religion eludes us. This strange slipping away is no mere disappearance but a withdrawal that allows appearances to appear. Though never here, what religion is about is not elsewhere.

The essays gathered in this book are more or less about religion. In some cases, this is obvious; in other cases, it is not. Since what religion is about is so slippery, we can never be sure where to look for it. Always a matter of surprise, religion is, I believe, most interesting where it is least obvious. Thus, I deliberately avoid the space of church, synagogue, and mosque in order to have time for art, literature, economics, science, and technology. Though these disciplines seem to share little, each, in a different way, raises new questions about religion. The relation between religion and culture is inevitably a two-way street. Not only do modern and contemporary art, literature, economics, science, and technology pose questions about religion, but the study of religion exposes religious dimensions of ostensibly "secular" culture, which usually remain undetected.

In an effort to sort out a broad range of contemporary critical issues that intersect in various disciplinary contexts, I repeatedly return to certain nineteenth-century thinkers and writers. I have followed this strategy for several reasons. The terms and boundaries of twentieth-century cultural debate were defined by leading philosophers, artists, and writers during the closing decade of the eighteenth century and opening decades of the nineteenth century. It is, therefore, impossible to appreciate the significance of current cultural discussions without an adequate understanding of their historical genealogy. But the nineteenth century is of more than historical interest. The creative interplay of religion, art, and philosophy that characterized the period between the publication of Kant's *Critique of Judgment* (1790) and Hegel's death (1831) continues to provide rich resources for both critical and constructive reflection. In many ways, the world that artists and philosophers imagined at the end of the eighteenth century has become the world in which we dwell at the end of the twentieth century.

It is obvious that we are living during a time of extraordinary transition: something is slipping away and something is beginning. The point is not merely that we are on the threshold of the millennium; something else, something whose significance remains obscure seems to be emerging. In an effort to understand what is occurring, we often try to describe this transition in terms that have become familiar. We are moving, many argue, from industrialism to postindustrialism, from modernism to postmodernism, from a manufacturing to an information economy. Far from clarifying our situation, however, this proliferation of terms underscores the uncertainty of what is passing away and what is arising in our midst. As I have considered this situation, I have concluded that the best way to look ahead is to cast a backward glance. When turning my gaze from the twenty-first to the nineteenth century, I rediscover the continuing relevance of Hegel's religio-philosophical vision.

Hegel, of course, has been out of fashion for nearly half a century. It is no exaggeration to say that Hegelianism is the significant other against which every major philosophical movement in this century has defined itself. From analytic philosophy and phenomenology to existentialism and poststructuralism, Hegel represents the position critics feel compelled to negate. But moving beyond Hegel is never as easy at it seems. Kierkegaard long ago realized that the attempt to negate Hegel actually confirms the dialectic he discovered. This is not to imply, of course, that all criticisms of Hegelianism are misguided. To the contrary, the critical engagement with Hegel's philosophy has disclosed noteworthy problems whose significance extends far beyond the printed page. Particularly important in this regard have been Kierkegaard's and poststructuralism's relentless criticism of Hegelianism's totalizing propensities. It is undeniable that Hegel's holistic vision sometimes leads to excesses that appear to be repressive. But the endless repetition of the mantra of singularity, difference, and otherness leads to excesses that are no less problematic. If Hegelianism's quest for the whole seems to undervalue difference, poststructuralism's obsession with difference tends to leave us with nothing in common. The challenge facing current reflection is to develop a third alternative, which values difference without devaluing commonality and pursues unity without repressing differences.

The need to rethink Hegel is not, however, merely a *philosophical* imperative. As I have indicated, emerging information and media culture bears an uncanny resemblance to the world envisioned in Hegel's system. From Hegel's point of view, religion, art, and philosophy are inextricably interrelated. Culture, moreover, is not only abstractly symbolic but concretely enacted and embodied in nature and history. Recast in terms of Hegel's system, nature and history appear to be the incarnation of the logical idea or, in theological terms, the Logos. For latter-day netizens who are thoroughly wired, such ontological and epistemological speculation is difficult to grasp and even more difficult to accept. Yet Hegel's complex ruminations are not as distant from our wired world as they initially appear. If Hegelian logic is reread through the notion of information and vice versa, the world that now is emerging is cast in a different light. Processes that have long seemed natural and relations that have long seemed material now appear to be information processes and virtual realities. In any reworking of Hegel, it is necessary to take into account the relevant criticisms of his system. Recent interpretations of complex adaptive systems and emerging self-organizing systems suggest ways in which Hegel's system can be opened to time and chance. A more complete elaboration of this line of analysis must await a later occasion. In order to prepare the way for a more comprehensive study of information and media society, it is necessary to reconsider cultural processes that have become so familiar that we rarely pause to study them.

In *About Religion: Economies of Faith in Virtual Culture,* I begin where it has long seemed impossible to begin—with God. The first two essays—"Discrediting God" and "Denegating God"—are meditations on the question of how to think God after the death of God. It is, of course, important not to confuse the question of religion with the question of God. Nonetheless, in the West, what religion is about is more often than not God. But for many thoughtful people today, it no longer seems possible to think about God responsibly. Faced with this dilemma, I turn not to contemporary theologians but to the most important writer America has yet produced—Herman Melville. While *Moby-Dick* is commonly acknowledged to be Melville's most theological work, *The Confidence-Man: His Masquerade,* which is often overlooked by critics, presents a remarkable exploration of the difficulties of faith in the modern, and by extension the postmodern, world. What makes Melville's analysis so extraordinary is his recognition of the intricate interplay of religion, economics, and semiotics. Over a century before money had become electronic, Melville recognized that neither gold nor God can put an end to the play of signs. The economy of faith as well as faith in the economy is a confidence game, which inevitably discredits God. Contrary to expectation, this discrediting opens a new space for theological—or more precisely a/theological—reflection. In "Denegating God," I attempt to rethink what once was called God in a way that eludes the traditional economy of faith that Melville discredits.

Even when cast in nontraditional terms, theology or quasi-theology makes many contemporary students of religion terribly uneasy. One of the most important developments in the postwar study of religion has been the dramatic split between theological and religious studies. Reacting to a field long dominated by Christian theological perspectives, many investigators rushed to embrace social scientific approaches to the study of religion. This has led to a widespread preoccupation with methodological and theoretical issues. Though these developments have, in many ways, been salutary, theoreticians frequently fail to turn their critical gaze back on their own presuppositions. Thus, they often end up being as "religiously" committed to antitheological perspectives as religious thinkers are to their theological positions. In "Politics of Theory," I examine the covertly religious and theological assumptions and implications of leading twentieth-century psychosocial theorists. As this analysis unfolds, it quickly becomes apparent that the formulation of so-called social scientific theories of religion in the early decades of this century is inseparable from the emergence of artistic modernism. Religion, art, and theory are mutually constitutive and hence inseparably related. "Minding the Brain" extends the theoretical debate about religion by considering recent efforts to establish "naturalistic" explanations of religious thought and practice. By appropriating insights from recent advances in evolutionary biology, cognitive psychology, and neurophysiology, I suggest how an extended notion of information makes it possible to develop nonreductive explanations of religious behavior.

Information is quickly becoming the currency of the realm. From neural networks to financial networks, the "substance" of the "realities" with which we deal is increasingly light. While for some, the expanding webs in which we are caught promise unprecedented fulfillment, for others, information society poses unparalleled dangers. In spite of their differences, prophets and critics agree that a New Age is dawning in which nothing remains the same. In chapters 5–7, I consider different aspects of recent versions of the age-old tale of the New Age. I begin by examining startling similarities between ancient metallurgical and alchemical rituals, on the one hand, and, on the other, visions and rituals in virtual culture. The psychosocial dynamics of burgeoning virtual culture are more about religion than either believers or nonbelievers realize. No longer limited to forges and crucibles, today's alchemists sublimate base matter into immaterialities on fiber-optic networks where everything is light. The line joining yesterday's occult sciences and tomorrow's virtualities passes directly through nineteenth-century speculative philosophy and its realization in the twentieth-century society of spectacle. Taking the popular film *Wall Street* as a point of departure, "Christianity and the Capitalism of Spirit" mixes low and high by approaching postindustrial capitalism through a rereading of Marx's analysis of money and Hegel's interpretation of the Christian notion of spirit. Returning to issues raised by Melville, I argue that, in today's world, money has become God in more than a trivial sense. Consumer capitalism generates a sacrificial economy, which eventually becomes all-consuming. Through a process approaching transubstantiation, thing becomes image in a symbolic exchange that renders all reality virtual. This virtualization of reality is reflected in Las Vegas.

Las Vegas brings to closure developments that began two hundred years ago in the small German town of Jena. When Schiller reinterprets Kant's analysis of the beautiful work of art in terms of an ideal social community, he defines what eventually became the task of the artistic avant-garde. As religious prophet gives way to creative artist, the challenge becomes the transformation of the world into a work of art. "The Virtual Kingdom" traces a trajectory that leads from the Jena of Schiller and Hegel through the artistic experiments in the Russian Revolution and at the Bauhaus, to pop art and consumer capitalism, which are displayed in the bright lights of the Strip. When viewed in the context of the displacement of religion onto art and the eventual transformation of the world into a work of art, which occurs in contemporary media culture, it appears that Las Vegas is, in effect, the realization of the Kingdom of God on earth. As the real becomes image and the image becomes real, the world becomes a work of art and our condition becomes transparently virtual. In the realized eschatology of the virtual kingdom, nothing lies beyond.

Emerging virtual culture is, in many ways, undeniably nihilistic. In the terminal space of Vegas, one has the sense that something is slipping away and nothing remains to take its place. It is not clear how either this nothingness or the nihilism it harbors is to be understood. For guidance in pondering matters that have become unbearably light, I turn to two contemporary sculptors—Fred Sandback ("Apprehension") and Richard Serra ("Learning Curves"). At first, the works of Sandback and Serra seem to have nothing in common. While Sandback creates art from delicately drawn strands of yarn, Serra produces massive objects from industrial steel. The longer one ponders these different works, the more it seems that *nothing* is precisely what they have in common. Sandback's works of yarn and Serra's works of steel are *about* nothing. Each in his own way draws on different strands of Japanese Buddhism to teach the wisdom of nothingness. By taking sculpture off its pedestal, Sandback and Serra open a pedestrian space in which art creates a world that transforms people who dwell in it.

About Religion concludes with "Indifference." Weaving together philosophical reflection and personal meditation, I return to some of the theological themes considered in the opening chapters. Though my questions are many, they all are more or less about a puzzle I have been pondering for many years: Can inevitable loss be embraced in a way that leads to creative engagement rather than the endless melancholy of interminable mourning?

We have barely begun to appreciate the myriad ways in which virtual culture is about religion. If we are not to be misled by the obvious, we will have to learn to think differently about both religion and our current cultural condition. The religion that today calls for reflection does not answer questions or provide meaning but abandons us in, and opens us to, worlds that are ever more complex. Forever turning toward what is always slipping away, we can never be certain what religion is about.

One

Discrediting God

"I don't know, I don't know," returned the old man, perplexed, "there's so many marks of all sorts to go by, it makes it a kind of uncertain."

HERMAN MELVILLE

Faith is a confidence game whose stakes are undeniably economic. There is an economy of faith that mirrors and is mirrored by faith in economics. The *speculum* in which this play of mirrors is staged is the space of speculation. But what does it mean to speculate? What are the stakes of speculation? Is it still possible to credit speculation or to have confidence in any economy? When the economy is theological—and what economy is not implicitly or explicitly theological?—do speculative systems credit or discredit the currency of belief? At this late date, might it be possible that the only remaining way to credit faith is to discredit what once was named God?

On September 14, 1993, students returning to Williams College were greeted by a full-page advertisement for a credit card, which read, in part:

> The psychology behind the Citibank Classic Visa card, and the emotional security of the Photocard. The Citibank Classic Visa instills in students feelings of safety, security, and general wellness not unlike those experienced in the womb. Therefore, it is the mother of all credit cards. . . . Some experts attribute these feelings to the Citibank Photocard, the only credit card with your photo on it. A voice inside says, "This is me, really me." . . . It's an immediate form of ID, a boost to your self-image. Of course, if your card is ever lost or stolen and a stranger is prevented from using it, you'll feel exceptionally good (showing no signs of Credit Card Theft Nervosa). . . . Special student savings are particularly therapeutic . . . Not to mention the low variable interest rate of 15.4%. . . . Suffice it to say, you'll have a credit card you can depend on while building a credit

history. . . . If we say that a sense of Identity is the first component of the Citibank Classic Visa card, a sense of Security is the second, and a sense of Autonomous Will from your newfound financial independence the third, don't be crazy . . . Call.

Like any good student paper, the ad summarizes its major points in what is explicitly labeled "The Monarch Notes Version: The Citibank classic card gives students peace of mind, protection against Freud—or rather fraud—a low rate and no fee. Apply today."

"Don't be crazy . . . Call." But if, as *The Confidence-Man* insists, "there's so many marks of all sorts to go by," to whom can we turn for advice? Where can we find a trustworthy investment counselor? Whom can we credit, in whom can we confide when every counselor appears to be a confidence-man?

Before calling an investment counselor, we must, of course, know what it means to invest. To invest is, among other things, to speculate by committing money or capital "in order to gain profit or interest, as by purchasing property, securities, or bonds." While investment is never without some risk, the responsible speculator always banks on a reasonable return. The prospect of return is what lends speculation its interest. Within a speculative economy, there is neither interest nor profit in disinterested speculation. The psychology of investment presupposes an interest in returns that secure credit.

As the ad suggests, there is a psychology "behind" economics, but as Freud teaches, there is also an economy "behind" psychology. Since every investment is made with the expectation of redemption, no cathexis (*Besetzung*) is without interest. The currency of psychological investment is the libidinal current whose flow is regulated by the constantly shifting *difference* between credit and debit. Though seeming to tend toward equilibrium, the psychic economy can operate only if books *do not* balance. When positive and negative, pluses and minuses cancel each other, the null point where eros becomes thanatos and being slips into nonbeing is reached. If we credit the psychic economy, it seems that, appearances to the contrary notwithstanding, Freud *is* a fraud. Those who invest in his theories eventually discover that their counselor is a confidence-man. The reason Freud is a fraud is that he shows—but how *can* this be shown?—that everything and everyone—even Sigmund himself—masquerades as something or someone other than what he, she, or it really is. Everyone, in other words, is an impostor. Freud discredits identity— all identity. Within the economy of psychoanalysis, there are no securities without exchanges that are inescapably insecure. Within this game, every

ID card turns out to be an id card that exposes players as jokers. When jokers are wild, as they usually are, charges tend to become excessive; the cards we play discredit the securities (on which) we bank. With such excessive expenditure, the system of credit breaks down and the economy falters. In the wake of this collapse or crash, it becomes possible—perhaps for the first time—to think the unthinkable by figuring the sacred uneconomically. While admittedly attempting to capitalize on the loss of faith, we nevertheless cannot have any confidence in the profitability of this nonspeculative venture.

In 1857, Melville, living in a family farmhouse named Arrowhead, located a few miles south of Williams College, completed what was to be the last prose work published during his lifetime—*The Confidence-Man: His Masquerade.* At the time, Melville was in ill health and was facing serious economic problems. After considerable difficulty locating a publisher, his opaque work proved a critical and financial failure. With little prospect of anything remotely resembling a reasonably profitable return on the effort he had invested in writing, Melville was forced to sell Arrowhead and move to New York City, where he worked as a customs inspector until his death in 1891. Though virtually ignored for nearly a century, *The Confidence-Man* is one of Melville's most challenging texts and remains one of the greatest works in the history of American literature.

Melville's preoccupations in *The Confidence-Man* are both theological and economic. With subtlety and deception, this double-dealing text probes, inter alia, the economy of faith and casts doubt on faith in every economy. In the century and a half since this work was written, Melville's prescient queries have become even more pressing than they were in his own day. As we rush toward the virtual realities of the next millennium, few writers are as current as Melville.

The time is April 1; the place, a latter-day ship of fools named *Fidèle,* sailing down the Mississippi from St. Louis to New Orleans; the characters, a motley crew, which, the narrator avers, resembles nothing so much as "Chaucer's Canterbury pilgrims." As the story opens, a young man who is deaf and dumb boards the ship. "His cheek was fair, his chin downy, his hair flaxen, his hat a white fur one, with a long fleecy nap. He had neither trunk, valise, carpet-bag, nor parcel. No porter followed him. He was unaccompanied by friends. From the shrugged shoulders, titters, whispers, wonderings of the crowd, it was plain that he was, in the extremist sense of the word, a stranger."[1] Though the identity of this seemingly innocent youth remains obscure, this description obviously evokes the image of the lamb whose sacrifice is essential to the economy of salvation. This impression is reinforced when, in the pages that follow, the youth repeatedly writes verses from 1 Corinthians 13 on a slate that he displays to the assembled passengers.

Between the innocent's initial appearance and his scriptural citation, Melville inserts an episode that provides the dramatic tension for the entire narrative. Making his way through the crowd on the lower deck, the youth "chanced to come to a placard nigh the captain's office, offering a reward for the capture of a mysterious impostor, supposed to have recently arrived from the East" (1). What follows is a catalogue of the disguises the alleged impostor is supposed to have assumed as well as a warning to passengers to beware of this trickster. Though apparently intended to counter doubts raised by the possible presence of an impostor, the actions of the Christlike figure leave the unavoidable impression that he himself might actually be a confidence-man. This suspicion grows as the next chapter of the drama unfolds.

In the midst of the clamor and confusion created by voyagers struggling to read the cautionary placard and charitable citations, the ship's barber prepared to open his shop for the day. Pushing people aside and

jumping on a stool, he hung over his door, on the customary nail, a gaudy sort of illuminated pasteboard sign, skillfully executed by himself, gilt with the likeness of a razor elbowed in readiness to shave, and also, for the public benefit, with two words not unfrequently seen ashore gracing other shops besides barbers':

"No TRUST." (3)

With the suspension of the barber's sign on the door as well as between quotation marks, it becomes clear that *The Confidence-Man* is not only a book whose plot hinges on the duplicity of signs but, more importantly, a text *about* signs. The work is simultaneously a narrative and a metanarrative whose textual strategies question themselves in their very deployment. In the first three chapters, the reader encounters three different signs, which are explicitly identified as such: the placard, the slate, and the gilded pasteboard sign. The sign that Melville names a sign is no ordinary sign, for it calls into question the very meaning and significance of signs. Were we to follow the counsel of the sign by refusing to trust, we would not have confidence in any sign. If, however, signs are not to be trusted, then we cannot even have confidence in the sign that reads

"No TRUST." The challenge of the sign creates a double bind: on the one hand, we are not supposed to trust signs, and on the other hand, the barber's sign bends back on itself to create a distrust of distrust. The sign, in other words, discredits itself by encouraging an attitude that is precisely the opposite of what it seems to promote. When we distrust distrust, it once again becomes possible to credit signs. Whether Melville is urging confidence or no confidence, belief or disbelief, trust or mistrust remains completely undecidable. This gilded sign and the paradoxes it engenders return later in the narrative to discredit accounts that once seemed settled.

It is significant that the sign upon which Melville's questions turn is "gilt." A gilded sign is *almost* as good as gold: its surface is gold but its substance a matter of little value. This play of surface and substance inverts the customary relation of signifier and signified to create a simulation whose value is uncertain. Throughout human history, gold is not so much a sign as the transcendental signified that is supposed to ground the meaning and value of other signs. Gold, in other words, is a sign constructed to erase its status as a sign. When understood in this way, the reasons for the intersection of economic and theological interests become obvious. God functions in a semiotic system in the same way that gold functions in the economic system. The go(l)d standard is the base upon which everything rests. When this foundation crumbles or becomes inaccessible, signs are left to float freely on a sea that has no shores.

From 1825 to 1875, debate about the gold standard raged throughout the United States. With increasing economic demands created by the approaching Civil War, pressures to forsake the gold standard became overwhelming. Nevertheless, many people were reluctant to lift anchor and set sail in the uncharted waters of floating signifiers. Concerns about the threat of the devaluation of currency, which the shift to paper not backed by gold seemed to pose, ranged across the political spectrum. In contrast to arguments about the gold standard in our own day, people on the left and the right ends of the political and economic spectrum defended the necessity of gold backing for paper currency. Analyzing the psychological stresses and social strains created by emerging capitalism, Marx has ominous visions of uncontrolled printing presses churning out banknotes that are not worth the paper on which they are printed.

> The only difference, therefore, between coin and bullion, is one of shape, and gold can at any time pass from one form to another. But no sooner does coin leave the mint than it immediately finds itself on the high-road

to the melting pot. During their currency, coins wear away, some more, others less. Name and substance, nominal weight and real weight, begin their process of separation.[2]

Though not expressed in semiotic terms, Marx's concern about the disjunction of name and substance or nominal and real weight expresses anxieties about the separation of the signifier from the signified. Several decades later, Nietzsche uses the image of the worn coin to explore the far-reaching semiotic and aesthetic implications of the economy of signs.

> What, then, is truth? A mobile army of metaphors, and anthropomorphisms—in short, a sum of human relations, which have been enhanced, transposed, and embellished poetically and rhetorically, and which after long use seem firm, canonical, and obligatory to a people; truths and illusion about which one has forgotten that this is what they are; metaphors that are worn out and without sensuous power; coins that have lost their pictures and now matter only as metal, no longer as coins.[3]

The issues raised in Nietzsche's acute observation are not only semiotic, economic, and aesthetic but, as we shall see, inescapably bound up with theological questions.

Nietzsche was not the first person to realize the aesthetic implications of problems of representation involved in economic and political developments. Many of his most telling insights were anticipated by several of America's leading nineteenth-century writers. For those with eyes to see, arguments about the gold standard cast doubt upon the value of writing and raised questions about the status of fiction. If we cannot have confidence in signs, then why write and why read? No one was more sensitive to these questions than Edgar Allan Poe. Fourteen years before the appearance of *The Confidence-Man,* Poe published "The Gold-Bug," which anticipates many of Melville's concerns as well as his literary strategy for addressing them.

In Poe's tale, an amateur entomologist, William Legrand, and his faithful Negro servant, Jupiter, who have recently moved from New Orleans to Sullivan's Island near Charleston, South Carolina, happen to find a gold bug. Describing the precious bug, Legrand observes:

> "It is of a brilliant gold color—about the size of a large hickory-nut—with two jet black spots near one extremity of the back, and another, somewhat longer, at the other. The *antennae* are—"
> "Dey aint *no* tin in him, Massa Will, I keep a tellin' on you," here interrupted Jupiter; "dey bug is a goole-bug, solid, ebery bit of him, inside and all, sep him wing—neber feel half so hebby a bug in my life."[4]

Truth—such as it is—is spoken by the fool. "Dey aint *no* tin in him."
All gold, no tin. The gold bug, Poe suggests, is no tin, notin, nothin,
nothing. As the story develops, the focus shifts from bugs and gold to
language and signs. While writing about gold, Poe makes it clear that his
interest is really language. Having been bitten by the gold bug, Legrand
becomes obsessed with finding buried treasure. In his quest for hidden
riches, the gold bug turns out to be less valuable in itself than as a sign
that points to even greater reserves of wealth. After tracing the outline
on a fragmentary parchment, Legrand notices an obscure image emerging on the underside of his drawing. Teasing out the hidden figure with
heat and moisture, he discerns a series of signs, which initially are unin-
telligible. In spite of the seeming arbitrariness of the signifiers, Legrand
believes in their profound significance and has confidence in his ability
to decipher it. Displaying skills as sophisticated as any contemporary
cryptographer, he eventually decodes the script and, following its instructions, unearths the treasure for which he longed. Legrand explains his
interpretive procedure:

> In the present case—indeed in all cases of secret writing—the first ques-
> tion regards the *language* of the cipher; for the principles of solution, so
> far, especially, as the more simple ciphers are concerned, depend upon,
> and are varied by, the genius of the particular idiom. In general, there is
> no alternative but experiment (directed by probabilities) of every tongue
> known to him who attempts the solution, until the true one be attained.
> But, as with the cipher now before us, all difficulty is removed by the
> signature. The pun on the word "Kidd" is appreciable in no other lan-
> guage than the English. But for this consideration I should have begun
> my attempts with the Spanish and French, as the tongues in which a secret
> of this kind would most naturally have been written by a pirate of the
> Spanish main. As it was, I assumed the cryptograph to be English. (587–
> 88)

Poe's irony is unmistakable. If Legrand's assumption proves correct and
the cryptograph *is* English, his decipherment of the message establishes
nothing or, in Jupiter's terms, no tin. Like the barber's sign, Kidd is a
joker whose code erases itself in its very inscription. If Kidd means kid,
then only a person who does not get the joke or is totally bugs would
have confidence in signs.

Legrand's faith in his cryptographic skills rests upon his assumptions
about the relationship between the mind and the signs it fabricates. "Circumstances, and a certain bias of mind," he admits, "have led me to take
interest in such riddles, and it may well be doubted whether human

ingenuity can construct an enigma of the kind which human ingenuity may not, by proper application, resolve" (587). In this version of the hermeneutic circle, Poe insists that human beings can always decipher the codes they create. But this leaves a critical question unasked: What if some signs are not created by human beings or are formed by an intelligence that does not remotely approximate the human mind? What if some signs or all signs are not created by any intelligence? What if signs are traces of notin?

Legrand's faith in signs and their comprehensibility seems to be confirmed by his discovery of long-lost treasures. Following the trail marked by Kidd's signs, he eventually discovers their referent, which turns out to be nothing other than gold. "There was not a particle of silver. All was gold of antique date and of great variety—French, Spanish, and German money, with a few English guineas, and some counters, of which we had never seen specimens before. There were several large and heavy coins, so worn that we could make nothing of their inscriptions" (579–80). Gold, pure gold; coins, some worn beyond recognition, others French, Spanish, German, and a few English guineas. If, however, Kidd is kidding, how are we to read these signs? What, after all, *is* a guinea? A guinea is, of course, a former British coin worth one pound and one shilling. But the currency named "guinea" sometimes takes forms other than precious metal.

Poe's text raises questions that take us back to the deck of the *Fidèle*. The young man peddling his scriptural wares disappears as suddenly as he appears. His place is taken by "a grotesque negro cripple, in tow-cloth attire and an old coal-sifter of a tamborine in his hand, who, owing to something wrong about his legs, was, in effect, cut down to the stature of a Newfoundland dog; his knotted black fleece and good-natured, honest black face rubbing against the upper part of people's thighs as he made shift to shuffle about, making music, such as it was, and raising a smile even from the gravest" (7). As white turns to black, the fleece seems to become a sign that is more diabolical than holy. Suspicions having been raised by the signs posted by the captain and barber, many of the passengers fear being fleeced by the confidence-man who is supposed to be roaming the ship.

> "What is your name, old boy?" said a purple-faced drover, putting his large purple hand on the cripple's bushy wool, as if it were the curled forehead of a black steer.
> "Der Black Guinea dey calls me, sar." (7)

Few passengers have confidence in the Guinea. When he attempts to defend himself by offering what he insists is indisputable proof of his identity, a fellow cripple explodes: "He can walk fast enough when he tries, a good deal faster than I; but he can lie yet faster. He's some white operator, betwisted and painted up for a decoy. He and his friends are all humbugs" (10). A credulous Methodist clergyman rushes to the defense of the poor Guinea by urging a more charitable response to his entreaties, but the master of suspicion remains unconvinced and responds:

> "Charity is one thing, and truth is another, . . . he's a rascal, I say."
>
> "But why not, friend, put as charitable a construction as one can upon the poor fellow?" said the soldier-like Methodist . . . "he looks honest, don't he?"
>
> "Looks are one thing, and facts are another," snapped out the other perversely; "and as to your constructions, what construction can you put upon a rascal, but that a rascal he is?" (11)

In an effort to resolve the conflict of interpretations created by the alternative constructions projected on the Black Guinea, an Episcopal clergyman, "with a clear face and blue eyes; innocence, tenderness, and good sense triumvirate in his air," intervenes to ask whether anyone on board can testify to the identity of the beggar. "Der Black Guinea" replies by listing many of the personae he later assumes. Seeing through the charade staged by the confidence-man, the person bearing the "true" prosthesis counsels the Episcopal priest not to waste his time on a "wild goose chase." The advice seems to be reliable because a search produces nothing.

But questions linger. The image of the elusive goose returns in the final chapter where the issue once again is the interplay between faith and economics. A cosmopolitan named Frank Goodman is deeply immersed in a theological conversation with an old man when a juvenile *marchand,* clad in a yellow coat, which "flamed about him like the painted flames in the robes of a victim in *auto-da-fe,*" interrupts him (210).[5] Playing on the elderly man's fear and distrust, the youth sells him a traveler's lock and a money belt to secure his possessions. As a bonus, he throws in a *"Counterfeit Detector."* Though insisting that he does not lack confidence in the economic system in which he has invested more than his hope, the old man nonetheless examines several of his bills "just to pass the time." Goodman, who takes considerable pride in his faith in other people, asks:

"Well, what say you, Mr. Foreman; guilty, or not guilty?—Not guilty, ain't it?"

"I don't know, I don't know," returned the old man, perplexed, "there's so many marks of all sorts to go by, it makes it a kind of uncertain. Here, now, is this bill," touching one, "it looks to be a three dollar bill on the Vicksburgh Trust and Insurance Banking Company. Well, the Detector says—"

"But why, in this case, care what it says? Trust and Insurance! What more would you have?"

"No; but the Detector says, among fifty other things, that, if a good bill, it must have, thickened here and there into the substance of the paper, little wavy spots of red. . . ."

"Well, and is—"

"Stay. But then it adds, that sign is not always to be relied on; for some good bills get so worn, the red marks get rubbed out. And that's the case with my bill here—see how old it is—or else it's a counterfeit, or else— I don't see right—or else—dear, dear me—I don't know what else to think."

"What a peck of trouble that Detector makes for you now; believe me, the bill is good; don't be so distrustful. . . ."

". . . Stay, now, here's another sign. It says that, if the bill is good, it must have in one corner, mixed in with the vignette, the figure of a goose, very small, indeed, all but microscopic; and, for added precaution, like the figure of Napoleon outlined by the tree, not observable, even if magnified, unless the attention is directed to it. Now, pore over it as I will, I can't see this goose."

"Can't see the goose? why, I can; and a famous goose it is. There" (reaching over and pointing to a spot in the vignette).

"I don't see it—dear me—I don't see the goose. It is a real goose?"

"A perfect goose; beautiful goose."

"Dear, dear, I don't see it." (213–14)

A real goose? A perfect goose? A beautiful goose? Since faith is a matter of vision, seeing is believing. But does Frank *really* see the goose? Does he believe because he sees, or does he see because he believes? If, as the Counterfeit Detector claims, "the sign is not always to be relied on," then is the search for faith based on vision, and vision based on faith a wild goose chase?

His confidence having been shaken, Goodman sought counsel and reassurance from the old man, who, though disbelieving, is nonetheless dubbed a "Master of Faith." In an effort to disprove the cynicism engendered by untrustworthy signs, Goodman enters into an agreement in which the barber, whose name we now learn is William Cream, promises to take down his "No TRUST" sign and serve his customers in good faith. Goodman, in turn, pledges to provide compensation for any losses resulting from this willing suspension of disbelief. To justify his insistence on the establishment of an escrow account as security against the possibility of lost income, Cream cites lines from "Wisdom of Jesus, the Son of Sirach": "I recalled what the son of Sirach says in the True Book: 'An enemy speaketh sweetly with his lips'; and so I did what the son of Sirach advises in such cases: 'I believed not his many words'" (202). Unwilling to believe that "such cynical sort of things are in the True Book," Frank seeks the wisdom of the elder who is absorbed in Scripture. The troubling words, the cosmopolitan discovers, are not precisely *in* the Bible, but are inside the book as a certain outside that is not truly incorporated. The words the barber cites are part of a textual supplement that falls *between* the Old and New Testaments and, as such, remain marginal to the text proper. "Ecclesiasticus or the Wisdom of Jesus son of Sirach" is part of the Apocrypha.

Apocrypha (Latin *apocryphys,* hidden, from Greek *apokruptein,* to hide away) was the Greek word used to designate writings that were so important that they had to be hidden from the general public and were disclosed only to initiates or the inner circle of believers. When used in a biblical context, *apocrypha* designates the books of the Septuagint included in the Vulgate but considered uncanonical by Protestants. The more general sense of the word reflects the biblical usage. *Apocryphal* also means "of questionable authorship; false, counterfeit." The status of the Apocrypha remains subject to dispute. While it is customarily composed of fourteen books, there is no universal agreement about which texts belong to the Apocrypha. The books designated "apocryphal" are not included in the Jewish Canon of the Hebrew Scripture. In 1534, Luther gathered a collection of apocryphal texts and published them in a separate section at the end of the Old Testament. The Reformed tradition was more suspicious of the Apocrypha. While the Geneva Bible omitted the Apocrypha after 1599, the Westminster Confession of Faith (1646–48) went so far as to identify these texts as "secular literature." In response to this exclusion, Catholics affirmed the Apocrypha and at the Council of Trent (1546) declared anathema anyone who did not accept the entire Vulgate as canonical.

Suspicions raised by this appendix are sometimes transferred to the book proper. Is Scripture canonical or heretical? true or false? genuine or counterfeit? Frank Goodman, it seems, is reassured by the discovery or rediscovery that the lines the barber quoted are apocryphal.

> I cannot tell you how thankful I am for your reminding me about the apocrypha here. For the moment, its being such escaped me. Fact is, when all is bound up together, it's sometimes confusing. The uncanonical part should be bound distinct. And, now that I think of it, how well did those learned doctors who rejected for us this whole book of Sirach. I never read anything so calculated to destroy man's confidence in man. . . . And to call it wisdom—the Wisdom of the Son of Sirach! Wisdom, indeed! What an ugly thing wisdom must be! Give me the folly that dimples the cheek, say I, rather than the wisdom that curdles the blood. But no, no; it ain't wisdom; it's apocrypha, as you say, sir. For how can that be trustworthy that teaches distrust? (209)

There is, however, a tremor of uncertainty in Frank's brave words of confidence: "Fact is, when all is bound up together, it's sometimes confusing." As the marginal between that both separates and joins the Old and New Testaments, the Apocrypha contains or attempts to contain doubt. But for thoughtful readers, the apocryphal doubt is uncontainable; the margin inevitably overflows its bounds and contaminates the whole book as if from within. Uncertainty about the Apocrypha discloses the undeniable arbitrariness of the text: sometimes included, sometimes excluded, and sometimes included as excluded. Once doubts about the authority of the book have been raised, only those whose faith is blind can fail to wonder whether every canon is apocryphal.

Though always shrouding his thoughts in duplicity, Melville appears to leave little doubt about his own doubt. On the penultimate page of the book, he returns to the exchange between Frank Goodman and the Master of Faith. Having just claimed to have had a vision of the goose that lays the golden egg by securing his confidence in the Vicksburgh Trust and Insurance Banking Company, Frank addresses the old man, who, in yet another reversal of roles, is now the one who needs reassurance.

> At length, seeing that he had given up his undertaking as hopeless, and was at leisure again, the cosmopolitan addressed some gravely interesting remarks to him about the book before him, and, presently, becoming more and more grave, said, as he turned the large volume slowly over on the table, and with much difficulty traced the faded remains of the gilt inscription giving the name of the society who had presented it to the boat, "Ah, sir, though every one must be pleased at the thought of the presence in public places of such a book, yet there is something that abates the satisfac-

tion. Look at this volume; on the outside, battered as any old valise in the baggage-room; and inside, white and virgin as the hearts of lilies in bud." (215)

This is the second time that a "gilt inscription" appears. The first, as I have noted, is the barber's gilded sign "No TRUST." By returning to the image of gold at the conclusion of his work, Melville extends the questions raised by the sign to the book as a whole. The Bible, like William Cream's sign, is not pure gold but is only gilded; its gold is perhaps fool's gold, which, though it might contain no tin, is nevertheless notin but a thin veneer that is utterly superficial. In his description of the Bible, Melville plays on the contrasts between surface and depth as well as inside and outside: "Look at this volume; on the outside, battered as any old valise in the baggage-room; and inside, white and virgin." How is such a book to be read? On the one hand, Melville implies that superficial corruption obscures a deeper purity. On the other hand, the worn cover and virgin pages suggest that the book is never opened and thus only surfaces matter.

But the Bible is not the only book contaminated by William Cream's duplicitous sign. Questions about the sign invade every book—even the book supposedly authored by Melville. Is *The Confidence-Man* a reinscription of the gilded sign that is notin? Can we bank on *Melville's* words? Does he attempt to credit faith or discredit confidence by counseling us to distrust trust and/or trust distrust? The book is prefaced with a brief inscription: "Dedicated to victims of Auto da Fe." *Auto-da-fé* refers to both "the public announcement of the sentences imposed on persons tried by the Inquisition" and "the public execution of these sentences by the secular authorities, especially the burning of heretics at the stake." Melville's book, then, appears to be dedicated to heretics who have died for their lack of confidence. But *auto-da-fé* can also be read in another way. The Portuguese phrase means act (*auto,* Latin *actus*) of (*da*) faith (*fé*). When read more "literally," which, in this case, means more literarily, Melville seems to dedicate his work to "victims of the act of faith." Is faith, then, the ultimate confidence game?

How is the exergue to be read? *Exergue,* it is important to note, means not only that which is outside of (*ex*) the work (*ergon*), but also "the space on the reverse of a coin or medal, below the central design." The underside of currency, we have discovered, is faith, and the currency of faith is an economy in which there is a profitable return on every investment. This is what redemption is all about. But what role does *The Confidence-Man* play in the economy of faith? Is Melville's missive sent to believers or heretics? Does he counsel confidence or doubt? Is *Melville's* book a gilded sign that reads "No TRUST"? Is it a narrative that is a metanarrative calling all signs—even the sign "No TRUST" into question? If the book is "inwardly" faulted in a way that discredits it, can we have confidence in Melville's work? Is his book the incarnation of words in which we can have faith? Is Melville a confidence-man, perhaps *the* confidence-man? Or is he the pale shadow of a confidence-man who never appears as such?

$ $ $

The psychoanalytic theory of money must start by establishing the proposition that money is, in Shakespeare's words, the "visible god," in Luther's words, "the God of this world."

NORMAN O. BROWN

In the years following the Civil War, the U.S. government restored the convertibility of paper currency to gold. By 1880, the gold standard had evolved into an international monetary system that was supported by all major countries. With the outbreak of World War I, however, wartime exigencies once again led to the suspension of the gold standard by many countries. While the United States maintained the gold convertibility of the dollar throughout the war, with the collapse of the banking system during the Depression, it became necessary to revoke the gold standard. The financial chaos resulting from this action plunged international trade and finance into confusion and decline that were not reversed until after the Second World War.

One of the major reasons for the postwar economic recovery was the development of an international monetary system. Several years before the end of the war, England and the United States began negotiations that eventually led to the 1944 Bretton Woods Agreement. In an effort to reestablish a semblance of order in international markets, fixed exchange rates were instituted by linking all major currencies to the U.S. dollar and reinstituting the convertibility of the dollar into gold at a specific price. This arrangement functioned reasonably well until 1971, when, in response to international pressures, President Nixon ended the convertibility of the dollar into gold. The efforts of the international community to preserve fixed rates of exchange in the absence of any vestige of the gold standard proved futile. In 1973, fixed exchange rates gave way to floating rates of exchange. With this development, it became undeniable that money is not the sign of a stable "transcendental signified" but is really "notin" but a sign of a sign. No longer bound to a secure referent, currency is a floating signifier whose value is relative to other floating signifiers. In this groundless economy, currency is the free flow of unanchored signs.

If, as the analysis of Melville's *Confidence-Man* suggests, there is an isomorphism between the semiotics of money and the economics of theology, then it should not be surprising that theological developments during this period mirror and/or are mirrored by currents circulating throughout the world of finance. While money was losing (its) ground, theology was becoming unmoored. Concurrent with the shift from an economy anchored in gold to an economy of floating signifiers was the emergence of the so-called death of God theology. The declaration of the death of God was not, of course, new news. Though the phrase was first used by Luther, who also insisted, without realizing the stakes of his claim, that money is "the God of this world," it was left for Hegel and Nietzsche to formulate and elaborate the theological significance of the death of God. The death of God theology of the 1960s takes its inspiration from the writings of Hegel and Nietzsche. There is, however, an important difference between nineteenth- and twentieth-century versions of the death of God theology. In the course of the twentieth century, the death of God is historically enacted and embodied in society and culture. The telos of this process is postmodernism and its extension in virtual culture, which exposes the presuppositions and implications of "the society of the spectacle."

Contrary to widespread misunderstanding, postmodernism, as it is generally understood, *does not* represent a decisive break with modernism but effectively realizes its fundamental tenets. As mechanical means of production and reproduction give way to electronic means of reproduction, ideality becomes reality in which everything is mediated as well as mediaized. When everything is always already mediaized, image becomes real and reality becomes imaginary. In this postmodern culture of images and simulacra, all reality is, in effect, virtual reality.[6] In different terms, everything is encoded in an imaginary register that functions as an ever-shifting cultural a priori constituted and reconstituted by electronic networks whose reach always exceeds our grasp. Since the sign does not re-present the real but is always a signifier of another signifier, there appears to be nothing outside the play of signs. In the absence of a foundational signified, it's signs all the way down. This is Baudrillard's point when he insists on the "precession of simulacra." Simulation,

Baudrillard argues, "is no longer that of a territory, a referential being or a substance. It is the generation by models of a real without origin or reality: a hyperreal. The territory no longer precedes the map, nor survives it. Henceforth, it is the map that precedes the territory—PRECES-SION OF THE SIMULACRA—it is the map that engenders the territory and if we were to revive the fable today, it would be the territory whose shreds are slowly rotting across the map."[7]

The virtual culture of media and images might seem to be distant from and unrelated to religious and theological traditions of the past. But to insist that the culture of simulacra merely negates its theological past is to miss the duplicity of the negation that has created our worlds. Baudrillard is one of the few critics who realizes the theological implications of contemporary culture.

> But what becomes of the divinity, he asks, when it reveals itself in icons, when it is multiplied in simulacra? Does it remain the supreme authority, simply incarnated in images as a visible theology? Or is it volatilized into simulacra, which alone deploy their pomp and power of fascination—the visible machinery of icons being substituted for the pure and intelligible Idea of God? This is precisely what was feared by the Iconoclasts, whose millennial quarrel is still with us today. Their rage to destroy images rose precisely because they sensed this omnipotence of simulacra, this facility they have of effacing God from the consciousness of men, and the over-whelming, destructive truth that they suggest: that ultimately there has never been any God, that only the simulacrum exists, indeed that God himself has only ever been his own simulacrum.[8]

The question that lingers between the lines of Baudrillard's text is whether the effacement of the divine is the negation of God or is God's self-realization. In virtual culture, perhaps God *lives* by dying. Death, in other words, does not necessarily discredit God.

It is not easy to escape the system of credit that founds and funds theological reflection. Theology, it seems, is inescapably speculative, even when it is not identified as such. Speculation, I have noted, is not merely a matter of thought but also involves a certain economy and psychology. According to the fundamental principles of speculative calculation, there can be no expenditure or investment without the expectation of a profit-able return. Every system—be it philosophical, social, political, psycho-logical, or religious—is an economic structure that sustains and is sus-tained by networks of exchange. Though the currency varies, the laws governing such systems remain *structurally* constant. The breakdown of a system can occur in at least three ways: (1) operational principles can become dysfunctional; (2) one of the members or parts of the system can die or be destroyed; (3) perfect equilibrium or homeostasis can be attained. It is important to note some of the implications of the third possibility. While the establishment and maintenance of equilibrium might appear to be the aim of economic systems, the achievement of this purpose would actually result in the annihilation of the structure. The functioning of the system presupposes a *differential* distribution of currency. When differences get too far out of balance, a reversal occurs, which, in turn, becomes excessive and must be counterbalanced, and so on ad infinitum. The structure of structure or the metastructure of equilibrium systems is binary or dialectical opposition. Within the bounds of seemingly all-encompassing structure, opposites are *reciprocally* related in such a way that each mirrors and is mirrored by the other. This mirror play lends every system its speculative cast.

The basic principles of speculation become somewhat clearer when their operation is observed in particular systems and structures. In this context, I will focus on the economy of theology and religion. While not all theology is systematic, Christian theology tends to be speculative. The principles of speculation guide both divine and human activity. Even when it appears to be senseless, believers have confidence that God's activity is carefully calculated. Though God's ways are not always man's ways, God never acts without purpose. From a Christian perspective, the most important act of God is, of course, the Incarnation, which represents God's investment in the human race. One does not need the elaborate apparatus Anselm deploys in *Cur Deus Homo?* to discern the economic principles at work in incarnational theology. If God is the creator, we always live on credit; our lives are loans and our futures are mortgaged. When we spend without limit or fail to meet our payments, as we inevitably seem to do, we discredit not only God but also ourselves and thus incur a debt, which in a theological economy is guilt. *Schuld* (guilt) is *Schuld* (debt).

Having exhausted our credit by spending excessively, we no longer have the funds necessary to repay our debt. But the creditor to whom we owe everything is no ordinary creditor. Always the prudent speculator, God realizes that he has invested too much in the human race to allow the market to crash. So he intervenes *personally* to redeem his coupons: God becomes man in order to absolve human beings of their debt. Our interest in God's investment is obvious. Unable to balance our books, we need a further loan to pay off our debt. If this loan is not to exacerbate our dilemma, however, it must be a loan that we are not required to repay. In an apparent break with basic economic principles, God spends without any possibility of receiving repayment of the principle or deriving profitable interest from his investment. For the human race to be redeemed, God's act of incarnation has to be without interest, that is, completely dis-interested. If God were to act *for himself* rather than *for us,* he would become human in the worst sense and would thereby discredit himself.

To his credit, God acts disinterestedly. It is precisely this dis-interest that is supposed to distinguish divine *agape* from human *eros.* But is divine disinterest really so disinterested? *To his credit,* God acts disinterestedly. If disinterested action is to God's credit, then is it not really interested? God's loan of himself is short-term, for he necessarily returns to himself from what appears to be his own otherness. According to the economy of trinitarian theology, the relation of the Father to the Son is both specular and speculative. The Father sees himself reflected in the Son, and the Son sees himself reflected in the Father. Since neither is simply himself but each is at the same time the other, that is, the Father is the Son and the Son is the Father, the specular/speculative relation forms a perfect circle. Father passes into Son in order to return to himself, and Son passes into Father in order to return to himself. This synchronic relation is staged diachronically in "historical events" of incarnation, crucifixion, and resurrection. The Father descends in the Son to affirm his status as Father, and the Son rises in the Father to claim his identity as Son. The currency of this system is spirit, which, because it is the lifeblood of the system, is deemed divine.

Since the Father only becomes himself through the Son, the Son represents the Father's most important investment. Though temporarily painful, there is no ultimate risk involved in this investment. Both the principle and the interest are absolutely secure. God, therefore, knows in advance that his expenditure will result in a profitable return. Inasmuch as disinterested investment is what makes God God, God *needs* the Incarnation as much as the human race does. If, however, God profits from disinterested speculation, then his investment is not truly disinterested. Instead of a prudent speculator, God is a duplicitous confidence-man who only plays when the deck is stacked in his favor. While life is always a gamble for human beings, God knows that the House never loses. In this casino economy, the ultimate confidence game is the Incarnation in which God appears to be other than what he truly is.

Does this confidence game discredit God? In one sense, yes, but in another sense, no. If disinterested investment makes God God, then God's interest in disinterest would seem to discredit God. How can one have confidence in a duplicitous investment counselor who never is what he seems to be? And yet, who would have confidence in an investment counselor who did not follow sound economic principles by insisting that no investment should be without interest? Why would one believe an adviser who encouraged foolish spending? Faith, it seems, *is* a confidence game we are all too willing to p(l)ay. There are, of course, profits to be made in confidence games. For those who believe, life remains meaningful even when it seems senseless. While the tenets of faith might not be verifiable, they nonetheless are nonfalsifiable. The uncertainty created by nonfalsifiability can create an opening for faith as well as an occasion for doubt. When the stakes are so high, many argue, a person would be a fool *not* to wager everything. Nothing to lose, everything to gain. Perhaps. But what "is" the nothing we seem to lose in such confidence games? Does this nothing discredit God more radically than God discredits himself? Might this nothing be precisely what confidence games are designed to lose? Is there a discrediting of God that cannot be discredited?

Death discredits God—unless, of course, it is temporary. There was a moment, a brief moment that was a dark interval when God seemed to have died. Between crucifixion and resurrection even the most devout followers of Jesus lost confidence. They banked on a counselor who, it seemed, turned out to be nothing more than a confidence-man. Having invested everything, they received nothing in return. *Nothing.* For those who have faith, nothing is unbearable. Nothing, therefore, must be lost. If the confidence-man is to be believed, nothing *is* lost because loss is never really loss but is always implicit gain. This assessment of the human situation requires us to take a long-term rather than short-term view. Instead of selling too quickly when losses mount, seasoned investors increase their wagers precisely when things seem to have hit rock bottom. For those with confidence, Black Friday does not cause despair, for it prepares the way for a brighter day that promises a payoff beyond our wildest expectations.

Claims about the contrary notwithstanding, the Christian God dies repeatedly throughout history, and, while circumstances vary, the pattern remains the same. As crucifixion gives way to resurrection and negation is negated, short-term losses become long-term profits. Since recovery is not merely restoration but something more, the investment of belief returns with compound interest. In this way, the wager of faith always seems to pay handsome dividends, which are most profitable precisely when they are least obvious. Nowhere is the profit of faith less apparent than when God seems to die.

The twentieth century, as I have suggested, is framed by the death of God. Proclaimed by Nietzsche at the beginning of the century and reformulated by leading theologians at midcentury, the death of God is historically enacted during the latter half of the twentieth century. Virtual culture realizes Nietzsche's vision of a world in which every ostensible transcendental signified is apprehended as a signifier caught in an endless labyrinth of signifiers. Translating theology into semiology, God dies and is reborn as a sign that points to *nothing* beyond itself.

In ways more radical than modernists ever dreamed, postmodernism negates what Christian believers affirm. Negation, however, is not necessarily denial. If the negation enacted in images and simulacra is understood speculatively, it remains within an economy that is inescapably Christian. Speculative dialectics create the possibility of recuperative readings in which loss becomes gain. From this point of view, the greatest loss provides the occasion for the greatest gain. When negation is doubled, it generates a *coincidentia oppositorum* in which apparent opposites are truly identical. For the speculator who invests in this basic economic principle, loss is never final and death—even the death of God—loses its devastating power.

Within the economy of speculative theology, death does not discredit God but is actually the climax of divine self-realization. Through a kenoic process, God's transcendence becomes an immanence in which the divine is *totally* present here and now. The death of the transcendent signified effectively divinizes the web of images and simulacra that constitute postmodern culture. When there is nothing beyond the sign, image is all. Height, depth, and interiority collapse in an infinite play of surfaces. In the midst of this superficiality, nothing remains profound.

The speculative economy in which everything is always already redeemed reflects the dream of sacrifice without sacrifice. Though blood might be spilt, there is never expenditure without return. If understood in this way, postmodernism involves a realized eschatology in which God dies and is reborn in the Magic Kingdom where we enjoy Tomorrowland today. In this Fantasyland, everyone lives on credit. At least until the market crashes.

If the discrediting of death is ultimately to God's credit, then it seems impossible *not* to play the confidence game. When explicit negation is implicit affirmation, every gesture of resistance turns out to support precisely what it is designed to oppose. To break the spell of the confidence-man, it is necessary to expose his confidence game as a charade by thinking an unthinkable gift. The unthinkable gift is the gift that can be neither given nor received yet renders all giving and receiving possible. Always falling "outside" the circuit of exchange, which it simultaneously sets in motion, the gift subverts every economy as if from "within."

If all theology is in some sense economical and all economies are implicitly theological, then the gift discredits God. For the gift to elude the structure of reappropriation, recovery, and redemption that speculation inevitably entails, it must interrupt the system of exchange in which credit and debit are reciprocally related. Since discredit cannot create credit, the gift must be an expenditure without return. If, however, the reception of the gift *as gift,* that is, as that which requires *nothing* in return, negates the donation it is intended to acknowledge, then how can the system of credit ever be discredited?

The only alternative to the confidence game that is designed to reclaim (the) all would seem to be a certain forgetting—not just any forgetting but the forgetting, which we have discovered is virtually "primal." Primal oblivion doubles forgetting without negating negation. When one forgets yet remembers that he or she has forgotten, speculation returns to remember what once was lost but now is found. To break the tie that binds, it is necessary not only to forget but to forget that one has forgotten. If forgetting is radical, re-membering is impossible. When re-membering is impossible, dis-membering has always already occurred and redemption can never take place. In this case, the lack of redemption does not render one guilty. Since the gift eludes every economy, it demands nothing in return. *Nothing.* To return nothing is to forget the gift without which we can neither give nor receive, be nor be not.

In virtual culture, the forgetting of forgetting makes it possible to lose loss yet gain nothing. In this case, forgetting does not transform absence into a simple presence that can be enjoyed here and now but traces something like a primordial loss, which is no longer experienced as a lack that might be filled. The lack of primal oblivion perpetuates a becoming that rests upon nothing beyond itself. When nothing lies beyond, everything is transformed. Height, depth, and interiority give way to a play of surfaces that is no longer superficial but is impossibly complex. Metaphoric substitution yields to metonymic displacement that knows no end. In the absence of ends, everything is as purposeless as the gift that is "without why" (*ohne warum*).

While making wagers unavoidable, virtual culture discredits every confidence game. The dilemma is no longer how to recover confidence but to learn how to live without it. " 'I don't know, I don't know,' returned the old man, perplexed, 'there's so many marks of all sorts to go by, it makes it a kind of uncertain.' " So many marks . . . it makes it kind of uncertain. Unavoidably uncertain. Such uncertainty renders erring inescapable. The place or nonplace of erring is the desert—the desert that opens with the gift whose giving is a desertion. In the sands of this desert, where every location is a dislocation, life becomes infinitely nomadic. Never lingering long enough to settle down, the nomad invests everything but receives nothing in return. *Nothing*. Always nothing. To err endlessly, to err purposelessly, to err without why in the desert of signs that are forever losing ground, is to discredit God by realizing nothing. Absolutely no tin . . . notin . . . nothing.

Two

Denegating God

It calls
Calls daily
Calls nightly
Calls (from) without
Beginning or end

A whisper so feint
A rustle so slight
A murmur so weak

When to respond
Where to respond
How to respond
To a call that approaches (from) beyond
Without ever arriving

I thought I was done with God—or that God was done with me. But I suppose I am not, at least not yet. And I am beginning to fear not ever. *Erring* was to have ended it all but it has not. To the contrary, from the beginning messages arrived—some written, some telephonic, some electronic—telling me what I was doing and what I was not doing. I did not really need to be told that something else, something other was stirring between the words of the text; it had always been all too clear and all too unclear. From my admittedly partial point of view, most of the messages seemed to miss the mark. The most intriguing missives struggled to explain what I was doing in my not doing or to show how what I was doing was a certain doing not. I did not respond to these messages, and thus the circuit of communication remained incomplete. But I listened, wondered, pondered. Letters and reviews alone would not have moved me to reply had not certain events or nonevents intervened. When sickness and death approach—only approach for they can never finally arrive—it is impossible not to respond to their provocation. Yet it is also impossible to respond without closing the circle that cancels the call. To respond/to respond not—this is the double bind that constitutes re-ligion by deconstructing everything once believed religious.

One day, the call, the letter I had long dreaded arrived. It was from friends to whom I knew I would have to respond. What made the letter so dreadful was my irrepressible sense that their words were not merely their own but echoed a whisper, a rustle, a murmur that rendered the unavoidable unavoidable. They wanted me to write once again about God or, more precisely, "God, as a category in [my] work or in the discipline [I] represent." When to respond? Where to respond? How to respond? I avoided responding as long as I could but realized from the beginning that it would be impossible not to respond. In recent years, it seemed I had reached the point where not responding had become a response. My response, in other words, had become to respond not. The challenge my friends posed was not simply not to respond but to inscribe the not that does not respond or responds by responding not.

Where to begin? How to begin? Perhaps with the letter—not only their letter but any letter, every letter. What spell does the letter cast? What shadow lies between the lines? What not does the word not say or say by saying not? And what does this spell, this shadow, this not have to do with God?

"God"—not God but "God"—"the concept of 'God' as a category." The words of the letter presuppose precisely what needs to be questioned. *Is* God a concept or a category? *Is* "God" a concept or a category? Or, perhaps, is God that which eludes conceptualization and categorization? Might "God" be the name for that "in" language that does not belong to language—the name, in other words (always in other words), for that which language can never name or cannot avoid naming the unnamable? Questions linger, calling us to linger with the question.

To God we have become unaccustomed; of God we have become unaccustomed to speak, even to think, especially to write. If we slip and find ourselves thinking, speaking, even writing of God, it seems embarrassing, horribly embarrassing—even when our inquiry is critical. All of this God stuff was supposed to have been over a long time ago. When someone ventures a word otherwise, the page tends to become a confessional without walls where our most intimate thoughts and unthoughts stand revealed for all to see and hear. Faced with the prospect of such exposure, we grow modest and withdraw. Devising strategies of avoidance in an effort not to think and not to say what nonetheless we cannot not think and cannot not say, we turn to history, politics, economics, literature, art. If it is no longer professionally and socially acceptable to speak of God, perhaps we can continue to think about what really matters by examining other forms of cultural expression. Thus, critics repeat—usually without realizing or wanting to realize what they are doing—the nineteenth-century gesture of translating theology into philosophy and art. Why do we still search, still probe, still question? What calls us to respond? What disrupts the present? Unless our work is "academic" in the worst sense of the word, something else haunts the search that is our research. What is this "something else" and why will it give us no rest?

When the urgency of the question makes it impossible not to respond—even while realizing that, in responding, one responds not—every strategy of avoidance becomes ineffective. Delay and deferral no longer suffice, for provocation cannot go unanswered forever. Though no text is original, there *is* a difference between couching one's thoughts in analyses of the works of others and witnessing to an other in words that appear to be one's own. With painful awareness of the immodesty of pronouns that once seemed personal, "one" becomes "I," even if I am never one. There is something frightfully unprofessional about the "I." Having spent many years learning not to say and not to write "I," the utterance of this most proper of pronouns marks, paradoxically, a transgression of the rules of propriety. Thus, *I* can speak of "God" only improperly, which is to say transgressively, by avoiding the avoidance to which I have become accustomed.

While I no longer believe in God, I can no longer avoid believing in the sacred. Belief in God becomes impossible and belief in the impossible unavoidable when a certain "piety of thinking" brings one to the edge ~~sacred~~ of the unthinkable where the sacred approaches by withdrawing and withdraws by approaching. The sacred "is" the denegation of "God," and God is the denegation of the sacred. To reinscribe the sacred in the midst of the so-called concept of "God" is to perform a paleonymic gesture that seeks to re-cover the shadow of the word. According to the "logic of paleonymics," it is strategically necessary to borrow an old name to deploy a new concept. While the old is never adequate to the new, the "sacred" deepens the incommensurability between the said and the unsaid by grafting the unnamable onto a nonconcept. The sacred, which, as we shall see, does not exist and yet is not nothing, is what the concept of God is (unknowingly) constructed *not* to think.

The paradox of denegation must not be confused with the dialectic of double negation. In double negation, opposites are reciprocally constituted in and through a process in which difference is maintained while identity is secured. Negation, as such, is negated in a higher affirmation, which is supposed to reconcile opposites. Though apparently preserved, such negation is actually penultimate, for it always remains in the service of a "higher" affirmation. When effective and working properly, negation becomes self-reflexive by negating itself. Denegation, by contrast, is a negation that denies itself and, by so doing, repeats the negation it apparently negates. To de-negate is to un-negate; but this un-negation remains a form of negation. More precisely, denegation is an un-negation that affirms rather than negates negation. The affirmation of negation by way of denegation subverts the negation of negation effected by way of dialectical negativity. Denegation, therefore, entails *negation without negation.* In the odd play of denegation, nothing remains even; opposites are not reconciled but are held together in their belonging apart. The complicity of the nots entailed in denegation issues in neither synthesis nor fragmentation but an alternative relation, which is always at the same time a non-relation.

When denegation involves God and the sacred, the intricate operation of negation without negation becomes even more complex. God and the sacred are not merely opposites, nor are they exactly the same. Though different, their difference is of a different order than the difference that is the opposite of identity. Eluding every oppositional structure, the sacred is the condition of the possibility of opposition as such. Thus, the sacred is that which allows God to be God by enabling God to be other than everything that is not God. God, in other words, is an after-effect or symptom of the sacred. In this way, the denegation of the sacred is not simply negation but is the un-negation without which God cannot exist. While negation without negation is undeniably negative, it is, more importantly, at the same time radically affirmative.

If we are to understand the nonreciprocal, nonoppositional interplay of God and the sacred more adequately, it is necessary to consider in greater detail the God that the sacred denegates. Even when discourse becomes personal, "my" voice is never really my own. Every position is, in some sense, an ex-position constituted by exposure to views and voices of others one attempts to displace. To mark the space of any constructive alternative, it is necessary to articulate the margin of difference along which one writes by defining the other or others with and against whom one thinks.

To think theologically at the end of the twentieth century is necessarily to think in the wake—the interminable wake of the death of God. This thinking must be a rethinking of what the thought of the death of God traditionally leaves unthought. In its *modern* version, the death of God leaves unthought the impossibility of *not* thinking God as unthinkable. Throughout much of the Western theological tradition, God has been interpreted as the Logos and hence reason has, in effect, been deemed divine. When viewed as the discipline charged with articulating the logos of theos, theology becomes the tautological effort to define the logos of the Logos. Far from a shortcoming, the circularity of such theological argumentation is taken to be a mark of superior achievement. Whether explicitly or implicitly, ontotheology pursues a systematic ideal in which beginning and end, presuppositions and conclusions, join to form a totality whose completion represents the fullness and perfection of God. The most exhaustive attempt to fulfill this systematic ideal is, of course, Hegel's speculative philosophy.

For Hegel, God is not only completely and absolutely knowable but is nothing other than the Concept itself. The Concept (*der Begriff*) is the category of categories, which is the condition of the possibility of all thought and being. In other words, the Concept is both an epistemological structure and an ontological ground. The insistence that God *is* the Concept brings the ontotheological tradition full circle and thereby marks its closure by realizing the death of God in his Word. Hegel is the first and most important *modern* death of God theologian. Within Hegel's all-inclusive scheme, the death of God is brought about by a double negation in which divine otherness is negated and the divinity of humanity is affirmed. In this way, the death of God extends the incarnational process by universalizing the truth revealed in the individual figure of the historical Jesus in such a way that it comes to include not only the entire human race but the natural cosmos as a whole. The incarnation is complete when the Kingdom of God is realized *here and now* in nature and history. In the *fullness* of time, transcendence is negated, otherness overcome, and opposites reconciled. When God is truly omnipresent, every vestige of absence disappears and presence becomes *total* presence undisturbed by anything other than itself. From this point of view, the death of God is the condition of the possibility of Parousia, that is, the appearance of essence that leaves nothing obscure. Theologically understood, Hegel's onto-logic represents a radically realized eschatology; philosophically interpreted, it is the fulfillment of the metaphysics of presence. Recent critics of ontotheology ignore the *theological* dimensions of the metaphysics of presence and, thus, present a partial and misleading account of the tradition they claim to find so disturbing.

According to the principles of ontotheology, being is presence and presence is most fully actualized in and through self-consciousness. The ontological argument, which purports to demonstrate the unity of thought and being, is nothing other than a conceptual articulation of the belief that the primal origin and creative ground of being is self-consciousness. Expressed in the traditional language of faith, God is the creator and sustainer of the world. In the appendix to his *Lectures on the Philosophy of Religion,* Hegel suggests that his entire philosophy is, in effect, an extended ontological proof of God's existence. Yet the Hegelian system is at the same time the philosophical enactment of the death of God. The God whose existence Hegel's system supposedly demonstrates is not a transcendent center of creative self-consciousness but the immanent structural ground of the cosmohistorical process, which gradually becomes self-conscious in the course of its own development. This foundation is the Logos and, as I have suggested, the Logos is the Concept, which, in its complete articulation, is the Hegelian Idea.

Hegel defines the *structural* foundation of his system in the *Science of Logic,* which opens with "The Doctrine of Being" and closes with "The Absolute Idea." By carefully unfolding a complex archeoteleological argument, Hegel attempts to demonstrate that, inasmuch as the Logos constitutes everything that exists, being and thought are one. In different terms, reason is neither merely transcendent nor only subjective but is *in* the world as the very substance of reality. When fully deployed, the Hegelian Idea defines the categorical conditions of the possibility of existence for every entity from the most particular to the most general. The Logos described in his *Logic,* however, remains disembodied and therefore is still abstract. The fulfillment of the Logos presupposes its incarnation. When properly comprehended, nature and history are the self-embodiment of God in which the transcendent divine dies and is reborn in humankind's absolute knowledge of its own self-becoming. Perfect self-consciousness comes to completion in the last two parts of Hegel's system: *Philosophy of Nature* and *Philosophy of Spirit.*

The achievement of transparent self-consciousness completes the circle of knowledge by joining *arche* and *telos* to secure the unity of thought and being. The structure of human self-consciousness is revealed by the inner life of the divine. Borrowing Augustine's analogical interpretation of the Trinity, Hegel argues that divine and human self-consciousness are isomorphic. In orthodox theology, the Logos is, of course, interpreted as the Son, who is both identical with and different from the Father.

The third person of the Trinity, the Holy Spirit or Holy Ghost (*der Heilige Geist*), constitutes the relationship between the Father and Son in such a way that distinction is maintained while unity is preserved. Hegelian *Geist* is "*pure* self-recognition in absolute otherness." "God is this," Hegel argues, "to differentiate himself from himself, to be an object to himself, but in this differentiation, to be absolutely identical with himself." The Son is at once other than and one with the Father, and the Father is at once other than and one with the Son. In this thoroughly specular relation, each sees himself in the other and becomes himself through the other. The relation to the ostensible other is actually a mediate self-relation that is necessary to self-identity. Though Hegel repeatedly insists that his goal is to reconcile identity and difference as well as union and nonunion, he sometimes tends to privilege identity and unity at the expense of difference and nonunion. In Hegel's dialectical vision, the other is always the other *of the same.* Put differently, the Son is the Father's *own other* and vice versa.

As logic remains abstract until it is realized in space (nature) and time (history), so the intratrinitarian life of God is incomplete apart from its incarnation. Human self-consciousness perfectly mirrors God's self-consciousness. In becoming self-conscious, the subject first objectifies itself by setting itself over against itself, and then proceeds to reappropriate this *internal* difference as a condition of its own identity. In the dialectic of human self-consciousness, the self-as-subject is the image of the Father, the self-as-object the image of the Son, and the unity of subject and object is the image of Spirit.

The God in whose image human beings are made is not, as we have seen, transcendent and self-contained. To the contrary, God is, in the final analysis, identical with the self-referential *totality* of reality. The intratrinitarian life of God is fully realized when human self-consciousness re-cognizes itself as the incarnation of the divine. If God is All-in-All, human self-consciousness can only be complete when it comprehends its *proper* place within the divine totality. The importance of this pivotal point in Hegel's argument is usually overlooked. Presence becomes *totally* present only when it is re-presented in self-consciousness, which is simultaneously human and divine. Instead of an extraneous supplement to immediate and self-sufficient presence, re-presentation is necessary to the complete actuality of presence as such. The full enjoyment of absolute presence here and now brings the Hegelian system to completion. Alpha and omega become one in the self-awareness of the divine-human Logos.

In the moment of transparent self-consciousness, which Hegel labels absolute knowledge, difference is taken up into identity and otherness is subsumed by the same.

But even at the end of the system, questions remain. Indeed, some questions can arise only *after* the advent of absolute knowledge. Why is Hegel so uneasy about difference and otherness? What does he dread? What provokes his anxiety? What does the Hegelian Idea leave out? What does his philosophy—or any other philosophy or theology—want to avoid? What has Hegel failed to think? What is his system constructed *not* to think?

At the very moment of Hegel's apparent triumph, something begins to stir that disrupts his system. It is difficult to know what to name this something, for every name seems inadequate. It is not just another difference awaiting a dialectical negation that will take it up within the system. Rather, it is something far more unsettling—something strange, different, other—something that not only remains unthought but seems unthinkable. In a curious way that is hard to determine, this unthinkable is not the opposite of thought; nor is it exactly outside the system as something that could be negated and thereby internalized. To the contrary, the unthinkable is the limit that forever shadows thought as its impossible condition. Thought constitutes itself by *not* thinking this limit and, in so doing, "includes" an exteriority it cannot incorporate. Such interior exteriority or exterior interiority faults thought *as if* from within, leaving every structure and system wanting. This unthinkable something is unavoidable; it can be neither denied nor negated. Every negation— especially when it is double—turns out to be a denegation through which the repressed returns to disturb, disrupt, and dislocate. The possibility of the return of the repressed drives Hegel mad.

What Hegel dreads, Kierkegaard solicits. In his philosophical fragments and unscientific postscripts, Kierkegaard struggles to think the unthinkable that Hegel's system is constructed to avoid. From the outset, Kierkegaard realizes that his thinking or unthinking is inseparably bound to Hegel's thought in a nondialectical relation that cannot be expressed in terms of classical structures of opposition. Kierkegaard's fragmentary writing denegates the denegation of the Hegelian system. This denegation of denegation subverts the negation of negation by turning thought toward that which forever turns away from reflection. Kierkegaard deliberately attempts to become the "other" that the Hegelian system can neither bare nor bear. He does not attack the system from without but, like a mole devoted to counterintelligence activities, burrows within the structure in a way that hollows out the very ground upon which the entire edifice rests. Through writerly strategies that are more literary than philosophical—if such a distinction makes sense—Kierkegaard uses irony and parody to expose the folly of Hegel's claim to have achieved transparent self-consciousness and absolute knowledge. Kierkegaard's criticism is never direct but always oblique or, in his own terms, "indirect." There are two basic reasons for Kierkegaard's use of indirect communication. First, he realizes that to attack Hegel directly is to enter into a relation of opposition, which is subject to negation and appropriation within the very system he is attempting to dismantle. Efforts to the contrary notwithstanding, to *oppose* Hegel is to side with him. The challenge facing the critic of Hegel is to develop a nonoppositional critique from a position that is not an op-position. Second, Kierkegaard realizes that the other that Hegel tries to avoid is never present and thus cannot be re-presented. *If* the other speaks—and it always remains uncertain whether such speech takes place—it *must* be indirectly. The unanswerable question Kierkegaard repeatedly asks is, How can the other speak and be heard without ceasing to be other? To probe the paradoxes involved in the question of the other, Kierkegaard devises a style of indirection intended to clear the space for the word of the other by speaking in a voice that is never his own.

But who or what is this other that haunts Kierkegaard's nonsystem? As I have suggested, it is difficult, perhaps impossible, to name the remainder the system cannot incorporate. Nonetheless, Kierkegaard improperly names the unnamable with the proper name "God." Contrary to Hegel's claim that God is the Concept, Kierkegaard insists that God resists all conceptuality and escapes every categorization. As such, God is what Kierkegaard sometimes describes as "the absolutely different" (*det Absolut Forskjellige*), "an infinite and qualitative difference" (*en unendelig Qualitets-Forskjel*), or "qualitative heterogeneity" (*qvalitative Ueensartethed*). Infinite, absolute difference or qualitative heterogeneity is not a difference that is the opposite of identity or sameness but is a more radical difference that cannot be comprehended within any dialectical or binary structure. This difference, which is different from but not opposed to other differences and identities, is absolutely singular.

Kierkegaard consistently distinguishes the individual (*individet*) from the singular (*enkeltet*). As the synthesis of universality and particularity, individuality is thoroughly rational and completely comprehensible. While Hegel has no trouble thinking the individual, the singular is something else—something altogether other. Since it is irreplaceable and unrepeatable, singularity remains unthinkable. The singular inevitably withdraws from thought, leaving the concept to trace its disappearance. Kierkegaard identifies two asymmetrical inscriptions of singularity: anthropological and theological. Anthropologically considered, singularity designates the most complete realization of human subjectivity. While usually associated with the individualism characteristic of existentialism, Kierkegaard insists that individuality is the penultimate form of human life. Through the responsible exercise of freedom in the enactment of the moral law, a person becomes an individual by concretely exemplifying the universal principles of practical reason. Beyond the sphere of ethical individualism, however, lies the domain of religious singularity. The individual becomes the singular one in relation to the absolutely singular whose pseudonym is "God." God is the infinitely and qualitatively different, the absolutely different that provokes the individual by calling from a beyond that forever approaches without ever arriving. The word of this other does not re-present presence but traces an absence that is not the absence *of* presence and thus can never be re-presented— even as absent. Since finite singularity unavoidably echoes absolute singularity, every subject is haunted by an other it can never know. *Nothing is ever itself.* Absolute heterogeneity "infects" everything and everybody as if from within, thereby transforming all seemingly proper names into pseudonyms and rendering all authorship pseudonymous. Even when we try to avoid it, we end up witnessing to altarity. This, Kierkegaard suggests, is what Hegel says by not saying, writes by not writing, thinks by not thinking. To think otherwise than Hegel is to think the not he does not think and yet cannot not think.

The debate between Hegel and Kierkegaard directly and indirectly sets the terms for all significant twentieth-century theology and defines the parameters for relevant cultural analysis in our era. The most important theological controversy running throughout this century reenacts the dispute between Hegel and Kierkegaard. In 1918, a previously unknown Swiss Reformed pastor named Karl Barth published *The Epistle to the Romans* in which he argued that the liberal *Kulturprotestantismus* that dominated the theological landscape during the opening decades of the century could not adequately address the horrors of a world torn apart by war on an unprecedented scale. In an effort to depict the depths to which modernity had fallen, Barth returned to the letters of Paul and reread them through Kierkegaard's long-forgotten writings. Barth's theology revolves around two interrelated poles: human sin and divine transcendence. Borrowing Kierkegaard's claim that God is "infinitely and qualitatively different," Barth argues that God is "wholly other" (*ganz Ander*). Man, by contrast, is mired in sin and cannot overcome his dilemma without divine intervention. Nothing could be farther from Barth's vision of God and the world than Hegel's principles of divine immanence and realized eschatology. Barth actually goes so far as to trace the disasters of the early twentieth century to the idolatry he believes to be implicit in every form of immanentism. When Barth pronounces his epoch-making "*Nein!*" he passes judgment on the entire culture of modernity. Sometimes labeled neoorthodoxy, sometimes dialectical theology, Barth develops a position in which the affirmation of God entails the negation of man, and the negation of man involves the affirmation of God. In Barth's dialectic, opposites are not synthesized but are joined in such a way that irreconcilable differences become unmistakable.

But, as any good dialectician should realize, opposites are inherently unstable and inevitably tend to negate themselves. Various brands of neoorthodoxy governed theological discourse until the death of God theology erupted in America during the 1960s. While Barth's *Epistle to the Romans* resulted from a return to Kierkegaard, Thomas J. J. Altizer's *Gospel of Christian Atheism* represented a resurrection of Hegelianism. Altizer interprets modernity as the historical enactment of the death of God. The God who dies in Altizer's theology is the transcendent God Kierkegaard describes as "absolutely different" and Barth names "the wholly other." While Barth criticizes Hegelianism by returning to Kierkegaard, Altizer criticizes Barth by returning to Hegel. In Altizer's apocalyptic vision, the death of God is the fulfillment of the divine. Through a radically kenotic process, God empties himself of himself to become totally present in the present. This present is the gift of salvation, which can be enjoyed here and now.

Altizer's death of God theology is every bit as dialectical as Barth's neoorthodoxy. Furthermore, the interrelation between Altizer's "gospel of Christian atheism" and Barth's neoprotestantism is itself thoroughly dialectical. Each theological position becomes itself in and through the negation of *its own* other. To move beyond the impasse that has plagued modern theology from Hegel and Kierkegaard to Altizer and Barth, it is necessary to develop a nondialectical a/theology that is postmodern rather than modern. Postmodern a/theology seeks the margin of difference *between* Hegel and Kierkegaard by rethinking the death of God as the *impossibility* instead of the realization of the Parousia. In an effort to indicate a difference that can be comprehended *neither* by Hegel's both/and *nor* by Kierkegaard's either/or, a/theology is driven beyond the precincts of theology properly so-called to the province of literature and literary criticism.

Though usually unrecognized, poststructuralism's critique of structuralism involves something like a Kierkegaardian criticism of Hegelianism. When approached from the perspective of twentieth-century French intellectual history, Hegelianism can be understood as protostructuralism and structuralism as a latter-day version of Hegelianism. In formulating assessments of the possibilities and limitations of structuralism, critics unwittingly return to many of the questions Kierkegaard raised about Hegel's system. The reappearance of Kierkegaardian issues does not, however, lead to a direct appropriation of his insights. To the contrary, Kierkegaard returns indirectly and with a critical difference. Though Kierkegaard searches for an absolute difference that is not subject to dialectical negation, he sometimes formulates his heterology in oppositional terms. Thus, while insisting that God is infinitely and qualitatively different, Kierkegaard often appears to be calling for a return to classical transcendence in which God is other than and opposed to self and world. If Kierkegaard's qualitative heterogeneity is read from a poststructural perspective, it is possible to overcome this shortcoming. More specifically, when Kierkegaard's infinite and qualitative difference is interpreted in terms of Derrida's *différance* and vice versa, the alternative space of a/theology opens.

A/theology is not the opposite of theology and must not be identified with atheism. Neither exactly positive nor negative, a/theology draws on the resources of deconstruction to develop a nonnegative negative theology that seeks to think what Western ontotheology leaves unthought. By so doing, a/theology traces the limits of theology in a way that displaces classical concepts of God. There are two interrelated aspects of the a/theological enterprise, which roughly correspond to the distinction between historical and constructive theology. The first task of the a/theologian is to reread the theological tradition against the grain in an effort to discern the unsaid in the midst of the said. This is the deconstructive moment of a/theology. Second, it is necessary to move beyond deconstruction sensu strictissimo to reconfigure theological notions in an a/theological register. At this point, more radical implications of a/theology begin to emerge. To appreciate the theological stakes of deconstructive a/theology, it is necessary to return to the question of the sacred.

The sacred, I have argued, "is" the denegation of God, and God is the denegation of the sacred. As negation without negation, denegation creates the possibility of a nonnegative negative theology that nevertheless is not positive. Inscribed along the irrepressible margin of difference, the sacred neither exists nor does not exist; it is neither being nor nonbeing. Moreover, the sacred is not a "God beyond God," for it is neither a God nor the other of God but is an other that is precisely not *of* God. More ancient than every God, the sacred "is" the other in whose wake all gods emerge and pass away. If understood in a non-Hegelian way, this wake mourns the endless death of God. The mourning of God's death is an impossible mourning through which one realizes that lack is insurmountable. When working through fails to work out, mourning becomes as interminable as death itself. Death—the death of presence—is one of the disguises or masquerades of the sacred.

Neither present nor absent, the sacred is that which is "set apart." The setting apart of the sacred is a withdrawal that marks, without representing, the approach of the unapproachable. Always already having withdrawn, the sacred forever draws near as the future that never arrives. Through the withdrawal of the sacred, what appears is that *nothing appears.* In ways that will be determined more extensively in what follows, the nothing that appears is neither nonbeing nor nonexistent but is the no-thing that clears the space and leaves the time for all things to appear and disappear. The revelation of nothing is a concealment and the concealment of nothing is a revelation. Since revealing concealment and concealing revelation are absolute, the sacred can "show" itself only by not showing itself or by showing not.

The not of the sacred is the secret, which, though it cannot be told, is, nevertheless, said in all saying. The withdrawal of the sacred creates a secret (*se,* apart, + *cernere,* to separate) that resists all telling and makes it impossible to tell (the) all. The sacred is not, of course, just any secret but is the secret of secrets that tolls in all telling. Yet the secret—even the sacred secret or the secret of the sacred—is not completely opposed to saying. An absolute secret could not even be recognized as such. Paradoxically, secrecy presupposes a certain saying that is a saying not. The secret, therefore, unsays itself in the very saying that constitutes its secrecy. Conversely, the secret that *cannot* be told unsays all saying by leaving an empty space that renders all words hollow. The secret, in other words, denegates itself. The nonplace of this empty space of unsaying is something like a crypt.

When not construed in terms of the metaphysics of presence, the death of God points to the crypt of the sacred. This crypt is the empty tomb whose nonabsent absence displaces every place. In the space of this tomb, God, whose name is presence, is kept alive *as dead.* The void of the crypt is not the sign of resurrection, which overcomes death by negating negation, but the inescapable trace of death, which always approaches without ever arriving. Amid the shadows of this tomb, the death of God appears as the *impossibility* of appearance in which presence is ever absent.

Never presenting itself or presenting itself only as the no-place that haunts every place, the secret of the crypt leaves everything and everyone cryptic. It is important to realize that the crypt is not always elsewhere but figures the strange archetexture of the subject. When possessed by a secret (*Ge-heim*) that cannot be decrypted, the self itself becomes uncanny (*un-heim-lich*). Forever doubled by another that is not itself, the subject never speaks simply for itself but always also speaks in the name of an other that is never known. The ghost that turns everything inside out and outside in, while revealing nothing, is neither *der Heilige Geist* nor an alter ego but something else, something more enigmatically other. Sealed "within" as an unfathomable "exteriority," the *atopos* of the crypt renders all discourse tropological (*tropos,* turn). The encrypted sacred turns toward by turning away, thereby turning away all turning toward. In the space of this turning, which is a re-turning that promises no return(s), communication becomes unavoidably indirect. Though not immediately apparent, there is a genesis of secrecy in which the secret secretes by its very nontelling. Indeed, saying is impossible apart from a certain not saying; to say, in other words, is always to say not. The saying-not implicit in all saying is of at least three orders. On the first and most obvious level, to say A is not to say B. It is impossible to assert anything without not saying something else. Second, all consciousness is shadowed by unconsciousness. As mirror images of each other, consciousness and the unconscious stand in a virtually dialectical relation in which affirmation is denial and denial is affirmation. There is, however, a third, more obscure secret, which is more radically heterogeneous to saying than the unconscious that is the opposite of consciousness. This secret is the sacred that secretes discourse by withdrawing from language. Older than the Logos, the sacred is the condition of the possibility and impossibility of all saying and saying not.

It should be obvious that, when reinscribed in the logic of paleonymics, the sacred is no longer associated with the excess of primal plenitude or undifferentiated totality. Far from holding the promise of mystic fusion, the crypt of the sacred opens a space that makes fusion impossible and unity secondary rather than primary. The excess of the sacred can be traced to something like an "originary" lack. This lack, which is neither the absence of a presence nor the presence of an absence, is not an *arche* but an *anarche* that re-moves the ground that once seemed secure. This unground that undercuts every *Urgrund* is always lacking and hence is ungraspable and incomprehensible. It resists the grip (*der Griff*) of the Concept (*der Begriff*). Never conceptualizable, the incomprehensible is "known" in a non-knowing that is a knowing not. To know not is to know nothing. This learned ignorance is not the opposite of knowledge but is the knowledge of ignorance that knows it does not know. Rather than announcing salvation, the non-knowledge of the sacred brings the awareness of the impossibility of cure.

Since I am always lacking, the I is always wanting. This lack and this want, which are never my own, are gifts of the sacred. The gift of the sacred, however, is no ordinary gift; it falls outside the circuit of exchange yet sets every economic system in motion. The sacred gives giving and receiving without precisely giving and certainly never receiving. As that which is never present, the gift of the sacred must always be a non-giving that is a giving not. In this way, the sacred gives not. The not that the sacred gives is the trace of its retreat that allows whatever is, to be present and whatever is not, to be absent. In this sense, the gift of the sacred is a present, a present that is nothing—nothing less than the condition of the possibility and impossibility of the present as such. To give what makes the present possible is to give time. When traditionally conceived, time, which appears to comprise three different tenses, actually involves three modalities of one tense: the present of things past, the present of things present, and the present of things to come. As that which gives time, the sacred itself is not temporal; nor is it eternal. The sacred is *in* time as that which is always already past and, therefore, always yet to come. Terrifyingly ancient and dreadfully remote, the sacred is, in a certain sense, more radically temporal than the time of tensed presence. Through a metaleptic reversal, the past that was never present eternally returns as the future that never arrives to dislocate repeatedly the present that never is. In this way, the sacred remains a gift that is not (a) present.

A gift that is never (a) present cannot be received. When it is a question of the gift, to receive is to receive not. If the gift is received, a reciprocal relation is established that cancels the gift by returning it to the sender as having been received. Paradoxically, the gratitude that acknowledges the gift is the ingratitude that rejects it by accepting it. For a gift to be a gift, it must be prodigal, extravagant, excessive; it must, in other words, be an expenditure without return. The very possibility of return introduces an element of calculation that annuls the gift. The gift is no investment—psychological or otherwise—and thus bears no interest. From an economic point of view, the disinterested giving of the gift is madness. The incalculable folly of the gift harbors a paradox that borders on the absurd. The gift can be a gift only if it is not accepted as such. But is it possible not to accept a gift—especially if it is the gift of the sacred? Non-acceptance seems to be as impossible as acceptance. While the acceptance of the gift is its non-acceptance, the non-acceptance of the gift is its acceptance. Our non-acceptance of the sacred is (impossibly) our acceptance of the gift of the present that is a present we can neither receive nor possess.

Always disinterested, the gift is without why. Giving without asking why appears as loving—loving unconditionally. The giving that gives without demanding anything in return is agape. Agape is unmotivated, purposeless, indifferent. Even when appearing as agape, the sacred is not a subject that loves and can be loved in return. Agape involves the absolute paradox of loving without either lover or beloved. Though *no one* loves or is loved, there is, *es gibt, il y a* loving. When interpreted in this way, the difference between agape and eros becomes unmistakable. While erotic love, in all of its manifestations, presupposes an economic relation that is *mutually* beneficial and thus thoroughly sensible, agape is a nonreciprocal nonrelation that eludes every economy and thus is senseless. Agape is not opposed to eros but is the giving not that leaves the gap eros ceaselessly longs to fill. The filling of the gap would be the closing of the ring that weds opposites. But such a wedding can never really take place, for the very gift that brings the couple together also holds its members apart.

Encompassable within no system, containable within no structure, the giving of the sacred is beyond reason without being irrational. Agape, which can never be comprehended, is utterly gratuitous. The gratuity of the gift is the prevenient trace that is the offering of the sacred. This offering is always already pre-sent without ever being present. The presending of the sacred is a prescinding that gives by withdrawing. The withdrawal of the sacred is not a negation but an affirmation. Indeed, the arriving departure of the sacred is the most radical affirmation that can be imagined. This affirmation is the for(e)giving of all being and every being. Such for(e)giveness offers the incalculable gift of being—and nonbeing.

Far from beautiful, the offering of the sacred is sublime. Surrounded by the aweful aura of the numinous, the "sublime offering" of agape is simultaneously attractive and repulsive. The irreducible ambiguity of the sacred is what makes it so endlessly fascinating. Its draw is a withdrawal that is always excessive. The sublimity of the sacred is its informality and unpresentability. Whereas beauty involves form that is present and presence that is formed, the sublime offering is the unpresentable presentation of presentation, which takes place without taking (a) place. Far from creating a sense of ease, the informality of the sacred is nothing less than monstrous. Love is not always reassuring but can be overwhelming—especially in the indifference of its nonoccurrence. The excess of agape is not a plenitude that overwhelms by overflowing all form. To the contrary, sublime excess astonishes by tracing the edge of form where *no-thing appears*. The void of nothing is not the abyss of nihilism but a clearing that creates the space for a yes-saying so radical that it can even joyfully embrace no. To say yes to no is to follow the sacred by denegating God.

To follow the sacred—and everything as well as everybody inevitably *follows* the sacred—is to err. Erring is the gift of the sacred's of(f)-erring. The non-place or no-where of erring is the desert created by the desertion of the sacred. The sacred offers by offing in a resignation that is infinite. Its offing is the desertion or abandonment that lets be by letting go. Never a standing-by that is a constant presence, agape entails a release so radical that it is, in a certain sense, indistinguishable from indifference. Nothing is more difficult than letting go—especially when one cares deeply. Yet love requires nothing less than letting go—letting go totally, completely, even to the point of abandonment. When loving requires desertion, it appears as loving not.

Abandoned, deserted, the boundless space of the desert is no longer the place where God is encountered or the sacred experienced. The sacred abandons all encounter, deserts all experience, leaving only limitless sands where one is pushed to the limit that is never experienced. In the sands of this desert, where every location is a dis-location and every place a dis-place, life becomes endlessly nomadic. The withdrawal of the sacred releases one into the infinite migration of error where meaning is unrecoverable and direction undiscoverable. Erring is a destiny that is no longer common. In the infinite space of the desert, we share the impossibility of sharing. More precisely, what "we" share is an abandonment that is a bond without bond of a bind that is a non-bind. When all sharing is a sharing not, every community becomes "inoperable" and "unavowable." The binding that binds not is the gift—the impossible gift of the sacred.

Is it really possible to give or receive a gift—especially the gift of the sacred? It seems not. There is no gift without bond, bind, ligature; yet there is no gift with bond, bind, ligature. By annulling the very relation it is supposed to secure, the tie that binds is its own undoing. When love is the issue, there are no strings attached. If the unconditional for(e)giving of the prevenient trace is an abandonment that releases rather than binds, the gift of the sacred creates neither debt nor guilt, neither *Schuld* nor *Schuld*. To incur debt, to fall guilty is to become tangled in an economic relation that implicitly or explicitly requires compensation. If repayment is demanded, however, the gift is destroyed. In giving, the sacred "says": "You owe nothing. You owe *nothing!*" Yet how can nothing be repaid? Perhaps by forgetting—forgetting so thoroughly and so completely that the gift disappears in an oblivion that is virtually primal. The forgetting of the forgetting of the sacred is not a double negation that is a re-membering or re-collection but a denegation that reinscribes the immemorial as that "in" memory that can be neither re-membered nor re-collected. In this case, remembering, paradoxically, dismembers the subject by insinuating within its innermost precinct a memorial to the immemorial that is never there.

Primal oblivion is not merely a forgetting but a forgetting of forgetting. The forgetting of the forgetting of the gift constitutes the ingratitude that responds by responding not to the indifference of the sacred. But forgetting, even when it seems absolute, inevitably remains secondary to and a symptom of the for(e)getting whose trace can never be completely erased. The for(e)giving of the sacred opens the gap of for(e)getting through which agape leaves the self agape. The gap that splits the subject is the tear that creates an opening for the play of passion. Never merely erotic, the passion of subjectivity is a passivity that knows not depth. This passivity engenders the response-ability that makes responsible activity possible. I suffer—the I always suffers—before I act. And when "I" act, it is never I alone who act, for my words and deeds always bear witness, albeit indirectly, to an other I cannot name. When to respond? Where to respond? How to respond to this other that calls daily, calls nightly, calls (from) beyond without beginning or end?

To respond/to respond not—this is the double bind that constitutes re-ligion by deconstructing everything once believed religious. The *re* of *religion* repeats the *ligare,* which binds yet bonds not, to create a double bind: respond/respond not. The double bind of religion is the existential enactment of the denegation of God. Even in death—especially in death (God's death as well as what is sometimes called "my own")—God continues to haunt from a distance that grows ever more proximate. To be done with God would be a solution every bit as reassuring as the belief in God's abiding presence. Unlike God, whose eternal presence some believe delivers satisfaction, the sacred, which is never present without being absent, brings dissatisfaction that knows no rest. In the wake— the interminable wake of the death of God, the desertion of the sacred creates a lack that leaves us wanting. "My" want is not my own but is the want of an other I can never know.

If the other forever remains other, how *can* I respond? To respond is to respond not, for all correspondence cancels the call by returning it to its presumed sender. But, of course, not to respond is, in a certain sense, a response that receives by receiving not. Agape, which neither demands nor allows response, nonetheless rend(er)s me infinitely response-able. I *must* respond yet I cannot respond. Caught in this impossible double bind, I respond by responding not.

> It calls
>   Calls daily
>   Calls nightly
>   Calls (from) without
>   Beginning or end
>
>   A whisper so feint
>   A rustle so slight
>   A murmur so weak
>
>   When to respond
>   Where to respond
>   How to respond
>   To a call that approaches (from) beyond
> Without ever arriving[1]

Three

Politics of Theory

Primal Scenes

Scene 1: Picasso's Brothel

1907. The curtain is drawn, the veil lifted by a hand, a strange hand in the upper left-hand corner that seems to come from nowhere to reveal the scene: *Les Demoiselles d'Avignon.* Hardly ladies proper, les Demoiselles are whores—not just any whores, but whores who are monsters. Several of the figures wear masks, African masks with Oceanic coloring. Five years earlier, Picasso had frequented l'Hôpital Saint-Lazare to study prostitutes who were infected with syphilis. In June 1907, he visited Musée d'Ethnographie du Trocadéro, where he experienced a "shock" and "revelation" while gazing at tribal masks. "At that moment," he later recalled, "I realized what painting was about." His revelation surfaces in *Demoiselles,* where he inscribes the so-called primitive on the body of woman.

Demoiselles is, of course, one of the most important paintings in twentieth-century art. For generations, critics have interpreted *Demoiselles* as a protocubist work that marks a decisive turn to the self-referential abstraction definitive of modern art. While not disputing such formal innovations, Leo Steinberg insists that *Demoiselles* must also be read as a "confrontation with the indestructible claims of sex." Drawing on insights advanced in *The Birth of Tragedy,* Steinberg argues that "few works of art impose the kind of esthetic experience which the young Nietzsche called 'a confrontation with stark reality.' And this, surely, is why Picasso strove to make his creation a piece of 'wild naked nature with the bold face of truth.' He wanted the orgiastic immersion and the Dionysian release."[1]

Picasso's visits to the syphilitic prostitutes in l'Hôpital Saint-Lazare suggest that there are other traces hidden in *Demoiselles.* In sketches leading up to this work, two additional figures appear: a sailor seated in the

FIGURE 1   Pablo Picasso, *Les Demoiselles d'Avignon,* 1907

midst of the whores, and a medical student who approaches on the left of the painting. In some of the drawings, the medical student is carrying a book, in others a skull. When read through these erased sketches, *Demoiselles* appears to mark the site where eros and thanatos intersect on the body of the "primitive woman."

Scene 2: Freud's Consulting Room

Berggasse 19. Down a dark corridor, up two flights of stairs, through the waiting room . . . the door opens to reveal The Consulting Room. It is dark and excessive, cluttered with late Victorian furniture, books, and artifacts, hundreds of antique artifacts—statues, figurines, fragments, vases, seals, paintings, drawings, etchings, and photographs from Egypt, Cyprus, Pompeii, China, Japan, Syria, Greece, Rome, and elsewhere. Every corner is crammed full, every space overflowing with figures and images. At the center of the far wall is the couch, which, like the floor, is covered with an Oriental rug.

At the foot of the couch, two objects are displayed: a reproduction of Ingres's painting of Oedipus questioning the Sphinx, and a plaster cast of the *Gradiva*. "The girl on the relief," Rita Ransohoff explains,

> was the inspiration for a book by a popular novelist, Wilhelm Jensen, a contemporary of Freud's. The book, in turn, stimulated Freud to write a paper which he called "Delusions and Dreams in Jensen's *Gradiva*," a pioneering essay in the psychoanalysis of literature. Jensen's novel . . . was made to order for Freud. The hero, Norbert Hanold, is an archeologist, a man who has "buried" a part of his own past, his youthful love for a girl named Zöe, or "life." She disappeared, "died" in Hanold's unconscious, only to reappear in the figure of "Gradiva . . ." on the marble bas-relief, to which he is mysteriously drawn.[2]

Zöe, the figure in whom life and death meet, fascinates not only the archeologist Norbert Hanold but also the archeologist Freud. Throughout his career, Freud repeatedly uses archeological metaphors to describe psychoanalysis. Freely admitting a "partiality for the prehistoric," he associates the archaic with the primitive and the child. To rediscover the lost origin, one must travel downward and backward—south and east. "Strange secret yearnings rise in me," Freud confesses, "perhaps from my ancestral heritage—for the East and the Mediterranean and for a life of quite another kind: wishes from late childhood never to be fulfilled."[3]

To the left of the couch, Freud's chair. Beside the chair, a fragment of a papyrus, bearing images of the Egyptian gods of the underworld: Horus, Anubis, and Osiris. Above the chair, more fragments of paintings: a centaur and Pan. Pan, god of shepherds and flocks who originated in Arcadia, was endowed with extraordinary sexual power. Son of Hermes and of the daughter of Dryops, this monstrous child terrified his mother, thereby forcing his father to take him to Olympus where he entered the service of Dionysus. The name "Pan" is derived from the Greek word for all, and was used by later mythographers and philosophers to designate the god who was "the embodiment of the Universe, the Totality."[4] Half man–half goat, Pan was a satyr. "For the Greek," Nietzsche points out, "the satyr expressed nature in a rude, uncultivated state. . . . the satyr was man's true prototype, an expression of his highest and strongest aspirations. He was an enthusiastic reveler, filled with transport by the approach of the god [Dionysus]; . . . a prophet of wisdom born out of nature's womb; a symbol of the sexual omnipotence of nature, which the Greek was accustomed to view with reverent wonder."[5]

In Freud's "museum," the primitive and the child (the primitive as child and the child as primitive) hold the key to unlocking the mystery of the madness that haunts everyone. The figure of this mystery is woman—or more precisely the mother in whose body eros and thanatos intersect.

Primitivism of Theory

Not-so-free associations—THE PRIMITIVE: Garden, Eden, Arcadia, natural, primal, original, pure, simple, unrepressed, intuitive, irrational, naïve, immediate, animal, dreamy, harmonious, whole, total, unified, fulfilled, timeless, prehistoric, undifferentiated, uncivilized, raw, monstrous, violent, horrifying, savage . . . childhood, madness, woman . . . colonialism, racism, sexism, anti-Semitism.

Derived from the Greek *theorein* (to view), a theory is "a scheme or system of ideas or statements held as an explanation or account of a group of facts or phenomena; a hypothesis that has been confirmed or established by observation or experiment, and is propounded or accepted as accounting for the known facts; a statement of what are held to be the general laws, principles, or causes of something known or observed."[6] Central to most accepted definitions of theory is the notion of disinterested observation and speculation. The construction of an adequate theory, it is argued, presupposes an effort to approximate objectivity as far as possible by setting aside special interests and prejudicial assumptions. The failure to bracket or suspend judgment results in a partiality of vision that yields more blindness than insight.

In the past several decades, students of the humanities and social sciences have become obsessed with theory. Whether one is "for theory" or "against theory," theory has become unavoidable.[7] As the interest in theory has spread, questions about its disinterestedness have grown. The issue is not merely the unattainability of objectivity and the unavoidability of partiality and prejudice. More important, through a rigorous deconstruction of the theoretical impulse, critics have begun to unravel the complex interplay between theoretical reflection and certain foundational tenets of Western philosophy. It is rarely noted, however, that theory is often implicitly theo-logical and that the theology grounding theory harbors political implications that are deeply troubling.

Rel. Stud. & Theory

Jonathan Z. Smith argues that what unites the fragmented field or nonfield of religious studies is a shared interest in theory. For many in religious studies, the concern with theory, which often takes the form of a preoccupation with methodology, arrived just in time to avert a potentially paralyzing professional identity crisis. Having entered the field at a time when the approach to the study of religion was primarily theological and often implicitly or explicitly Christian, many teachers and scholars gradually became uneasy about the assumptions grounding their work. Though the reasons for the emergence of criticisms of theological approaches to the study of religion are complex, two factors are particularly important: a growing appreciation for the richness and vitality of different religious traditions, and the impact of teaching and writing in the context of secular colleges and universities. In an effort to overcome the impasse created by privileging theology in general and Christianity in particular, many students of religion turned to the social sciences for guidance. Claiming to have freed themselves from the limitations imposed by religious interpretations of religion, analysts enthusiastically embraced social scientific methods. Henceforth any responsible approach to the study of religion would have to be theoretically self-conscious and methodologically sophisticated. All too often, however, these interpreters failed to assess their newfound theories with the same critical rigor they directed toward the methods they had left behind. Thus they remained blind to the philosophical, theological, and political implications of the positions they developed. In this way, belief and ideology were not left behind but merely changed their names.

Protests to the contrary notwithstanding, theory is *never* disinterested. Knowledge, interest, and power form a nexus that is historically determinate and politically determinative. The very word *theoria* is embedded in a metaphorics of vision and sight that is inextricably bound to certain presuppositions of Western philosophy and theology. The theoretician is the spectator/speculator whose omnipresent/omnivorous gaze exposes phenomena. The presence/absence of Picasso's drawn curtain and the location of Freud's analytic chair are unthinkable apart from the metaphorics of vision and the gaze implied by the word *theory*. To theorize is to speculate and the wager of speculation is mastery. That which is effectively subjected to the gaze of theory is supposed to be mastered, controlled, disciplined, dominated, even colonized.

Nowhere are the interests of theory more evident but less recognized than in the work of the major social theorists who were writing at the beginning of this century: Nietzsche, Durkheim, and Freud. Though nearly a century old, the insights of these dominant figures continue to inform the ways in which many analysts understand the nature and function of religion. Given the abiding significance of their work, it is important to appreciate the philosophical, theological, and political concerns that guide their inquiries.

Nietzsche, Durkheim, and Freud formulated their theories of religion at the exact moment that artistic modernism was bursting upon the historical scene (*The Birth of Tragedy*, 1872; *The Interpretation of Dreams*, 1899; *Totem and Taboo*, 1913; *The Elementary Forms of the Religious Life*, 1912).[8] While not immediately evident, their theoretical reflections share many of the presuppositions of modern art and literature. Perhaps the most significant assumption they hold in common is the belief in what modernists describe as "the primitive." Modernism presupposes primitivism; indeed, they are two sides of the same coin.[9] The primitive is a deliberate fabrication in contrast to which the modern defines itself. Like the sacred, whose substitute it becomes, the primitive is highly charged and consequently overdetermined. On the one hand, the primitive represents *illo tempore* in which life is harmonious, whole, unified, and fulfilled; on the other hand, the primitive refers to prehistory in which life is uncivilized, violent, horrifying, and savage. It is precisely the polyvalence of the primitive that makes it so fascinating. Simultaneously attractive and repulsive, the primitive is that for which one longs yet cannot bear.

Whether affirmed or denied, expressed or repressed, the primitive is always inscribed within a historical trajectory that is definitively formulated in romantic poetry and philosophy. From a romantic point of view, the primitive is the archaic, primal, or original, which is the first moment in a dialectical development that eventually issues in modernity. Modernity, however, does not merely negate the primitive; to the contrary, the full realization of the modern presupposes the return to, or of, the original. Since the arche is also the telos, history is an archeoteleological process in which beginning returns as end. From this point of view, the origin is the end for which modernity longs. *The primitive, in other words, represents the desire of the modern.*

While desire is the pulse of life, it can quickly become the stroke of death. There is something demonic about modernity's desire for the primitive. The interplay of ritual and sacrifice, violence and the sacred, blood and soil suggests a strange and disturbing complicity between modernism and fascism: Ezra Pound addressing the Allies on Italian radio, Wyndham Lewis writing in *Blast,* Filippo Marinetti praising Mussolini, Martin Heidegger lecturing at the University of Freiburg, Mircea Eliade joining the Iron Guard. There are others—many others. As we will see, the puzzling bond between modernism and fascism becomes somewhat clearer when one recognizes the implications of modernity's desire for the primitive. If, as I have suggested, the theories that still inform leading interpretations of religion are grounded in the tenets of modernism, then the political consequences of these theories might be more problematic than their proponents are willing to admit.

In the following pages, I will explore questions raised by the intersection of theory, theology, politics, and primitivism in the writings of Durkheim, Freud, and Nietzsche. In addition to these three well-known theorists, I will also consider the lesser-known but no less significant work of Georges Bataille. Theory, I will argue, is still, indeed, perhaps always, in a primitive state. When we acknowledge the primitivism of theory, we discover that theory is, in Nietzsche's terms, yet another lingering shadow of the God we thought had died.

Elementary Forms

Durkheim's theory of rel.

Durkheim is commonly acknowledged to be the "founding father" of Western sociology and social anthropology. His pioneering work in the early decades of this century set the course later generations of investigators have followed. From Durkheim's perspective, religion (or its substitute) plays an essential role in the formation and maintenance of society. Indeed, he goes so far as to argue that "god and society are only one."[10] Durkheim reaches this conclusion through a lengthy investigation of what he describes as the "primitive" societies of Australian Aborigines and North American Indians. The opening paragraph of *The Elementary Forms of the Religious Life* summarizes the methodological principles guiding his inquiry.

> In this book we propose to study the most primitive and simple religion that is actually known, to make an analysis of it, and to attempt an explanation of it. A religious system may be said to be the most primitive that we can observe when it fulfills the two following conditions: in the first place, when it is found in a society whose organization is surpassed by no others in simplicity; and secondly, when it is possible to explain it without making use of any element borrowed from a previous religion. (13)

The elementary is the primitive and the primitive is both simple and original. In different terms, the elementary or the primitive is undifferentiated and hence inarticulate. The movement from the primitive to the modern involves a process of development from the simple to the complex, or the undifferentiated to the differentiated. Durkheim frequently uses the analogy of biological evolution to explain his view of social progress. "Biological evolution has been conceived quite differently ever since it has been known that monocellular beings do exist. In the same way, the arrangement of religious facts is explained quite differently, according as we put naturism, animism or some other religious form at the beginning of evolution" (16). According to this model of inquiry, to understand something, it is necessary to comprehend its origin. Durkheim admits that "the study we are undertaking is therefore a way of taking up again, *but under new conditions,* the old problem of the origin of religion" (20). To discover the origin of religion, it is necessary to reverse the process of evolution by moving from the complex to the simple. The primitive is not of intrinsic value to Durkheim but is of interest only insofar as it illuminates the dynamics of complex modern society. "What we want to do," Durkheim avers, "is to find a means of discerning the ever-present causes upon which the most essential forms of religious thought and practice depend. . . . These causes are proportionately more easily observable as the societies where they are observed are less complicated. That is why we try to get as near as possible to the origins. It is not that we ascribe particular virtues to the lower religions. On the contrary, they are rudimentary and gross" (20). The primitive, then, is not historically distant but lies hidden *beneath* the modern. Sociological inquiry is, in effect, an archeological enterprise: to go back is to dig down, and to dig down is to inevitably go back.

The origin, which is primitive, I have noted, is simple or undifferentiated. In the absence of social differentiation, individuals are not yet clearly defined. While sometimes expressing misgivings about what Lévy-Bruhl eventually defines as "la mentalité primitive," Durkheim nonetheless insists that in "inferior societies *[les sociétés inférieures]* . . . the lesser development of individuality, the slight extension of the group, the homogeneity of external circumstances, all contribute to reducing the differences and variations to a minimum. The group has an intellectual and moral conformity of which we find but rare examples in more advanced societies. Everything is common to all" (18).[11] Since individual self-consciousness has not yet evolved, mental representations tend to be "collective." Religion, for Durkheim, is a paradigmatic "collective representation."

In order to discover the origin of the collective representations that lie at the foundation of religion, Durkheim examines the genesis of totemism. The totem reflects the society that it represents. Since primitive society is characterized by the absence of individuality, the totem is the embodiment of "anonymous and impersonal force." "No one possesses it entirely and all participate in it. It is so completely independent of particular subjects in whom it incarnates itself, that it precedes them and survives them" (217). The totem originates in collective gatherings or festivals, designed to renew societies by bringing together members at regular intervals to perform ritual activities. The concentration of the group releases what Durkheim describes as a "creative effervescence" that ineluctably leads to "a genuinely wild and savage scene" (249). Wildness and savagery of this scene result from the inability of primitives to control their emotions. Durkheim argues that "since the emotional and passional faculties of the primitive are only imperfectly placed under the control of his reason and will, he easily loses control of himself" (246). Drawing an explicit parallel between the primitive and the mad, Durkheim describes ritual excesses in graphic detail.[12]

> [The primitive] is seen running here and there like a madman, giving himself up to all sorts of disordered movements, crying, shrieking, rolling in the dust, throwing it in every direction, biting himself, brandishing his arms in a furious manner, etc. . . . As such active passions so free from all control could not fail to burst out; on every side, one sees nothing but violent gestures, cries, veritable howls, and deafening noises of every sort, which aid in intensifying still more the state of mind that they manifest. . . . This effervescence often reaches such a point that it causes unheard-of actions. The passions released are of such an impetuosity that they can be restrained by nothing. . . . The sexes unite contrarily to the rules governing sexual relations. Men exchange wives with each other. Sometimes even incestuous unions, which in normal times are thought abominable and are severely punished, are now contracted openly and with impunity. (246–47)

As this passage makes clear, rituals create the space and time for the return of the repressed. Durkheim identifies the primary passions released during the festival as violence and sexuality, which, in different ways, transgress or violate boundaries. When carried to the limit, such transgression leads to the loss of differentiation. "This state of indistinction," Durkheim maintains, "is found at the base of all mythologies."

Once released, sentiments are "transferred" or "projected" onto the totem (265–66, 251, 261).

> Religious force is only the sentiment inspired by the group in its members, but projected outside of the consciousnesses that experience them, and objectified. To be objectified, they are fixed upon some object that thus becomes sacred; but any object might fulfill this function. . . . Therefore, the sacred character assumed by the object is not implied in the intrinsic properties of this latter: *it is added to them.* The world of religious things is not one particular aspect of empirical nature; *it is superimposed upon them.* (261)

While Durkheim insists that the totem does not originate in dreams, nonetheless the processes he describes bear a striking similarity to Freud's account of dream work. Since the totem is overdetermined, there is a distinction between its manifest and latent content. Ostensibly an animal or a plant, the totem is actually the incarnation of violent and erotic passions unleashed during the ritual excesses of the festival.

Once formed, the totem serves two closely related functions. On the one hand, it is a mnemonic device, which serves to recall the collective sentiments that form the glue of society; on the other hand, the sense of collective identity embodied in the totem represents the ideal that the group struggles to realize in its day-to-day activities. Durkheim insists that society is not a product of natural processes but must be constantly constructed and reconstructed. Since collective rituals provoke the sentiments and generate the ideals necessary for social cohesion, religion (or its substitute) is essential to the formation and maintenance of society. In this account of the idealizing function of collective rituals, Durkheim remains strangely forgetful of the excessive violence in which religious representations supposedly originate. Social order, it seems, harbors savage disorder, which always threatens to erupt.

As these remarks suggest, Durkheim's attitude toward religion is deeply ambivalent. In describing his interpretive task, he frequently uses medical analogies to compare religion with disease and hallucination. By the end of his study, however, he admits that "there is something eternal in religion that is destined to survive all the particular symbols in which religious thought has successively enveloped itself" (474). Religion's capacity to explain phenomena does not endure, for this activity is progressively taken over by science; what persists is religion's social function. No society can continue to exist without regular periods of renewal and revitalization. Moreover, the integrity of society depends upon symbols that originate in rituals that create collective effervescence.

In the closing pages of *Elementary Forms,* Durkheim finally turns from his analysis of the primitive to reflect upon the modern. While repeatedly associating religion with disease, infantilism, and madness, he is nevertheless drawn to the primitive and distressed by the modern. As he moves from the past to the present, he becomes surprisingly nostalgic.

> If we find a little difficulty today in imagining what these feasts and ceremonies of the future could consist in, it is because we are going through a stage of transition and moral mediocrity. The great things of the past that filled our fathers with enthusiasm do not excite the same ardour in us, either because they have come into common usage to such an extent that we are unconscious of them, or else because they no longer answer to our actual aspirations; but as yet there is nothing to replace them. . . . In a word, the old gods are growing old or already dead, and others are not yet born. (475)

This gloomy assessment of modernity does not, however, leave Durkheim discouraged. To the contrary, casting a glance toward the future, he anticipates a period of renewal that will revitalize society.

> A day will come when our societies will know again those hours of creative effervescence, in the course of which new ideas arise and new formulae are found that serve for a while as a guide to humanity; and when these hours shall have been passed through once, men will spontaneously feel the need of reliving them from time to time in thought, that is to say, of keeping alive their memory by means of celebrations that regularly reproduce their fruits. (475)

Though not immediately obvious, there is a dark side to Durkheim's hope, which comes to light when we recall that the collective sentiments released by the concentration of the group are unavoidably violent. "A very intense social life," Durkheim acknowledges, "always does a sort of violence to the organism, as well as to the individual consciousness, which interferes with its normal functioning" (259). Durkheim does not seem to realize that in looking forward to future "hours of creative effervescence," he inevitably welcomes the violence that social collectives sometimes generate. There are, however, hints of what lies ahead scattered throughout his book. At one point, Durkheim describes the dynamics of the relationship between a leader and a group.

> This is why all parties political, economic or confessional, are careful to have periodic reunions where their members may revivify their common faith by manifesting it in common. To strengthen those sentiments which, if left to themselves, would soon weaken, it is sufficient to bring those

who hold them together and to put them into closer and more active relations with one another. This is the explanation of the particular attitude of a man speaking to a crowd, at least if he has succeeded in entering into communion with it. His language has a grandiloquence that would be ridiculous in ordinary circumstances; his gestures show a certain domination; his very thought is impatient of all rules, and easily falls into all sorts of excess. It is because he feels within him an abnormal plethora of forces which overflow and burst forth from him; sometimes he even has the feeling that he is dominated by a moral force that is greater than he and of which he is only the interpreter. It is by this trait that we are able to recognize what has often been called the demon of oratorical inspiration. (241)

It is difficult to imagine a more apt description of the rituals that were later acted out in Nuremberg, Berlin, and elsewhere.

Primary Processes

Psychoanalysis is the archeology of the mind. The arche for which the psychoanalyst searches is the primary, primal, primitive, that is never destroyed but remains as the ever-present substratum of the psyche. In the realm of the mind, Freud argues,

> what is primitive is so commonly preserved alongside of the transformed version which has arisen from it that it is unnecessary to give instances as evidence. When this happens it is usually in consequence of a divergence in development: one portion . . . of an attitude or instinctual impulse has remained unaltered, while another portion has undergone further development. . . . Let us try to grasp what this assumption involves by taking an analogy from another field. We will choose as an example the history of the Eternal City. . . . If he knows enough—more than present-day archaeology does—he [an imaginary visitor "equipped with the most complete historical and topographical knowledge"] may perhaps be able to trace out in the plan of the city the whole course of that wall and the outline of the *Roma Quadrata*. . . . There is certainly not a little that is ancient still buried in the soil of the city or beneath its modern buildings.[13]

For Freud, as for Durkheim, to dig down is to go back. The distinction between the latent and manifest content of the psyche implies the temporal difference between the early and late, or primitive and modern. Since what is earlier is more fundamental, the primal or primitive explains what comes later or the modern. Adapting the biological principle according to which ontogeny recapitulates phylogeny to the realm of the mind, Freud maintains that later individuals repeat the phases of development enacted by earlier members of the species. The life of the primitive, in other words, is reenacted in the child.[14] The experiences of the primitive and the child are characterized by the predominance of desire expressed in the relatively free exercise of the pleasure principle. Like children, "primitive men . . . are *uninhibited:* thought passes directly into action."[15] History, Freud believes, involves a process of gradual civilization in the course of which desire is repressed as the pleasure principle is forced to adapt to the reality principle. To discover the desires that govern all experience in their raw state, it is necessary to return to the origin of life in the "savage" and the infant.

When Freud plumbs the depths of the personality, he discovers two fundamental instincts: eros and thanatos. Though apparently opposite, these drives are dialectically related in such a way that each tends to turn into the other. An instinct, Freud argues, *"is an urge inherent in organic life to restore an earlier state of things* that the living entity has been obliged to abandon under the pressure of external disturbing forces."[16] The instincts find expression in the pleasure principle. Pleasure, according to Freud, is the reduction of tension created by conflicting forces. If carried to completion, the elimination of tension would create a homeostasis in which differences would be reduced to identity, and, thus, the flow of energy or play of forces would cease. With the cessation of vital functions, organic life returns to "an earlier state of things." In this archaic state, differences are neutralized and distinctions erased; self and world, subject and object collapse into undifferentiated identity. This condition repeats or reactualizes the "law of participation" that characterizes the life of both the primitive and the infant. Recapitulating the evolution of life, the fetus, during intrauterine existence, is literally at one with its world. Even after birth, however, differentiation emerges only slowly; at the oral stage, child and world remain essentially indistinct. Differentiation does not occur until reality impinges upon the infant through a delay in the satisfaction of desire. This deferral engenders a discontent that leads to the longing to return to the (undifferentiated) origin.

The course Freud charts is obviously circuitous. Since the beginning of life is at the same time its end, progression becomes regression. The end of this process is, of course, death. In his analysis of the development of the personality, Freud argues:

> Those instincts are therefore bound to give a deceptive appearance of being forces tending towards change and progress, whilst in fact they are merely seeking to reach an ancient goal by paths alike old and new. More-

over, it is possible to specify this final goal of all organic striving. It would be in contradiction to the conservative nature of the instincts if the goal of life were a state of things that had never yet been attained. On the contrary, it must be an *old* state of things, an initial state from which the living entity has at one time or another departed and to which it is striving to return by the circuitous paths along which its development leads. If we are to take it as a truth that knows no exception that everything living does for *internal* reasons—becomes inorganic once again—then we shall be compelled to say that *"the aim of all life is death"* and looking backwards, that *"inanimate things existed before living ones."*[17]

Yet the desire for death is rarely expressed directly but is usually diverted from self to other in the form of aggression. In this way, aggression becomes the displacement of thanatos toward the other. But aggression is also a form of identification and thus entails a unification with the one against whom it is directed. When the unitive function of aggression is recognized, the inseparability of eros and thanatos becomes clear. Freud discovers the erotic dimension of thanatos in sadism.

> But how can the sadistic instinct, whose aim it is to injure the object, be derived from Eros, the preserver of life? Is it not plausible to suppose that this sadism is in fact a death instinct which, under the influence of the narcissistic libido, has been forced away from the ego and has consequently only emerged in relation to the object. It now enters the service of the sexual function.[18]

Eros lies at the heart of thanatos, and thanatos is inherent in eros. Inasmuch as eros involves the urge to unite, its radical realization would result in the loss of individual selfhood. Complete or perfect union would be death in which identity eliminates difference. If understood in this way, Freud's interpretation of the life cycle reinscribes a characteristic romantic dialectic of development. Individual, as well as racial, history "progresses" from undifferentiation through differentiation, which eventually leads to tension and conflict that result in a collapse back into a state of undifferentiation. When eros and thanatos become one, the beginning becomes the end.

Since instincts are both universal and unconscious, Freud is driven to postulate a "collective mind." Contrary to popular misconception, the difference between Freud and Jung is not that one posits a personal and the other a collective unconscious, but that the former describes multiple archetypes and the latter identifies only two archetypes. For Freud, as for Durkheim, the collective mind is characterized by sexuality (eros) and violence (thanatos). These sentiments or instincts form the foundation of all mental life and, by extension, all cultural institutions, including religion.

Rather than developing a single theory of the origin and function of religion, Freud stresses the importance of different aspects of psychic life for religious thought and practice: wish fulfillment, illusion, guilt, obsessional neurosis, Oedipus complex. In the opening pages of *Civilization and Its Discontents,* for example, he responds to the suggestion that the *fons et origo* of religion is an "oceanic feeling" in which one experiences "an indissoluble bond, of being one with the external world as a whole" by attempting "to discover a psychoanalytic—that is, a genetic—explanation of such a feeling." Drawing on his interpretation of certain "pathological" conditions, he concludes:

> [O]riginally the ego includes everything, later it separates off an external world from itself. Our present ego-feeling is, therefore, only a shrunken residue of a much more inclusive—indeed, an all-embracing—feeling which corresponded to a more intimate bond between the ego and the world about it. If we may assume that there are many people in whose mental life this primary ego-feeling has persisted to a greater or less degree, it would exist in them side by side with the narrower and more sharply demarcated ego-feeling of maturity.... In that case, the ideational contents appropriate to it would be precisely those of limitlessness and of a bond with the universe—the same ideas with which my friend elucidated the "oceanic" feeling. (15)

Freud is, however, reluctant to trace the origin of religion to the oceanic feeling. Repeating conclusions reached in *The Future of an Illusion,* he insists that religion derives from the helpless infant's longing for a powerful father figure. Nonetheless, he leaves open the possibility of an origin more primal than the desire for/of the father. Though Freud never explicitly admits it, this primal origin might be the desire for/of the mother, which reappears in the longing for the oceanic feeling.

Freud develops his most sustained analysis of the origin of religion in *Totem and Taboo: Some Points of Agreement between the Mental Lives of Savages and Neurotics.* Like Durkheim, Freud builds much of his analysis on anthropological reports about the Australian aborigines.[19] Again like Durkheim, he is not interested in "aborigines" or "primitives" for their own sake but only insofar as they help him to understand modern experience. In the opening paragraph of *Totem and Taboo,* Freud writes: "There are men still living who ... stand very near to primitive man, far nearer than we do, and whom we therefore regard as his direct heirs and representatives. Such is our view of those whom we describe as savages or half-savages; and their mental life must have a peculiar interest for us if we are right in seeing in it a well-preserved picture of an early stage of our own development" (1). Just as Freud analyzes the child to understand the adult, so he studies the primitive to comprehend the modern. There is, however, a problem with Freud's method, which is rarely acknowledged: he does not, in fact, base his arguments on the analysis of children but analyzes adults and then projects what he finds back into childhood to create the appearance of causal explanation for events in the lives of mature people. The same circularity is evident in his account of primitive experience. Freud uses the results of the analysis of his patients to interpret the experience of so-called savages, and then proceeds to use primitives to explain moderns.

criticizing F.

Nowhere are the difficulties with Freud's method clearer than in his reading of totemism in *Totem and Taboo.* In the pivotal essay "The Return of Totemism in Childhood," Freud argues that any adequate theory of totemism must account for its two basic taboos: the prohibition against killing the totem and the prohibition against sexual relations between members of the same totem (i.e., exogamy). Following the principle according to which prohibition presupposes desire, Freud insists that a taboo signals the inclination to perform the forbidden deed. In an effort to explain the relation between totem and taboo, he once again draws a parallel between the primitive and the child. "There is a great deal of resemblance," Freud claims, "between the relations of children and of primitive men towards animals. Children show no trace of arrogance that urges adult civilized men to draw a hard-and-fast line between their own nature and that of other animals" (126–27). Developing his interpretation of totems by extending his analysis of animal phobia from childhood experience to primitive ritual practices, he explains the etiology of little Hans's horse phobia as the displacement of the child's feelings about his father onto an animal.

Analysis is able to trace the associative paths along which this displacement passes. . . . Analysis also enables us to discover the *motives* for the displacement. The hatred of his father that arises in a boy from rivalry for his mother is not able to achieve uninhibited sway over his mind; it has to contend against his old-established affection and admiration for the very same person. The child finds relief from the conflict arising out of this double-sided, this ambivalent emotional attitude towards his father by displacing his hostile and fearful feelings onto a *substitute* for his father. (129)

When this line of analysis is extended from the animal phobia to totemism, it appears that totemism originates in the Oedipus complex. This
insight enables Freud to interpret the latent content of the taboos associated with totemism as the prohibition against killing the father and sexual relations with the mother.[20] Not satisfied with this conclusion, Freud
proceeds to combine anthropological data, derived from Frazer and Robertson Smith, with Darwin's theory of the primal horde to construct a
myth of origins, which involves the historical enactment of the Oedipus
conflict. Sons, who are sexually repressed by a domineering father, join
together to slay and then eat the father in order to win the females of
the tribe. But these deeds prove only marginally successful. While admiration for the father resurfaces and leads to guilt and remorse, the persistent desire for the mother issues in conflict among the sons, which must
be controlled. Thus, further prohibitions are inevitably imposed, thereby
creating additional tensions that must be released periodically. The occasion for this release is the festival.

> But the mourning [of the slain father] is followed by demonstrations of
> festive rejoicing: every instinct is unfettered and there is license for every
> kind of gratification. Here we have easy access to an understanding of
> the nature of festivals in general. A festival is a permitted, or rather an
> obligatory excess, a solemn breach of a prohibition. It is not that men
> commit the excesses because they are feeling happy as a result of some
> injunction they have received. It is rather that excess is of the essence of
> a festival; the festive feeling is produced by the liberty to do what as a
> rule is prohibited. (140)

Freud's festival obviously repeats Durkheim's collective ritual. In the violence and sexuality of the festival, boundaries are transgressed and cultural differences collapse in a unity where opposites mingle. Though horrifying, the return to undifferentiation nevertheless is our deepest desire.

Primitive . . . child . . . mad . . . woman. The ultimate site of undifferentiation is the body of the mother where eros and thanatos meet. The
mother is "uncanny" (*unheimlich*). Like Rudolf Otto's holy, which is also
unheimlich, Freud's mother is simultaneously attractive and repulsive.
She represents the "home" (*Heim*) from which we come and to which
we both long and dread to return. Simultaneously womb and tomb, the
mother is the primal origin we profoundly desire yet cannot bear. After
considering multiple examples of the uncanny, Freud summarizes his
conclusions:

> It often happens that neurotic men declare that they feel there is something
> uncanny about the female genital organs. This *unheimlich* place, however,

is the entrance to the former *Heim* of all human beings, to the place where each one of us lived once upon a time and in the beginning. There is a joking saying that "Love is home-sickness"; and whenever a man dreams of a place or a country and says to himself, while he is still dreaming: "this place is familiar to me, I've been here before," we may interpret the place as being his mother's genitals or her body.[21]

Within the Freudian psychic economy, the mother is the savage origin that is our end. As such, she appears standing before us wearing nothing but a monstrous mask, exposing our most primitive desires.

Genealogy of Art

Freud once admitted that he refused to read Nietzsche because he feared being too influenced by him. This anxiety of influence is well-founded, for Nietzsche anticipates many of Freud's most important insights. Had Freud been willing to read his powerful precursor, he would have discovered not one but many Nietzsches. In the midst of the multiple strands of Nietzsche's tangled texts, several stand out as relevant to the questions with which Freud wrestles. One of Nietzsche's most telling texts concludes his posthumous *Will to Power:*

> This world: a monster of energy, without beginning, without end . . . a becoming that knows no satiety, no disgust, no weariness; this, is my *Dionysian* world of the eternally self-creating, eternally self-destroying, this mystery world of the twofold voluptuous delight, my "beyond good and evil," without goal, unless the joy of the circle is itself a goal. . . . *This world is the will to power—and nothing besides!* And you yourselves are also this will to power—and nothing besides.[22]

The figure of Dionysus, whom Nietzsche also names the Anti-Christ, embodies the conflicting forces Freud labels eros and thanatos. When slowly slipping into madness, Nietzsche goes so far as to sign his last texts and letters "Dionysus." Who or what is this Dionysus incarnate in Nietzsche's life and works?

Dionysus is, of course, the god of wine and mystic ecstasy, who, for Nietzsche, is inseparable from Apollo. Apollo represents the sun, music, and poetry and, as such, is the divine image of the "god of individuation and just boundaries." As "the marvelous divine image of the *principium individuationis,*" Apollo embodies the "freedom from all extravagant urges" and the moral demands of "self-control" (22, 21, 34). Dionysus, by contrast, represents "the shattering of the *principium individuationis*" in an ecstasy "whose closest analogy is furnished by physical intoxication" (22). While Apollo is "reasonable" and "controlled," Dionysus is "excessive" and "extravagant." Apollo and Dionysus are not, however, merely hostile opposites. Like Durkheim's social order and disorder, and Freud's ego and id, these contending gods are inextricably interrelated. Apollo is "the interpreter of dreams" who weaves "a thin veil hiding . . . the whole Dionysiac realm" (32, 28). While Apollo derives energy from Dionysus, Dionysus requires the guise of Apollo to appear. This unity-in-difference of Apollo and Dionysus is dramatically staged in ancient Attic tragedy.

The problem Nietzsche poses in *The Birth of Tragedy* is, to borrow a phrase from Heidegger, the question of "the origin of the work of art." Nietzsche fashions his response by developing a genealogy of Greek tragedy. Following suggestions initially advanced by Schiller, he argues that the origin of tragedy can be traced to the satyr chorus. As I have noted, Nietzsche believes that

> [f]or the Greek the satyr expressed nature in a rude, uncultivated state. . . . the satyr was man's true prototype, an expression of his highest and strongest aspirations. He was an enthusiastic reveler, filled with transport by the approach of the god; a compassionate companion re-enacting the sufferings of the god; a prophet of wisdom born out of nature's womb; a symbol of the sexual omnipotence of nature. . . . Here archetypal man was cleansed of the illusion of culture, and what revealed itself was authentic man, the bearded satyr jubilantly greeting his god. (52–53)

To greet Dionysus is to become immersed in the creative-destructive origin from which all arises and to which everything returns. Nietzsche describes this origin with a variety of richly suggestive images and metaphors, all of which presuppose a fundamental distinction between nature and culture. "The contrast between this truth of nature and the pretentious lie of civilization is quite similar to that between the eternal core of things and the entire phenomenal world" (53). While culture is the realm of opposition and alienation, nature is the domain of unity and oneness.

> Not only does the bond between man and man come to be forged once more by the magic of the Dionysiac rite, but nature itself, long alienated or subjugated, rises again to celebrate the reconciliation with her prodigal son, man. . . . Now that the gospel of universal harmony is sounded, each individual becomes not only reconciled to his fellow but actually at one

with him—as though the veil of Maya had been torn apart and there
remained only shreds floating before the vision of mystical Oneness. (23)

The "original Oneness," which Nietzsche also describes as "the primordial One," is "the ground of Being." This ground is not inert but is
the dynamic essence of "the True Subject," which expresses itself in and
through all reality (32, 24). Though omnipresent, this essence remains
obscure; it is a dark "chthonic realm" that can never be illuminated. In
a summary of the difference between Apollo and Dionysus, Nietzsche
invokes a particularly revealing image of the primordial One: "Apollo
embodies the transcendent genius of the *principium individuationis;*
through him alone is it possible to achieve redemption in illusion. The
mystical jubilation of Dionysos, on the other hand, breaks the spell of
individuation and opens a path to the maternal womb of being" (97). To
his followers, Dionysus cries out: "Be like me, the Original Mother, who
constantly creating, finds satisfaction in the turbulent flux of appearances!" (102).

To be like Dionysus, it is necessary to identify with the original, primordial One, ground of Being, True Subject, chthonic realm, maternal
womb, or Original Mother where eros and thanatos are one. Like the
"contagious" sentiments unleashed in Durkheim's ritual and Freud's festival, the ecstasy triggered in Nietzsche's "bacchanalian revel" is "epi-
demic" (56). Though joyful, ecstasy is also terrifyingly painful. "The original Oneness, the ground of Being" is "ever-suffering and contradictory"
(32). To be united with this Original Mother is to endure "the truly
Dionysian suffering" of "dismemberment" (66). The followers of Dionysus undergo a process of "un-selving" in which individual differences
collapse into undifferentiated unity (39). This "de-individuation" of
unique selves is the realization of universal identity. In this way, the
death of individual subjects is the birth of universal subjectivity (64). This
experience of death and rebirth is supposed to be redemptive.

Redemption, for Nietzsche, takes place through art. As a "sorceress
expert in healing," art holds out the promise of "eventual reintegration"
(52, 67). Yet art is undeniably "illusory." The chthonic realm to which
one is reconciled in tragedy is "fictive" rather than actual or real (50).
Artistic fiction serves as a substitute for, or supplement to, a reality that
can never be truly represented. This is why Dionysus cannot appear directly but must be revealed indirectly through Apollo.

This substratum of tragedy irradiates, in several consecutive discharges,
the vision of the drama—a vision on the one hand completely of the

nature of Apollonian dream-illusion and therefore epic, but on the other hand, as the objectification of a Dionysiac condition, tending toward the shattering of the individual and his fusion with the original Oneness. Tragedy is an Apollonian embodiment of Dionysiac insights. (56–57)

The interplay of Dionysus and Apollo enacts a revelation that is a concealment and a concealment that is a revelation. The masks worn by the actors indirectly imply something beyond tragedy. When carried to completion, Nietzsche's genealogy discloses the way in which religion gives birth to art.

The origin of tragedy, Nietzsche concludes, is "purely religious" (47). The religion that lies beneath tragedy is not the moralistic and repressive religion of Christian Europe but a barbaric paganism in which transgression knows no limits. Nietzsche insists that there is "a profound gap separating the Dionysiac Greeks from the Dionysiac barbarians."

> Throughout the range of ancient civilization . . . we find evidence of Dionysiac celebrations which stand to the Greek type in much the same relation as the bearded satyr, whose name and attributes are derived from the he-goat, stands to the god Dionysos. The central concern of such celebrations was, almost universally, a complete sexual promiscuity overriding every form of established tribal law; all the savage urges of the mind were unleashed on those occasions until they reached that paroxysm of lust and cruelty which has always struck me as the "witches' cauldron" *par excellence.* (25–26)

Accordingly, the barbarian is a savage who is unable to control the basic urges of lust and cruelty, love and aggression, sexuality and violence. What savages act out in life, Greeks act out on stage. In the work of art, thought is a substitute for deed. Tragic drama, in other words, is the sublimation of the basic drives embodied in religious festivals of cruelty. Nietzsche might well have used the words with which Freud concludes *Totem and Taboo* to describe these festivals: Primitive men . . . are *uninhibited:* thought passes directly into action. With them it is rather the deed that is a substitute for the thought. And that is why, without laying claim to any finality of judgment, I think that in the case before us, it may safely be assumed that 'in the beginning was the Deed' " (161).

The barbarism of Dionysian festivals is terrifying. The figurative dismemberment of the tragic hero is but a faint echo of the literal dismemberment of the possessed reveler. As we have come to expect, this savage frenzy is curiously attractive. "[W]hat is the significance, physiologically speaking," asks Nietzsche, "of that Dionysiac frenzy which gave rise to tragedy and comedy alike? Can frenzy be viewed as something that is *not* a symptom of decay, disorder, overripeness?" (8). Nietzsche's answer is an unequivocal Yes! The radical affirmation of Dionysian frenzy, with all the pain, suffering, and violence it entails, is the sign of not only health but of "superabundance." This embrace of Dionysus is not the destiny of mere mortals but awaits the arrival of the *Übermensch.* At the time Nietzsche wrote *The Birth of Tragedy,* he still entertained the dream that the German people might give birth to such a superman.

> And yet there have been indications that the German spirit is still alive, and marvelously alive, like a knight who sleeps his enchanted sleep and dreams far underground. From out of these depths a Dionysiac song rises, letting us know that this German knight in his austere enchantment is still dreaming of the age-old Dionysiac myth. Let no one believe that the German spirit has irrevocably lost its Dionysiac home so long as those bird voices can clearly be heard telling of that home. One day the knight will awaken, in all the morning freshness of his long sleep. He will slay dragons, destroy the cunning dwarfs, rouse Brünnhilde, and not even Wotan's spear will be able to bar his way. (144)

In a certain sense, Nietzsche's dream came true. A German knight did awaken, but he slayed more than dragons. Brünnhilde and Wotan are, of course, leading characters in Wagner's *Ring.* Throughout his life, Nietzsche had a complicated and tumultuous relation to Wagner and his wife, Cosima. *The Birth of Tragedy* bears a preface in which Nietzsche dedicates the work to Richard Wagner.

> [A]nybody judging these pages to be a mere antidote to patriotic frenzy would judge amiss; they are more than a sportive fancy rising airily from a scene dedicated to bloody horror and military virtue. Upon a serious perusal of the essay my readers should become aware, with a sting of surprise, that I have been grappling with a crucial German issue—an issue situated at the very center of our hopes and aspirations. But it may well be that these same readers will feel shocked at seeing an esthetic issue taken so seriously, especially if they are in the habit of looking at art merely as a merry diversion, a light carillon sounding on the edges of earnest pursuits, easily dispensed with—as though they did not know . . . what such a confrontation with "stark reality" *really* implies. (16–17)

In the years following Nietzsche's death, it has become terribly clear that sometimes art is more than a diversion. Dionysus returned not as a Greek, but as a savage barbarian. The festivals acted out artistically on the stage at Bayreuth were acted out actually on the battlefields of Europe and beyond. Though longing for the savage they nonetheless abhor, it is doubtful that either Nietzsche or Wagner could have anticipated the extent of the sacrifices their barbaric German knight would demand of Western culture.

Hyperreality of Sacrifice

Sacrifice creates a spectacle that is surreal. Not only a chapter in modern art, surrealism is increasingly a pervasive cultural condition. The French writer, critic, and theorist Georges Bataille was for many years deeply involved in the surrealist movement. A person of unusually broad interests, Bataille moved freely among fields as diverse as philosophy, theology, art, literature, psychology, sociology, and anthropology. From 1937 to 1939, he was the leader of an informal organization known as Le Collège de Sociologie. This Collège, which traced its origin to the pioneering work of Marcel Mauss and Durkheim, brought together a group of highly influential artists and writers. At one time or another Roger Caillois, Michel Leris, Pierre Klossowski, Denis de Rougemont, Georges Duthuit, and Jean Wahl addressed the Collège.[23] It is not insignificant that during these same years, Alexandre Kojève, who also participated in the Collège, was delivering his highly influential lectures on Hegel. Much of the work of members of the Collège can be understood as an extended dialogue with and criticism of Hegel. But it was not only the intellectual climate of Paris that provided the context for the Collège; world events also contributed rich material for the critical reflection. In March 1938, Hitler annexed Austria and a year later entered Czechoslovakia. For members of the Collège, the coincidence of the outbreak of fascism and a preoccupation with Hegel was no accident, for Hegelianism, they believed, inevitably leads to totalitarianism. As the work of the Collège unfolded, however, many of its members fell prey to the very excesses they deplored in others. The Collège reportedly dissolved when Bataille urged the group to perform a human sacrifice. The question raised by this bizarre proposal is whether Bataille's actions contradict or confirm his theory of the origin and function of religion.

From its inception, the College of Sociology was preoccupied with the problem Goethe once posed: "What is the sacred?" In responding to this question, Bataille draws extensively on the work of Durkheim, Nietzsche, and Freud to formulate a theory of religion that illustrates some of the most problematic political implications of theories based on the distinction between modernism and primitivism. Bataille's analysis of religion rests upon his fundamental distinction between the sacred and the profane, which effectively echoes Durkheim's sacred/profane, as well as Freud's conscious/unconscious contrast and Nietzsche's Dionysus/Apollo binary or polarity. The profane, Bataille contends, designates the "real order," which is characterized by "discontinuity." Discontinuity is the condition in which contrasting objects, various subjects, and subjectivity and objectivity are decisively differentiated. As such, the profane world is the world where reason articulates the differences and distinctions necessary for clear consciousness and transparent self-consciousness. Reason is the condition of the possibility of the purposeful activity realized in work, which is utilitarian activity that represses desire and deters gratification for the sake of what is regarded as useful production. In every profane economy, reason is productive and production is reasonable. Extravagance and excessive behavior, therefore, are avoided at all costs. The cost of such avoidance, however, eventually proves to be too high, and unreasonable compensation must be sought.

The real world, as Bataille conceives it, is not original but emerges from an obscure primal "world" that he describes as sacred. Always harboring a faint recollection for the archaic world that has been left behind yet dwells within, so-called modern man longs to return to the ground from which he originally arose. The function of religion (*re-ligare*) is to bind believers back to the sacred origin.

[margin note: function of rel.]

> Man is the being that has lost, and even rejected, that which he obscurely is, a vague intimacy. Consciousness could not have become clear in the course of time if it had not turned away from its awkward contents, but clear consciousness is itself looking for what it has itself lost, and what it must lose again as it draws near to it. Of course what is lost is not outside it; consciousness turns away from the obscure intimacy of consciousness itself. Religion, whose essence is the search for lost intimacy, comes down to the effort of clear consciousness that wants to be a complete self-consciousness: but this effort is futile, since consciousness of intimacy is possible only at a level where consciousness is no longer an operation whose outcome implies duration, that is, at the level where clarity, which is the effect of the operation, is no longer given.[24]

The sacred, in contrast to the profane, is the domain of intimacy or "immanence" where clear differences and articulate distinctions are lacking. Recalling Nietzsche's Dionysian world, Bataille maintains that "the immanent immensity, where there are neither separations nor limits . . . has the passion of an absence of individuality" (42, 50). The sacred is most obvious because least repressed in the life of "archaic man." Like

Freud's child, Bataille's primitive identifies more closely with animals than do either moderns or adults. In a manner reminiscent of Freud, this identification is fraught with ambivalence.

> There is every indication that the first men were closer than we are to the animal world; they distinguished the animal from themselves perhaps, but not without a feeling of doubt mixed with terror and longing. The sense of continuity that we must attribute to animals no longer impressed itself on the mind unequivocally (the positing of distinct objects was in fact its negation). But it had derived a new significance from the contrast it formed with the world of things. This continuity, which for the animal could not be distinguished from anything else, which was in it and for it the only possible mode of being, offered man all the fascination of the sacred world, as against the poverty of the profane tool (of the continuous object). (35)

The terror that the sacred provokes is the result of the violent destruction of the individual in the state of intimacy. Violence and the sacred join in sacrifice.[25]

As an act that is neither reasonable nor useful, sacrifice breaks with the economy regulating the profane order. In sacrifice, one performs a deed of "uncalculated generosity" that involves what Bataille describes as "an expenditure without return." While reason demands a return on every investment (be it economic or psychic), religion requires excessive prodigality. In developing this account of sacrifice, Bataille brings together Mauss's influential account of the gift (*le don*) and Nietzsche's interpretation of art. A genuine gift must be given selflessly, that is, without self-interest or in the absence of any expectation of personal profit or benefit. From this point of view, every gift is, in effect, a self-sacrifice. "Sacrifice," Bataille argues, "is the antithesis of production, which is accomplished with a view to the future; it is consumption that is concerned only with the moment. This is the sense in which it is gift and relinquishment, but what is given cannot be an object of preservation for the receiver: the gift of an offering makes it pass precisely into the world of abrupt consumption" (49). Since the most radical form of self-sacrifice is, of course, the sacrifice of the self, every sacrifice harbors a faint trace of the ultimate sacrifice, which ends in death. "Paradoxically, intimacy is violence, and it is destruction, because it is not compatible with the positing of the separate individual. If one describes the individual in the operation of sacrifice, he is defined by anguish. But if sacrifice is distressing, the reason is that the individual takes part in it. The individual identifies with the victim in the sudden movement that restores it to immanence (to intimacy)" (51). Like Greek tragedy, Bataille's sacrifice is a substitute for the literal dismemberment of the individual. By identifying with the victim, the sacrificer vicariously experiences a return to intimacy without actually dying. But the forces unleashed in sacrifice cannot always be controlled; the sacred is, as Durkheim and Freud realized, "contagious" and sometimes runs wild.

> The sacred is that prodigious effervescence of life that, for the sake of duration, the order of things holds in check, and that this holding changes into a breaking loose, that is, into violence. It constantly threatens to break the dikes, to confront productive activity with the precipitate and contagious movement of a purely glorious consumption. The sacred is exactly comparable to the flame that destroys the wood by consuming it. (53)

The release of this prodigious effervescence takes place during the festival, which, Bataille explains, "is the fusion of human life. For the thing and the individual, it is the crucible where distinctions melt in the intense heat of intimate life" (54). The heat that transforms differences into identity is generated by transgressive acts that violate the boundaries separating individual subjects and things. Forever beyond good and evil, "crimes" of violence and eroticism open the realm of divine intimacy. In his deliberately provocative book *Death and Sensuality: A Study of Eroticism and the Taboo,* Bataille claims that "the final aim of eroticism is fusion, all barriers gone."[26] This fusion is a *coincidentia oppositorum* in which eros is thanatos and death is life.

> Death actually discloses the imposture of reality, not only in that the absence of duration gives the lie to it, but above all because death is the great affirmer, the wonder-struck cry of life. The real order does not so much reject the negation of life that is death as it rejects the affirmation of intimate life, whose measureless violence is a danger to the stability of things, an affirmation that is fully revealed only in death. The real order [i.e., the reality principle] must annul—neutralize that intimate life and replace it with the thing that the individual is in the society of labor. But it cannot prevent life's disappearance in death from revealing the *invisible* brilliance of life that is not a *thing.* (46–47)

The invisible brilliance of death becomes unmistakably visible in the sacrificial flame. "To sacrifice," Bataille concludes, "is to give as one gives coal to the furnace" (49).

In one of its guises, this furnace is, of course, an oven. Bataille was not unaware of the social and political implications of his interpretation of the sacred. In an important essay entitled "The Psychological Structure of Fascism," he explains that the sacred/profane polarity is a subset of the more general distinction between heterogeneity and homogeneity. Homogeneity signifies those aspects of human society that are governed by established codes and fixed rules. "Production is the basis of a social *homogeneity. Homogeneous* society is productive society, namely, useful society. Every useless element is excluded." The heterogeneous is precisely what the homogeneous excludes; as such, it is "something *other* . . . incommensurate.*" Bataille associates heterogeneity with "*unproductive* expenditure" (i.e., waste products of the human body, erotic acts, trash, vermin, etc.), as well as the "*violence, excess, delirium, madness,*" of mystics, primitives, dreams, and the unconscious.[27] The example Bataille offers to illustrate his understanding of heterogeneity underscores the close connection he sees between primitivism and fascism.

> If these suggestions are now brought to bear upon actual elements, the fascist leaders are incontestably part of heterogeneous existence. Opposed to democratic politicians, who represent in different countries the platitude inherent to *homogeneous* society, Mussolini and Hitler immediately stand out as something *other*. Whatever emotions their actual existence as political agents of evolution provokes, it is impossible to ignore the *force* that situates them above men, parties, and even laws: a *force* that disrupts the regular course of things, the peaceful but fastidious homogeneity powerless to maintain itself (the fact that laws are broken is only the most obvious sign of the transcendent, *heterogeneous* nature of fascist action).

The force of fascism is the will to power, which, once released, spreads like wildfire. "In theory, what is started in the operation of sacrifice is like the action of lightning: in theory there is no limit to the conflagration" (53). In Bataille's reading of the sacred, modern ovens appear to rekindle primitive sacrificial fires that once were deemed religious.

Aestheticization of Politics/Politicization of Aesthetics

In his historically informed and philosophically sophisticated book *Heidegger, Art, and Politics,* Philippe Lacoue-Labarthe argues that the political model of National Socialism is the *Gesamtkunstwerk*.[28] The "*Gesamtkunstwerk*," he explains, "is a political project, since it was the intention of the *Festspiel* of Bayreuth to be for Germany what the Greater Dionysia was for Athens and for Greece as a whole: the place where a people, gathered together in their State, provide themselves with a representation of what they are and what grounds them as such."[29] Following the well-established theory of history advanced by the Romantics, Lacoue-Labarthe associates Greece with an ideal political community in which organic relations promote individual and social unity. As the drama of Dionysus is enacted in the modern state, its violence spreads. Lacoue-Labarthe examines the way in which Heidegger's philosophy and politics grow out of and extend the pernicious complicity between violence and the sacred.

Insisting on the inseparability of religion, art, and politics, Heidegger traces the unprecedented problems of the twentieth century to an unexpected source—the absence or forgetting of God. "The era is defined," he insists,

> by the god's failure to arrive, by the "default of God." . . . Because of this default there fails to appear for the world the ground that grounds it. The word for abyss—*Abgrund*—originally means the soil and ground toward which, because it is undermost, a thing tends downward. But in what follows we shall think of the *Ab-* as the complete absence of the ground. The ground is the *soil* in which to strike root and to stand. The age for which the ground fails to come, hangs in the abyss.[30]

Heidegger's ground is the soil or earth, whose absence creates a longing to return to the lost origin; the theological name for this ground or *Ab-grund* is "God." Philosophically conceived, the ground that grounds and the earth in which everything is rooted is Being—the Being of beings that is the ground of Being. Throughout the history of Western onto-theology, God and Being tend to be interpreted as one—or more precisely the One. In a text whose significance extends far beyond the printed page, Heidegger explains:

> The *eon,* being, of the *eonta,* beings as a whole, is called the *hen,* the unifying One. But what is this encircling unifying as a fundamental trait of being? What does Being mean? *Eon,* "in being," signifies present, and indeed present in the unconcealed. But in presence there is concealed the bringing on of unconcealedness that lets the present beings occur as such. But only Presence itself is truly present—Presence that is everywhere as the Same in its own center and, as such, is the sphere. . . . The sphericity of the unifying, and the unifying itself, have the character of unconcealing lightening, within which present beings can be present. . . . The well-rounded sphere is to be thought of as the Being of beings, in the sense of the unconcealing-lightening unifying. . . . We must never represent this sphere of Being in its sphericity as an object. Must we then present it as a nonobject? No; that would be a mere flight to a manner of speaking.

> The spherical must be thought by way of the nature of primal Being in
> the sense of unconcealing Presence.[31]

Before presence, more ancient than beings and more primordial than
being is *lightening*. But what is "lightening"? What does it illuminate
and what does it obscure? Heidegger's philosophical musings entail far-
reaching theoretical and practical consequences. Perhaps this Heideggerian lightening reflects the lightning of a limitless conflagration
sparked by sacrifice to the One? To explore this troubling possibility, it
is necessary to turn first to theory and then to practice.

In the course of this investigation, it has become clear that major theorists discern a close relationship between religion and primitive behavior.
While modernity seems to have left the primitive behind, the light of
reason is always shadowed by primal urges that never disappear. Their
considerable differences notwithstanding, Durkheim, Freud, Nietzsche,
and Bataille all agree that the most fundamental human desire is the
desire for unity. Unity, in turn, is associated with the origin from which
everything derives and to what it longs to return. While not immediately
obvious, the theoretical speculations we have been tracing indirectly reen-
act the very religious quest they are designed to theorize. The aim of
theoretical machinations is, of course, to understand phenomena. Within
a theo(-)retical economy, to under-stand is to grasp what stands under
by comprehending the sub-stance of things. By stripping away the manifest or laying bare appearances, it seems possible to penetrate the latent
and, thus, discover the origin, which is not only simple but, more important, primitive. This primitive origin, which is never left behind but remains as a "presence that is everywhere the same," is the "unifying One"
for which theory relentlessly searches. From this point of view, theo-ry
is really theo-logical or, in Heidegger's terms, ontotheological. The logos
of theory, in other words, is theos, and in the West, God is One and
One is God. Within the context of ontotheology, theory is the search for
an overarching or underlying unity that unites multiple data. The gaze
of the theorist strives to reduce differences to identity and complexity to
simplicity. When understood in this way, the shift from theology to theory does not, as so many contemporary theorists think, escape God but
exchanges overt faith for covert belief in the One in and through which
all is understood.

Our inquiry leads us to suspect that theory is never innocent but always has important practical and political consequences. The politics of
Heidegger's philosophy suggest one of the outcomes of the theoretical

trajectory we have been charting. In one of his richest and most provocative essays, "Bread and Wine," Heidegger returns to Nietzsche by way
of Hölderlin. "And what," he asks, "are poets for in a destitute time?"
Citing Hölderlin, Heidegger claims that poets keep alive the possibility
of turning from destitution by following "the trace of the fugitive gods."

> But they are, you say, like the wine-god's holy priests,
> Who fared from land to land in holy night.[32]

This wine-god is, of course, Dionysus. "In Hölderlin's experience," Heidegger explains, "Dionysus, the wine-god, brings this trace down to the
godless amidst the darkness of their world's night. For in the vine and
in its fruit, the god of wine guards the being toward one another of earth
and sky as the site of the wedding feast of men and gods. Only within
reach of this site, if anywhere, can traces of the fugitive gods still remain
for godless men."[33] The "cure" the poet brings is a cruel cure, for, as
Nietzsche teaches, Dionysus's terrifying presence is disclosed in tragedy.

It is rarely noted that the interpretation of tragedy that Nietzsche develops in *The Birth of Tragedy* can be traced directly to the writings of
Hölderlin. Hölderlin draws a distinction between the organic and the
aorgic, which parallels Nietzsche's contrast between the Apollonian and
Dionysian. "By 'aorgic,' " Josef Chytry explains, "Hölderlin means 'undifferentiated substance,' or passive, sensuous, unshaped, while to him 'organic,' or subject, is the active element, or that which shapes and creates,
which posits. In humans the aorgic is present as the intuitive or sensuous
element, whereas the organic is egoistic self-identification. It then follows,
according to Hölderlin's reasoning, that the aorgic typically is not found
without the organic, nor the organic without the aorgic."[34] In the course
of human and social development, the organic (i.e., the individuated and
differentiated) and the aorgic (i.e., the universal and undifferentiated)
come into conflict. As egoistic tendencies increase, uncontrollable sensuous impulses are unleashed. When this opposition reaches its maximum,
the organic collapses into the aorgic; the human returns to the natural,
and individuals dissolve into the undifferentiated substance from which
they originally emerged. This return to the origin is the death of the
self. In the moment of dismemberment, the disappearing subject experiences an ecstatic feeling of pure unity, which Hölderlin labels "Innigkeit."[35] This "infinite union" is, in Nietzsche's terms, "the shattering of
the *principium individuationis*" that constitutes the essence of tragedy.

For Hölderlin, as for Wagner and Nietzsche, the tragic poet is the
"ultimate educator." As the holy priest of Dionysus, the poet serves the

"Fatherland" by lighting the way to the primal origin where all differences are overcome. Through a not-so-holy act of transubstantiation, "Bread and Wine" becomes "Blood and Soil," and the community becomes *das Volk*. From this point of view, the *Gesamtkunstwerk* that results when the *Festspiel* of Bayreuth is enacted on the parade grounds of Nuremberg is a *Trauerspiel*. From Hölderlin to Wagner, from Wagner to Nietzsche, from Nietzsche to Heidegger, tragedy presupposes a "will to immediacy," which is original, archaic, primitive.

Primitivism, we have discovered, is a psychosocial construction upon which modernism projects its most profound desires as well as its deepest fears. Suffering the pain of fragmentation, differentiation, and isolation, the modern subject both longs and fears to return to the totality from which he or she came. When theory becomes practice—when tragedy leaves the stage and enters history—the longing for totality can become totalitarian. With this turn of events, dream becomes nightmare and savagery becomes actual. Echoing Bataille, Lacoue-Labarthe argues:

> the *Gesamtkunstwerk* is a political project . . . that finds its truth in a "fusion of the community" (in festival or war) or in the ecstatic identification with a Leader who in no way represents any form of transcendence, but incarnates, in immanent fashion, the immanentism of a community. And this is also why a will to immediate effectuation or self-effectuation underlies national-aestheticism. This will to immediacy is precisely what has been caesura-ed, for it was, ultimately, the crime—the boundless excess—of Nazism.[36]

Is this conclusion inevitable? Are all theories theological? Is every theology sacrificial? If, from the beginning, primitivism is the end of modernism, then are theories that fashion themselves modern any longer acceptable? Or can theory be a/theological?

Scenes of Writing

Return to Berggasse 19. This time proceed through The Consulting Room to The Study. Do not stop; do not lie down; do not expose yourself to the hidden gaze of the father/analyst. Like the other rooms, The Study is filled with books and artifacts. Beside the window, facing a wall of books, is Freud's desk—the desk where he wrote almost all of his works. The figures crowding the desk leave barely enough room for a writing tablet. The Egyptian Amun-Re; a Chinese tomb figure; Osiris; Isis nursing Horus; a Roman Janus head depicting Silenus and Minerva; Aphrodite; Ptah, creator-god of Memphis; Bastet, Egyptian cat-headed goddess; Nefertum, son of Ptah; Sakmet, the Egyptian lioness-headed goddess and wife of Ptah. Standing at the back corner of the desk is the marble statue of a baboon. Friends and colleagues with whom Freud met in his study late into the night report that he was particularly fond of this figure and would frequently stroke it. The marble baboon represents Thoth.

Thoth, the Egyptian god of wisdom and patron of the scribes, is the inventor of writing who created hieroglyphs, which are *mdw-ntr* (god's words). But Thoth is also the moon god and, as such, is the companion of the sun god, Re. From light to dark and writing to wisdom, Thoth cannot be easily classified in terms of the contrasts and oppositions that traditionally structure thought and life. "The system of these traits," Derrida argues,

> brings into play an original kind of logic: the figure of Thoth is opposed to its other (father, sun, life, speech, origin or orient, etc.), but as that which at once supplements and supplants it. Thoth extends or opposes by repeating or replacing. By the same token, the figure of Thoth takes shape and takes its shape from the very thing it resists and substitutes for. But it thereby opposes *itself,* passes into its other, and this messenger-god is truly a god of the absolute passage between opposites. If he had any identity—but he is precisely the god of nonidentity—he would be that *coincidentia oppositorum* to which we will soon have recourse again. . . . His propriety or property is impropriety or inappropriateness, the floating indetermination that allows for substitution and play. *Play,* of which he is also the inventor, as Plato himself reminds us. . . . He would be the mediating movement of dialectics if he did not also mimic it, indefinitely preventing it, through this ironic doubling, from reaching some final fulfillment or eschatological reappropriation. Thoth is never present. Nowhere does he appear in person. No being-there *[Dasein]* can properly be *his own.*[37]

So conceived, Thoth is never present; nor is he absent. In the "presence" of this absence" and "absence" of this "presence," the origin that is our end forever withdraws. To pursue the trace of the "god" of nonidentity, who is neither present nor absent, is to pursue a trace other than the One left by the god of identity. The trace of Thoth leads to no primitive origin; in the absence of origin, binding back (*religare*) does not bind together but binds us to an unbinding that can never be undone. If the origin is unrecoverable, theory, as it has traditionally been understood, becomes as impossible as classical theology. In the absence of the beginning that is the end, nothing hangs together. The task of thinking at the end of theory is to think this endless deferral repeatedly.

Four

Minding the Brain

Limiting Construction

The death of nature is as long and slow as the death of the God who once was believed to have been its creator. Every time nature seems to have disappeared, it returns to disrupt schemes and structures designed to exclude it. In recent years, the issue of nature has emerged at the heart of important theoretical and critical debates in the humanities and social sciences. As these discussions have unfolded, it has become clear that the question of nature is not merely a matter of theoretical interest but harbors important political implications. For many critics, the notion of nature entails an essentialism and a foundationalism, which seem to undercut the possibility of significant personal and social change. Deeply committed to transformative practice, these theorists maintain that, appearances to the contrary notwithstanding, there is nothing natural about nature. Far from something that is given apart from human striving, nature is a cultural construction fabricated to serve identifiable personal and social interests and to promote specific political programs. Nature, in other words, is culturally relative and, as such, has a history. The history of nature tells the story of efforts to authorize the deployment of power by representing contingent social arrangements as necessary structures of interaction. While the locus of sovereignty might shift from God to nature to the political ruler, the structure of domination and servitude remains fundamentally unchanged. To overcome bondage to laws long deemed natural, it is necessary, among other things, to denature nature by exposing the ways in which the "natural" is culturally constructed.

There are, however, certain contradictions inherent in this line of analysis. Though suspicious of universal principles that are supposed to be natural, cultural constructionists implicitly assume that world creation is a universal activity. As such, nothing seems more "natural" than the fabrication of nature. Apparently rejecting all universalism and every naturalism, cultural constructionists nonetheless cling to universal processes and natural propensities that tacitly form the foundation of their arguments. Furthermore, while maintaining that the essentialism intrinsic to the notion of nature collapses historical differences into ahistorical identities, the insistence on thoroughgoing cultural constructionism reduces the ostensible otherness of the objective order of things to the underlying sameness of creative subjectivity. In defending the psycho-socio-cultural construction of reality, critics unknowingly invoke the same thetic subject that, in other contexts, they charge with repressing differences and colonizing altarity. When the subject creates itself by positing apparent difference as implicit identity, otherness disappears in a speculative circuit, which returns everything to the same original source. In this way, social constructionism becomes a new version of subjective idealism.

But these inconsistencies are not what prove most troubling to outspoken opponents of social constructionism. Far more disturbing than covert appeals to universality and creative subjectivity is the resolute antifoundationalism of cultural constructionism. The claim that every foundational principle is actually created to advance the interests of individuals and groups entails a relativism that seems to lead ineluctably to nihilism. In the absence of transcendent norms or universal principles, everything is reduced to the ceaseless exercise of competing wills to power. Critics argue that, while social constructionists profess to resist the totalitarianism to which they think foundationalism inevitably leads, they actually espouse forms of idolatry that have led to this century's worst excesses. If everything is the expression of subjective will, nothing remains to resist the arbitrary deployment of power. In an effort to avoid what appear to be the devastating consequences of such nihilism, many call for a return to the very traditions that criticism seems to have rendered questionable. Though the traditions to which appeal is made differ, the argument remains more or less the same: human life is impossible apart from a bottom line that is given rather than made. These critics counter antifoundationalism with neofoundationalism.

Neofoundationalism, however, is as self-contradictory as antifoundationalism. While cultural constructionism unexpectedly reverts to the universalism it calls into question, neofoundationalism tends to issue in the idolatry it is supposed to reject. All too often the search for secure foundations ends in a fundamentalism that absolutizes a particular religious, intellectual, or cultural tradition as the privileged or even the sole bearer of universal truth. Accordingly, neofoundationalism is no more open to difference and otherness than cultural constructionism.

But not every version of neofoundationalism necessarily falls into this fundamentalist trap. A small but growing number of cultural theorists are arguing that both the cultural relativism of antifoundationalism and the traditional absolutism of foundationalism are misguided. To negotiate the oppositions and divisions that increasingly are tearing us apart, they argue, it is necessary to engage in reasoned discourse that both acknowledges differences and affirms commonalities. As technological innovations hasten the globalization of culture, the need to cultivate channels of communication that effectively cut across social and political boundaries grows ever more urgent. Only if we have something in common can we communicate and only if we communicate can we form the communities, ranging from the local to the global, without which we cannot survive.

The search for commonalities that make communication possible is creating renewed interest in efforts to establish a natural foundation for mental processes. Some of the most intriguing research currently being conducted in this area is devoted to the exploration of the complex interplay between the mind and the brain. As if to update the nescience of phrenology, neuroscientists are using the latest advances in imaging technology to determine the precise location of different mental activities in the brain.[1] Furthermore, the development of high-speed computers now makes it possible to simulate brain functions as well as mental activity. A picture of the brain and of the mind-brain relation is beginning to emerge, which calls into question assumptions that have guided reflection for several hundred years.

It is clear that the implications of this research extend far beyond neurophysiology. Philosophers and investigators like Daniel Dennett (*Consciousness Explained*), Francis Crick (*The Astonishing Hypothesis: The Scientific Search for the Soul*), Antonio Damasio (*Descartes' Error: Emotion, Reason, and the Human Brain*), and Roger Penrose (*The Emperor's New Mind: Concerning Computers, Minds, and the Laws of Physics* and *Shadows of the Mind: A Search for the Missing Science of Consciousness*) have been quick to point out that the intersection of developments in artificial intelligence, artificial life, on the one hand, and, on the other, neuroscience, brain research, and evolutionary biology, is recasting the mind-body dualism, which has plagued Western thought ever since Plato. Though seemingly immune to philosophical interests, some cognitive psychologists are also drawing extensively on neuroscience to recast their account of mental functions and their development. In many cases, these revisions tend to involve a crude reduction in which mental activity is regarded as an epiphenomenon of more rudimentary physical processes.

This interpretation of recent research, however, misses what is most revolutionary about the reconfiguration of the mind-brain and, by extension, the mind-body relation. Rather than trying yet again to reduce the mental to the physical or material or, conversely, to demonstrate that the material is an expression of the mental, a more promising approach recasts the distinction between the mental and the material in nonoppositional terms. This becomes possible with the recognition that research in a variety of fields is converging to suggest that the mental and the material are both *information processes.* Instead of opposites, which must be synthesized or conjoined, mind and brain appear to be interfaces of distributed processes that are all-pervasive yet do not form a closed system or constitute an integrated structure.

This account of information processes has important theoretical implications for our understanding of cultural production. If the interplay between the mental and the material is reconfigured through informational interfacing, the choice between antifoundationalism and neofoundationalism becomes a false alternative, which does little more than extend the binary structure that traditionally has grounded analytic reflection. To move beyond this impasse, it is necessary to develop an account of something like a nonfoundational foundation for cultural constructions. Such an open structure would create the possibility of nonreductive explanation, which would leave space for aleatory events.

One of the few fields in which the far-reaching ramifications of recent developments in neuroscience and cognitive psychology are beginning to register is anthropology. In the course of the ongoing struggle to free themselves from their religious moorings and thereby to secure the legitimacy that the social sciences supposedly bestow, analysts frequently turn to anthropology not only for insight into particular religious practices but, more important, for methodological principles to guide their overall investigations. In his influential study entitled *The Map Is Not the Territory,* Jonathan Z. Smith goes so far as to argue that "[i]n the West, we live in a post-Kantian world in which man is defined as a world-creating being and culture is understood as a symbolic process of world-construction. It is only, I believe, from this humane, post-Enlightenment perspective that the academic interpretation of religion becomes possible. Religious studies are most appropriately described in relation to the Humanities and the Human Sciences, in relation to Anthropology rather than Theology."[2] However, when one turns to anthropology, one finds a field no less divided and filled with self-doubt than religious studies. Surveying the discipline in 1984, Sherry Ortner writes:

> The field appears to be a thing of shreds and patches, of individuals and small coteries pursuing disjunctive investigations and talking mainly to themselves. We do not even hear stirring arguments any more. Although anthropology was never actually unified in the sense of adopting a single shared paradigm, there was at least a period when there were a few large categories of theoretical affiliation, a set of identifiable camps or schools, and a few simple epithets one could hurl at one's opponents. Now there appears to be an apathy of spirit even at this level. We no longer call each other names. We are no longer sure how the sides are to be drawn up, and of where we would place ourselves if we could identify the sides.[3]

While the sources of disagreement among anthropologists are many, much of the controversy in recent years has centered on what has been labeled "symbolic" or "cultural" anthropology. Perhaps predictably, it is precisely this branch of anthropology that has had the greatest impact on the study of religion. So far ignored in religionists' enthusiasm for cultural anthropology is the fact that the most suggestive appropriations of mind-brain research, evolutionary biology, and cognitive psychology have been developed to counter the very position they find so attractive. The debate between cultural anthropologists and their critics reenacts the arguments between cultural constructionists and cultural reductionists. In order to overcome the relativism inherent in cultural constructionism and account for perceived regularities in religious thoughts and practices separated by time and space, some anthropologists are attempting to rehabilitate the notion of nature. Whereas earlier efforts to describe "natural religion" usually bear persistent traces of Enlightenment philosophy, recent arguments about the "naturalness" of religion rely on what many regard as one of the most advanced and rapidly developing branches of science. Pascal Boyer develops the most complete and provocative formulation of this position to date in *The Naturalness of Religious Ideas: A Cognitive Theory of Religion*. Boyer begins by stating the premise of his analysis.

> Religious ideas can be called "natural" in (at least) two senses. "Natural" are those aspects of religious ideas which depend on noncultural constraints, like the human genome or the capacities of human brains or the properties of the world humans live in. Yet "naturalness" can be understood as describing a subjective quality, the fact that certain religious postulates are considered perfectly obvious, self-evident ideas by the people who hold them. In cultural anthropology, the natural aspects of religious

ideas, in the first sense, are generally viewed as either nonexistent or trivial, in any case irrelevant to anthropological theory. It is also generally assumed that people are led by socialization to find perfectly "natural," in the second sense, their religious systems; religious assumptions are seen as combining with other types of ideas in a seamless fabric of a worldview. Here I will try to show, on the contrary, (1) that the content and organization of religious ideas depend, in important ways, on noncultural properties of the human mind-brain, and (2) that, despite "socialization," they are perceived as intuitively unnatural by human subjects.[4]

When this remark is combined with the subtitle of the investigation (i.e., *A Cognitive Theory of Religion*), it becomes clear that Boyer attempts to ground the anthropological investigation of the naturalness of religion in the understanding of the mind-brain that has been developed in contemporary cognitive psychology. By so doing, he remains committed to neofoundationalism, albeit in a naturalistic guise. But such neofoundationalism is not the only conclusion that can be drawn from the effort to reinterpret cultural practices through insights developed in information processing, computer science, neuroscience, and evolutionary biology. Many of the problems critics have so thoroughly analyzed in other forms of neofoundationalism continue to plague Boyer's naturalism. In the face of these persistent problems, it is no longer helpful to declare yet again the historical relativity of cultural symbols. Instead of attempting to counter the claims of neofoundationalism by reasserting the indisputability of antifoundationalism, a more effective strategy is to undo the arguments of neofoundationalism as if from within by taking their claims even more seriously than they themselves do. In what follows, I will argue that, while Boyer's reading of the naturalness of religious ideas poses a suggestive alternative to the current orthodoxy of cultural constructionism, he has not carried his analysis far enough. Though Boyer tries to explain religious ideas by recourse to cognitive psychology, he does not adequately examine the connection between mental activity and certain neurophysiological processes. A more careful account of the informational character of neurological processes points to a nonfoundational foundation for cultural practices, which is no longer plagued by the specter of reductionism.

In order to appreciate what is at stake in the debate between constructionism and reductionism, it is necessary to understand the distinctive features of symbolic anthropology as it emerged in the early 1960s. While a variety of theoretical perspectives can be included under the heading "symbolic anthropology," the two major versions of this approach are defined in the work of Clifford Geertz, who extends the tradition of

Max Weber and Talcott Parsons, and Victor Turner, who was most influenced by Émile Durkheim and the tradition his work inaugurated.
Geertz, as Ortner explains, "clearly represents a transformation upon the
earlier American anthropology concerned mainly with the operations of
'culture,' while Turner represents a transformation upon the earlier British anthropology concerned mainly with the operations of 'society.' "[5]
This distinction does not, of course, imply an opposition but underscores
a difference in emphasis that makes the label "cultural anthropology"
more appropriate for Geertz than for Turner. Moreover, the assumptions and strategies of Geertz's analysis are the preferred target of Boyer's
criticism.

In his highly influential essay "Religion as a Cultural System," Geertz
offers a clear and concise definition of culture. Culture, he argues, "denotes an historically transmitted pattern of meanings embodied in symbols, a system of inherited conceptions expressed in symbolic forms by
means of which men communicate, perpetuate, and develop their knowledge about and attitudes toward life."[6] Several points in this definition
deserve emphasis. First, Geertz stresses the semantic aspect of culture.
Noting his agreement with Susanne Langer's contention that "the concept of meaning, in all its varieties, is the dominant philosophical concept
of our time" (641), Geertz devotes special attention to the cognitive dimension of culture. His preoccupation with the question of meaning is
evident when he defines *symbol* as "any object, act, event, quality, or
relation, which serves as a vehicle for a conception" (643). Symbols, he
elsewhere emphasizes, are "tangible formulations of notions" (644). This
is not to suggest that Geertz ignores the affective and volitional functions
of cultural symbols. As we shall see, he carefully formulates the ways in
which symbols instill moods and guide actions. But the centrality of the
problem of meaning and hence the priority of cognitive processes remains indisputable. Second, Geertz indicates that symbols form systems.
Though this point remains relatively underdeveloped in Geertz's analysis, the question of the systematicity of symbolic structures has been central to theoretical debates since the 1960s. Third, symbols constitute media through which people communicate. As such, symbols presuppose,
if not some kind of universality, at least a degree of commonality that
is both necessary and sufficient for cognitive exchange. And finally, the
symbols constituting cultural systems are "historically transmitted." If
this claim is to be persuasive, there must be discernible mechanisms that
facilitate cultural transmission.

Having established the overall parameters of culture, Geertz proceeds
to define religion as a specific system of symbols, "which acts to establish

powerful, pervasive, and long-lasting moods and motivations in men by formulating conceptions of a general order of existence and clothing these conceptions with such an aura of factuality that the moods and motivations seem uniquely realistic" (643). The interplay of the cognitive (conceptions), affective (moods), and volitional (motivations) dimensions of experience is mediated by symbols, which function as "models *of* and models *for* reality." Recalling the traditional distinction between theoretical and practical reason, Geertz maintains that "models of" entail "the manipulation of symbol structures so as to bring them, more or less closely, into parallel with the preestablished nonsymbolic systems." "Models for," by contrast, facilitate "the manipulation of the nonsymbolic systems in terms of the relationships expressed in the symbolic" systems (646). In other words, "models of" re-present "reality" in the medium of concepts, and "models for" function as programs for altering "reality" by changing moods and instilling motivations for action. "The transposability of models *for* and models *of,* which symbolic formulation makes possible," Geertz argues, "is the distinctive characteristic of our mentality" (647).

Though cultural systems are historically relative, they occur universally. Different societies "construct" alternative symbolic frameworks to render experience meaningful. The activity of cultural construction is neither arbitrary nor dispensable but is rendered necessary by the inherent limitations of human nature. In an effort to establish the necessity of cultural systems and to illustrate the way they function, Geertz has recourse to an analogy whose far-reaching implications provide unexpected resources for his most insightful critics. Cultural systems, Geertz maintains, can best be understood as something like a "genetic template." As genes provide the code by which the biological organism operates and replicates, so cultural symbols provide the program by which the psychosocial organism thinks and acts. Nature and culture are not unrelated because it is precisely the indeterminacy of the genetic code that makes the cultural code necessary. Though always already programmed, the human mind is not hardwired but operates with a variety of software programs written in different societies. While the content of cultural symbols varies, the information they encode is essential to human survival. Since the genetic analogy comes to play a crucial role in responses to this argument as well as in the thinking of other theorists, it is helpful to cite Geertz's formulation of this point at length.

> So far as culture patterns, i.e., systems or complexes of symbols, are concerned, the generic trait which is of first importance for us here is that they are extrinsic sources of information. By "extrinsic," I mean only

that—unlike genes, for example—the culture patterns lie outside the boundaries of the individual organism as such in that intersubjective world of common understandings into which all human individuals are born and in which they pursue their separate careers. Furthermore, culture patterns are extrinsic in that they persist after the human organism has died. By "sources of information," I mean only that—like genes—culture patterns provide a blueprint or template in terms of which processes external to themselves can be given a definite form. As the order of bases in a strand of DNA forms a coded program, a set of instructions, or a recipe, for the synthesization of the structurally complex proteins which shape organic functioning, so culture patterns provide such programs for the institution of the social and psychological processes which shape public behavior. Though the sort of information and the mode of its transmission are vastly different in the two cases, this comparison of gene and symbol is more than a strained analogy of the familiar "social heredity" sort. It is actually a substantial relationship, for it is precisely the fact that genetically programmed processes are so highly generalized in men, as compared with lower animals, that culturally programmed ones are so important, only because human behavior is so loosely determined by intrinsic sources of information that extrinsic sources are vital.(645)

Geertz's insight is considerably richer and more complex than he realizes. After offering the analogy between cultural systems and genes, he drops it, thereby leaving the impression that the relationship between the cultural and the biological, or, alternatively, between mind and body, or the mental and the material, is readily transparent. But this relation is not as obvious or as straightforward as Geertz assumes. Nor is it clear that the analogy will bear the weight of Geertz's argument without considerable explanation and elaboration. His use of terms is too imprecise and his indication of relations too loose. Curiously, it is just this imprecision and laxity that makes Geertz's argument attractive to so many humanists. If the analogy between cultural symbols and genes is to be anything more than a suggestive association, it is necessary to explore the tangled terrain where information theory, genetic biology, and evolutionary biology intersect.

Genes and Memes

Ever since the initial formulation of information theory, philosophers, mathematicians, and scientists have insisted on the relevance of cybernetics for the understanding of living organisms and mental activity. In

Cybernetics, or Control and Communication in the Animal and Machine (1948), Norbert Weiner develops an extended analysis of the ways in which information theory can be used to establish the isomorphism of nonliving and living systems. His arguments remained largely speculative until the remarkable advances in molecular biology in the middle of this century. Though he never makes the point directly, it is obvious that these developments in information theory and biology lie behind Geertz's use of the genetic analogy. In 1952, James Watson and Francis Crick forever changed the way in which human beings understand themselves by deciphering the genetic code. They successfully demonstrated that the genetic material in cells forms something like a blueprint for the entire organism. Each of the fifty to one hundred thousand genes in the cell nucleus makes up a segment of the DNA and possesses instructions for making a particular protein. These instructions are produced by varying the sequence of the four chemical bases that form what is, in effect, the alphabet of the organism's communication network: adenine (A), thymine (T), guanine (G), and cytosine (C). The functioning of the organism involves the coding and decoding of the messages composed from this rudimentary alphabet. Since each cell in the organism has all the DNA and thus contains a complete operational blueprint, cell specialization requires the restriction or self-regulation of genetic information. In this way, the body is similar to a cybernetic system in which information is managed by intricate feedback loops.

The force of the genetic analogy depends upon an exact definition of "information." When Geertz argues that cultural symbols function like genes by providing "extrinsic sources of information," which structure thought and direct action, he generalizes the notion of information to such an extent that it loses all precision. Furthermore, at pivotal junctures in his argument, Geertz simply asserts what he ought to demonstrate. As we have seen, his definition of culture includes the necessity of "historically transmitting" patterns of meaning embodied in symbol systems. At no point, however, does Geertz explain how or why this critical process of transmission occurs.

In order to address these difficulties, it is necessary to draw a distinction, which Geertz fails to note, between the genotype and the phenotype. *Genotype* designates the "genetic constitution of an individual organism, as distinguished from its physical appearance." *Phenotype,* by contrast, specifies the "genetically determined and observable appearance of an organism, especially as considered with respect to all possible genetically influenced expressions of one specific character."[7] While the genotype includes all the genes I have, that is, the composition of the DNA in my cells, the phenotype refers to those genes whose expression is externally visible. One of the abiding puzzles of genetics is the way in which the genotype is translated into the phenotype. It is precisely at this point that questions of transmission and reception become critical. What are the processes by which one gene is expressed and another is repressed?

The cultural implications of this biological conundrum become clear in the provocative theories of Richard Dawkins. In a certain sense, Dawkins's work is a mirror image of Geertz's argument. While Geertz starts with an analysis of culture and turns to genetics for analogies, Dawkins begins by investigating genetics and eventually develops analogies that enable him to extend his argument to culture. Dawkins forms his argument by bringing together insights from genetic biology with the most recent research in the new fields of artificial life and computational biology. Insisting that Watson and Crick are the Plato and Aristotle of our time, Dawkins stresses that the cracking of the genetic code proves beyond doubt that life is a *digital* information process or, more precisely, is a process of digital-information transfer. The digital structure of the genetic code implies a remarkable similarity in the way genes and computers function. Genes, Dawkins insists,

> are pure information—information that can be encoded, recoded and decoded, without any degradation or change of meaning. Pure information can be copied and, since it is digital information, the fidelity of the copying can be immense. DNA characters are copied with an accuracy that rivals anything modern engineers can do. They are copied down the generations, with just enough occasional errors to introduce variety. Among this variety, those coded combinations that become more numerous in the world will obviously and automatically be the ones that, when decoded and obeyed inside bodies, make those bodies take active steps to preserve and propagate those same DNA messages.[8]

The isomorphism between computer code and genetic code creates the possibility of using computers to investigate life.

Dawkins's controversial research is situated at the juncture where scientific theory and cultural theory are transforming our understanding of nature as well as culture. Life, it seems, is becoming more informational and information is becoming more lifelike. In the rapidly developing field of artificial life, computer scientists are generating information organisms, which are virtually alive. In a manifesto issued on the occasion of the first conference devoted to artificial life, held at Los

Alamos in 1987, Chris Langton, a leading investigator in the field, declares:

> Artificial life is the study of artificial systems that exhibit behavior characteristic of natural living systems. It is the quest to explain life in any of its possible manifestations, without restriction to the particular examples that have evolved on earth. This includes biological and chemical experiments, computer simulations, and purely theoretical endeavors. Processes occurring on molecular, social, and evolutionary scales are subject to investigation. The ultimate goal is to extract the logical form of living systems. Microelectronic technology and genetic engineering will soon give us the capability to create new life forms *in silico* as well as *in vitro*.

Langton's claim becomes considerably more plausible when one recognizes the basic assumption informing his analysis. "The leap you have to make," he stresses, "is to think about machineness as being the logic of organization. *It's not the material.* There's nothing implicit about the material of anything—if you can capture its logical organization in some other medium, you can have the same 'machine' because it's the organization that constitutes the machine, not the stuff it's made of." What Langton is suggesting is that life must be defined as a property of the organization of matter, rather than a property of the matter that is organized. From this point of view, "the stuff of life is not stuff. Life is a dynamic process, and, if you can duplicate those processes—enable them to 'haunt' otherwise inanimate material—you have created life. This can be done regardless of the materials. It could even be done in a computer."[9]

If life is understood in terms of the pattern and communication of information instead of the presence or absence of material, then computer-generated information organisms might be alive in more than a trivial sense. Within the womb of the computer, virtual organisms are born, reproduce, and die. Like other living organisms, these creatures are self-organizing and self-replicating. Furthermore, with the use of genetic algorithms, it is possible for these information organisms actually to "mate" and "evolve." The reproducibility of information organisms transforms the computer into a laboratory for experiments in evolutionary biology. The study of artificial life has led Dawkins to recast Darwin's theory of evolution in terms of the information processes of genetic coding.

Dawkins's rethinking of evolution results in a transformation in human self-understanding that is almost as radical as Darwin's original theory. Dawkins begins the preface to his highly controversial book entitled *The Selfish Gene* by declaring

This book should be read almost as though it were science fiction. It is designed to appeal to the imagination. But it is not science fiction: it is science. Cliché or not, "stranger than fiction" expresses exactly how I feel about the truth. We are the survival machines—robot vehicles—blindly programmed to preserve the selfish molecules known as genes.[10]

If, as Freud insists, the revolutions introduced by Copernicus, Darwin, and psychoanalysis wound human narcissism by undercutting man's "proclivity to regard himself as lord of the world" as well as driving home the uncomfortable but undeniable truth that *the ego is not master in its own house,* then Dawkins's neo-Darwinian view of life must be understood as inflicting yet another blow to humankind's self-esteem.[11] Not only are we descendants of slime and apes, but human beings are not even the most important product of the evolutionary process. Instead of genes having been created to promote human life, human beings seem to have developed to allow genes to replicate. From this point of view, the evolutionary process is directed to the perpetuation of the genetic code rather than to the promotion of individual organisms. Far from ends-in-themselves, individuals are the means by which information reproduces. In a recent work, Dawkins reformulates his guiding insight: "We—and that means all living things—are survival machines programmed to propagate the digital database that did the programming. Darwinism is now seen to be the survival of the survivors at the level of pure, digital code."[12] In an argument that unexpectedly recalls Hegel's analysis of the universal march of *Geist* in and through the lives of individuals, Dawkins maintains that "a river of information" flows through all living beings. This analysis of life obviously obscures the line between the living and the nonliving. As Hegel argues that nature and spirit are alternative embodiments of a common dialectical structure, so Dawkins suggests that living organisms and nonliving entities are contrasting inscriptions of shared digital codes and information.

The suggestion of noteworthy similarities between Hegel's absolute idealism, on the one hand, and, on the other, the most advanced information theory and evolutionary biology seems far-fetched until we realize that Dawkins extends his genetic analysis from natural organism to cultural systems. Though starting from an investigation of biology rather than culture, Dawkins comes to the same conclusion as Geertz: there is a strict parallel between cultural symbols and genes. Dawkins labels the cultural analogue of the gene a "meme." "A 'meme,'" Dawkins writes, is "a unit of cultural inheritance, hypothesized as analogous to the partic-

ulate gene, and as naturally selected by virtue of its 'phenotypic' consequences on its own survival and replication in the cultural environment."[13] The meme, in other words, functions in relation to the
individual human mind in the same way that the gene functions in relation to the individual human organism. As the gene reproduces itself
through the organism, so the meme reproduces itself through the mind.
Dawkins goes so far as to insist that "memes should be regarded as living
structures, not just metaphorically but technically. When you plant a
fertile meme in my mind you literally parasitize my brain, turning it
into a vehicle for the meme's propagation in the same way that a virus
may parasitize the genetic mechanism of the host cell."[14] As examples of
memes, Dawkins lists "tunes, ideas, catch-phrases, clothes fashions, ways
of making pots or of building arches." "Just as genes propagate themselves in the gene pool by leaping from body to body via sperms or eggs,
so memes propagate themselves in the meme pool by leaping from brain
to brain via a process which, in the broad sense, can be called imitation."[15]
If Dawkins's point is translated into Geertz's terms, the individual mind
appears to be the vehicle for a memetic conception. Echoes of Hegelian
Geist again can be heard in this formulation. While the Absolute Idea,
which is the universal Subject, unfolds in and through particular ideas
of individual subjects, so transpersonal memes replicate themselves in
and through ideas that seem to be personal.

For Dawkins, however, the relation between genes and memes is more
than analogical. Since they are different versions of common information
processes, biological and cultural systems are inextricably bound together.
The interplay of genetic and memetic processes creates "the extended
phenotype," which Dawkins defines as "all effects of a gene upon the
world. . . . The conventional phenotype is the special case in which the
effects are regarded as being confined to the individual body in which
the gene sits. In practice it is convenient to limit 'extended phenotype'
to cases where the effects influence the survival chances of the gene, posi-
tively or negatively."[16] With the introduction of the notion of the extended phenotype, the far-reaching cultural implications of Dawkins's
analysis finally emerge. Rather than dualistic opposites separated by an
unbridgeable Cartesian gap, nature and culture, body and mind, and the
material and the immaterial are interfaces of processes whose primary
purpose is to ensure the survival of information coded in genes. If life
is defined in terms of patterns of information instead of material entities
or organic substance, then the self-replication of certain information

codes is, in effect, the preservation of life. The extended phenotype includes not only cultural symbols, which are vehicles for conceptions, but the entire web of technology that human beings have created.

> Just like a bird's nest, a beaver's dam, or a groundhog's intricate set of underground tunnels, our technologies are now an integral part of our evolutionary fitness. In light of Dawkins's work, to be a scientist today and talk about human evolution divorced from technological evolution no longer makes sense. In the truest and most fundamental sense, human evolution is now inextricably bound with technological evolution. Taken to its natural conclusion, Dawkins's idea suggests that humankind is really co-evolving with its artifacts; genes that can't cope with that new reality will not survive into future millennia.[17]

This conclusion is at once radically new and surprisingly old. As Hegel long ago realized, nature and culture develop together because they are different phases of the same process. While Hegel assumes that this process is dialectical and Dawkins holds that it is digital, the *structure* of their analyses is virtually identical. Whether the river running through us is the Absolute Idea or the universal code, we are the embodiment of something like what might once have been described as the Word of God.

Having begun with anthropology and been led to something like a latter-day natural theology, let us now return to anthropology. The contributions of Dawkins and his colleagues seem to create the possibility of mediating the positions staked out by cultural constructionists and their critics. As we have seen, constructionists argue that the mind is not hardwired but is programmed by cultural symbols and systems that are historically relative. Though cultural systems bear a certain similarity to genetic codes, the former differ from the latter in their variability among different groups and mutability over time. For its critics, cultural constructionism is problematic for at least two reasons. First, they believe that the unavoidable relativism of constructionism undercuts the basis for rational judgment and thereby removes the foundation of cross-cultural and perhaps even interpersonal communication. Second, constructionism cannot account for the undeniable similarities displayed by cultural symbols separated by time and space.

In an effort to overcome both of these difficulties, some analysts are attempting to ground mental activity and, by extension, cultural production in universal natural processes. What cultural constructionists find most disturbing about this line of argument is its implicit essentialism and its inescapable reductionism. If certain aspects of human beings are natural rather than cultural, then some things about us can never be changed. As I have noted, cultural constructionists argue that the notion of nature has traditionally functioned to legitimate abusive social and political practices. The most persuasive accounts of the pernicious effects of naturalism have been developed in recent analyses of racism and sexism. If supposedly natural racial and sexual differences are unmasked as sociocultural constructions, they can be delegitimized and thus opened to transformation. Though closely related to the critique of essentialism, resistance to the reductive implications of naturalistic explanations reflects concerns that tend to be more theoretical than practical—if, indeed, such a distinction still makes sense. The implicit or explicit foundationalism of every effort to find a natural basis for mental activity renders culture epiphenomenal. When the universal morphological infrastructure is presented as immutable, causality becomes unidirectional (i.e., from ground to grounded) and all differences appear to be superficial manifestations of more essential realities.

Dawkins's reinterpretation of the nature-culture relation through the interplay of genes and memes points toward the possibility of mediating the positions of neofoundationalism and antifoundationalism. While explaining phenomena in terms of constitutive structures, the information codes that generate natural and cultural processes are neither fixed nor immutable. To the contrary, codes evolve and thus change over time. This process of evolution is no more essentially natural than it is merely cultural. Within the genetic-memetic web, "culture" influences "nature" as much as "nature" influences "culture." Accordingly, neither can be reduced to, or completely explained by, the other. All evolution is coevolution and, though this process is generally stable, nothing ever remains the same.

In spite of these noteworthy advantages over less sophisticated understandings of nature and evolutionary development, two problems continue to plague Dawkins's analysis. First, Dawkins is no more successful than Geertz in explaining the way in which culture is transmitted from person to person and generation to generation. Though genetic inheritance obviously provides the model for memetic self-replication, Dawkins is, as the following remark indicates, surprisingly vague when it comes to describing the mechanisms by which memes are relayed: "If a scientist hears, or reads about, a good idea, he passes it on to his colleagues and students. He mentions it in his articles and his lectures. If the idea catches on, it can be said to propagate itself, spreading from brain to brain."[18]

But is the process of memetic self-replication really so imprecise? Do memes pass from one brain to another in such an arbitrary way? If so, how are we to account for cultural continuity and stability? To begin to answer these questions, it is necessary to supplement Dawkins's notion of the extended phenotype with a notion of an extended genotype.

The second problem plaguing Dawkins's argument is his tendency to slip back into something like reductionism. While his analysis is not reductive in the usual sense, he remains infatuated by the dream of foundationalism. The parallels between the genetic-memetic process and the activity of Hegelian *Geist* suggest that the digital code driving nature and culture might be understood as the latest version of the logocentrism that has always tempted the Western imagination. As critics of logocentrism have repeatedly demonstrated, the problem with comprehensive systems and structures is their propensity to eliminate contingency and reduce difference to sameness. In Dawkins's work, it remains unclear whether the information processes embedded in genetic and cultural codes leave any room for the aleatory, which would be manifest in random mutagenesis. Are information systems seamless structures or can neural networks and data webs be understood as nonfoundational foundations, which create openings for the incalculable?

As I have noted, Pascal Boyer has developed a suggestive analysis of "the naturalness of religious ideas." One of the strengths of Boyer's work is that he is aware of, and conversant with, the developments in anthropology, information theory, genetics, and evolutionary biology that we have been considering. In mounting his critique of cultural constructionists, Boyer is intent on presenting a theory that can account for both the cross-cultural similarities of religious ideas and the historical transmission of cultural symbols. While Dawkins elaborates a highly provocative account of the extended phenotype, Boyer suggests, but does not develop, the way in which a cultural version of the genotype/phenotype distinction might form the basis of an adequate account of cultural transmission. It will be recalled that, whereas the genotype includes all the genes in an organism, the phenotype refers only to those genes that are actually expressed. The extended phenotype would, by analogy, represent all the memes that are actually expressed in a particular culture at a given historical moment. But if the analogy is to hold, the phenotype presumably would have to be the specification of the genotype. The question, then, becomes, How do the genotype and phenotype differ and how is the former translated into the latter? Boyer's argument is helpful at this point.

Modern biology replaced the notion of preformation with that of a genetic program, in which a DNA sequence carries, not a "copy" of an organism, but detailed instructions for the manufacture of proteins, a process that in most cases results in the growth of the normal adult organism. The central fallacy of a preformation account is to think that there must be a *structural similarity* between genotype and phenotype. Because there are long necks and four legs in adult giraffes, there must be some long-necked and four-legged aspects in the giraffe's reproductive cells.[19]

If, however, there is not a structural similarity between the genotype and the phenotype, then how is the difference between them to be explained? Most biologists agree that the genes that are actually expressed result from a combination of hereditary and environmental factors. Some genes influence other genes, and some aspects of the environment (i.e., the availability and quality of food, dietary practices, chemical pollutants, etc.) can modify genetic constitution. Though the details of genetic expression are extremely difficult to calculate with precision, matters are even more complex in the cultural domain. To determine the difference between the genotype and the phenotype, the analysis would have to be extended from genetic and environmental factors to a range of cultural influences whose limits are difficult, if not impossible, to establish.

The importance of this problem for cultural theory can be clarified by recasting the question of the relation of the genotype to the phenotype in terms of something like what Lacan describes as "the symbolic order." In this context, "the symbolic order" designates the entire set of psychosocial possibilities created by a given cultural symbol system and encoded in the unconscious of individuals. It is obvious that some of these possibilities will be realized (i.e., expressed) and others will remain latent (i.e., repressed). The symbolic order, then, forms something like the code or program that determines the subject positions available in a particular society at a particular time. One becomes a human subject by being born into the symbolic order, which exists prior to the birth and after the death of any given individual. The question that both Geertz and Dawkins leave unanswered is how the symbolic order (i.e., the genotype) is received in the psychosocial constitution of individual subjects (i.e., the phenotype).

Though he never poses the issue in exactly these terms, Boyer argues that cultural transmission and reception can be explained by grounding the anthropological investigation of cultural ideas in theories advanced by cognitive psychologists. The translation of the genotype into the phenotype obviously entails a process of selection. From Boyer's point of view, cultural constructionists cannot account for the transmission of symbols and ideas because they cannot explain how selection takes place.

> [C]ultural anthropology generally assumes a commonsense, implicit view of cultural acquisition, which is theoretically insufficient and conceals many important problems. I will call this view the theory of "exhaustive cultural transmission." The main assumption is that the anthropologically relevant aspects of the representations adult, competent members of a group entertain are entirely determined by what was given to them through cultural transmission. This is very much what is implied by recurrent elements of anthropological phraseology such as "cultural construction." What is studied by anthropologists is supposed to consist of representations created by human groups, in the absence of any relevant cognitive constraints. (22)

Boyer is convinced that there is an obvious flaw in this widely accepted and usually unexamined "anthropological theory of cognition." The insistence that cultural ideas are always mediated by other cultural ideas involves an infinite regress, which results in "nothing but a *magical* account of cultural transmission" (263). When culture is interpreted through culture, everything becomes tautological and nothing is actually explained.

In order to break out of the vicious circle created by this infinite regress, Boyer argues, it is necessary to identify natural, that is, noncultural, selective constraints, which function as something like intelligent agents or web browsers by filtering the massive quantities of information with which we are constantly bombarded.

> The notion of *constraint* plays a central role in a cognitive account of religious ideas. Selective models are based on the assumption that a set of general constraints can be described, such that they would constitute a plausible causal explanation for the observed recurrence and the patterns of transmission. They would explain, in our case, why certain types of cultural representations are more likely than others to be acquired, represented, and transmitted. . . . I will focus on two types of constraints, *evolutionary* and *cognitive*. Evolutionary constraints consist in those aspects of the selective pressure that can be said to have a direct effect on the range of religious ideas and practices found in human societies. . . . Cognitive constraints are universal features of the human mind-brain, which have a direct effect on the likelihood that certain ideas will be acquired, memorized, and transmitted. (14–15)

Throughout his analysis, Boyer concentrates more on cognitive constraints than on evolutionary ones. His consistent hyphenation of "mind-brain" underscores his denial of Cartesian dualism.

For readers whose knowledge extends beyond their own lifetime (it is not clear Boyer's does), it is obvious that in presenting his criticism of cultural constructionism, Boyer replays many of the debates between eighteenth-century empiricists and rationalists. From Boyer's perspective, cultural anthropology presupposes an empiricist epistemology in which the mind is a tabula rasa passively receiving data in a variety of forms.

> This "theory of cognition" includes two particularly implausible assumptions. One is that cultural transmission is, by and large, a *passive* process. Minds are conceived as containers of ideas, which are more or less empty at the outset of cultural acquisition and are gradually filled with whatever ready-made products are given by "the culture." The other assumption is that this filling process is *simple*. (22)

Boyer believes that if the mind is as passive and malleable as the cultural constructionists imply, we could never make sense of experience. Everything would remain, in William James's apt phrase, "a bloomin, buzzin confusion." The intelligibility of experience presupposes ordering structures, which are not themselves derived from experience. The mind-brain, in other words, is not a blank slate but is formed by a priori patterns, which might or might not be hardwired. "Prior cognitive structures," Boyer argues, "orient the subject's attention to certain aspects of the available stimuli and narrow down the range of possible generalizations. Some aspects of these constraints cannot be directly derived from the experienced stimuli; on the contrary, they are a necessary condition, if the experience in question is to have any cognitive effects at all" (26). While constantly deferring to cognitive psychology, Boyer presents what is, in effect, a transcendental argument intended to establish the conditions of the possibility of knowledge. Cognitive constraints provide channels through which experience is filtered so as to render some things possible and other things impossible. In this way, the selective constraints identified by cognitive psychologists might be able to mediate the extended genotype and the extended phenotype.

Boyer concludes that the selective cognitive constraints imposed by the mind-brain are adequate to account for the historical (i.e., diachronic) stability and the cross-cultural (i.e., synchronic) similarity of religious ideas. He stresses that one of the primary results of his study is "to show that we can reduce the apparent contingency of cross-cultural resemblance, and that of transmission, if we take into account the fact that universal cognitive processes limit the range of variation of cultural ideas" (5). Having been led to this conclusion, Boyer confronts a dilemma, which is the precise opposite of the difficulty he sees in cultural constructionism. While cultural constructionists can account for the differences but not the unity of cultural production, Boyer can explain the unity of religious ideas but has problems accounting for their differences. To his credit, Boyer recognizes this predicament and makes an effort to address it. But his response creates further difficulties for his position.

In the first place, Boyer argues, prior cognitive constraints limit but do not completely determine religious ideas. In a manner that recalls the process by which some genes are expressed and others repressed, Boyer maintains that specific religious symbols and concepts always result from the complex interaction of the mind-brain with the environment. "That a universal process exists," he argues, "does not imply that its outcome is necessarily the same in all possible circumstances. It is precisely the point of an explanatory theory to reduce diversity and to show in what manner it results from the encounter between general mechanisms, on the one hand, and many diverse circumstances, on the other" (7). If cognitive constraints might or might not be determinative in any particular situation, however, do they actually have the explanatory power Boyer attributes to them?

Second, and more problematic, Boyer unexpectedly contends that, while cognitive constraints are "the outcome of universal properties of the human mind-body," they are not necessarily innate.

> The first and main reason for positing prior, non-experience-driven cognitive structures is the argument from *under-determination*. It consists in showing that the information available to the learning subject, in a certain cognitive domain, is insufficient to infer the principles that govern adult competence. The input is amenable to indefinitely many structural interpretations, on the basis of which a simple inductive machine, tabulating recurrent patterns, could produce irrelevant principles. It must be noted that under-determination arguments, by themselves, do not entail that the cognitive structures in question are necessarily *innate*. They only entail that the acquisition process, for a certain cognitive domain, is constrained by structures that are already present, when or before that domain is acquired. (26–27)

What Boyer does not seem to realize or acknowledge is that, if the cognitive constraints of the mind-brain are not innate but are only actualized in certain situations, then their presence or absence is neither necessary nor universal but is contingent and relative. Efforts to the contrary notwithstanding, he ends up in a position of substantial agreement with the cultural constructionists he had set out to oppose.

Throughout the course of his investigation, Boyer repeatedly backs away from the most interesting implications of the arguments he advances. What he gives with one hand, he takes away with the other. Nowhere is Boyer's reluctance to carry his argument to its logical conclusion more apparent than in his failure to examine the relation between mind and brain upon which his entire argument depends. He asserts, without demonstrating, the unity of mind and brain. In different terms, Boyer never examines the interplay of cognitive and neurological processes. His reluctance to trace the connection between cognitive psychology and neuroscience is symptomatic of his lingering uneasiness with the reductionism inherent in neofoundationalism. If, however, one is willing to push Boyer's argument even farther by extending the analysis from genes and memes, as well as cognitive constraints, to the neurophysiological operation of information processes, a different kind of "foundation" begins to emerge. This "foundation" might create the possibility of nonreductive explanation.

Basic Bias

The structure and interaction of the mind and brain can be clarified by returning to the notion of the symbolic order. It will be recalled that in the course of discussing Dawkins's account of the phenotype, we had recourse to Lacan's description of the symbolic order, which is the entire set of psychosocial possibilities created by a given cultural system and encoded in the unconscious of individuals. In Lacan's famous phrase, "the unconscious is structured like a language." Lacan develops his theory of the unconscious by bringing together Hegel's analysis of consciousness and self-consciousness with Freud's reading of the unconscious, through an appropriation of Lévi-Strauss's structural anthropology. As Ortner points out, "structuralism, the more-or-less single-handed invention of Claude Lévi-Strauss, was the only genuinely new paradigm to be developed in the sixties. One might even say that it is the only genuinely original social science paradigm (and humanities too, for that matter) to be developed in the twentieth century."[20] Lévi-Strauss, in turn, draws on Saussure's linguistics to form an all-inclusive theory, which is supposed to account for the structure and interrelation of mind, society, and culture. Saussure's fundamental distinction between *la langue* (language) and *la parole* (speech) is central to Lévi-Strauss's argument. *La langue* designates the underlying system of language, which, as the totality of formal structures, supports and makes possible the actual speech events and concrete linguistic activities that Saussure labels *la parole*. Saussure explains that "in separating *langue* from *parole,* we are separating what is social from what is individual and what is essential from what is ancillary or accidental." In terms that evoke memories of transcendental philosophy, *la langue* is the condition of the possibility of *la parole*. Particular speech events are expressions of and, thus, reducible to universal structures, which, taken as a whole, constitute an atemporal system. Though actual linguistic practices vary, the structure that makes them possible is everywhere the same and does not change over time. Saussure discerns the metastructure shared by all languages in the most basic linguistic element—the sign. The constitutive structure of signs is binary opposition, which, predictably, is displayed in two fundamental relations. First, the sign is composed of the interplay between a signifier and a signified. Second, a sign assumes determinate identity by its interplay with other signs. In the best-known line in his *Course in General Linguistics,* Saussure states that, in the system of language, "there are only differences with no positive terms." Within the twofold binary structure of the sign, signifier refers to a signified, which, in turn, is defined by its relation to other signifiers.

It is important to note the formal similarities between Saussure's linguistics, on the one hand, and, on the other, perspectives as seemingly different as Hegelian philosophy, information theory, and genetic biology. In each case, particular phenomena and events are understood in terms of an underlying structure, which is general, if not universal. This structure is the generative grammar, logos, or genetic template without which nothing can exist. Furthermore, whether defined as binary, dialectical, or digital, the structure or metastructure of these ostensibly different structures is formally identical.

Lévi-Strauss creates structuralism by extending Saussure's linguistic theory to society and culture. Not only the unconscious but everything is structured like a language. Though not uninterested in psychological processes, Lévi-Strauss is, for the most part, primarily concerned to demonstrate the ways in which cultural systems mediate social relations. "In practice, structural analysis consists of sifting out the basic sets of oppositions that underlie some complex cultural phenomenon—a myth, a ritual, a marriage system—and of showing the ways in which the phenomenon in question is both an expression of those contrasts and a reworking of them, thereby producing a culturally meaningful statement of, or reflection upon, order."[21] Lévi-Strauss shares Boyer's preoccupation with explaining cross-cultural similarities but not his concern with accounting for cultural transmission. In classical structural terms, Lévi-Strauss brackets diachronic relations and concentrates on synchronic associations. By comparing and contrasting myths, symbols, and rituals in different cultures, Lévi-Strauss thinks it is possible to identify deep structural elements that are universal. Though they form the foundation of culture, these structures are, in Boyer's terms, noncultural. Moreover, since structural elements are, as Saussure demonstrates, diacritical, they form, when taken as a whole, a comprehensive system. Lévi-Strauss's systematic impulse is every bit as strong and persistent as Hegel's. The unspoken ambition of Lévi-Strauss's structural anthropology is to rewrite Hegel's *Encyclopedia of the Philosophical Sciences* as *The Encyclopedia of the Human Sciences*.

Lévi-Strauss realizes that the strength of his theory depends on his ability to establish the interconnection of the cultural, social, psychological, and biological dimensions of experience. His brief essay "The Effectiveness of Symbols" represents one of his clearest and most concise attempts to effect this integration. The purpose of this text is to explain a childbirth ritual practiced by the Cuna tribe in Panama by establishing its structural similarities with psychoanalytic practices. As the title implies, the question that drives Lévi-Strauss's inquiry is, How can symbols be effective? Since the problem to which the Cuna myth and ritual are addressed is a difficult childbirth, the question Lévi-Strauss actually poses is, What must be the relation between mind and brain or the mental and the material if cultural symbols are to have not only psychological but also physiological effects?

After a careful analysis of the details of the Cuna myth and a consideration of the interplay between myth and ritual in the curative rite administered by the shaman, Lévi-Strauss concludes that the condition of the possibility of the effectiveness of symbols is the isomorphism of conscious, unconscious, and biological processes. The conscious reenactment of the myth in the ritual is intended to trigger unconscious regulatory mechanisms, which, in turn, bring about physiological changes. In light of this argument, it appears that Lacan does not so much extend the structuralist argument from anthropology to psychoanalysis, as directly appropriate Lévi-Strauss's depiction of the linguisticality of the unconscious.

> The unconscious . . . is always empty—or, more accurately, it is as alien to mental images as is the stomach to the foods which pass through it. As the organ of a specific function, the unconscious merely imposes structural laws upon inarticulated elements, which originate elsewhere—impulses, emotions, representations, and memories. We might say, therefore, that the preconscious is the individual lexicon where each of us accumulates the vocabulary of his personal history, but that this vocabulary becomes significant, for us and for others, only to the extent that the unconscious structures it according to its laws and thus transforms it into language. . . . If we add that these structures are not only the same for everyone and for all areas to which the function applies, but that they are few in number, we shall understand why the world of symbolism is infinitely varied in content, but always limited in its laws. There are many languages, but very few structural laws which are valid for all languages.[22]

Though drawing on structural linguistics and psychoanalysis instead of cognitive psychology, this insight is completely consistent with Boyer's conclusion. But whereas Boyer fails to examine the interconnection between mind and brain, which he necessarily presupposes, Lévi-Strauss pushes his argument beyond the mental and psychological to the material and physiological. In his summary of the relation between the Cuna ritual and psychoanalysis, he attempts to establish the link between mind and brain.

> The analogy between these two methods would be even more complete if we admit, as Freud seems to have suggested on two different occasions, that the description in psychological terms of the structure of psychoses and neuroses must one day be replaced by physiological, or even biochemical, concepts. This possibility may be at hand, since recent Swedish research has demonstrated chemical differences resulting from the amounts of polynucleids in the nerve cells of the normal individual and those of the psychotic. Given this hypothesis or any other of the same type, the shamanistic cure and the psychoanalytic cure would become strictly parallel. It would be a matter, either way, of stimulating an organic transformation, which would consist of essentially a structural reorganization, by inducing the patient intensively to live out a myth—either received or created by him—whose structure would be, at the unconscious level, analogous to the structure whose genesis is sought on the organic level. The effectiveness of symbols would consist precisely in this "inductive property," by which formally homologous structures, built out of different ma-

terials and different levels of life—organic processes, unconscious mind, rational thought—are related to one another.[23]

For symbols to be effective, Lévi-Strauss insists, there must be a formal or structural identity among conscious, unconscious, and organic processes, which allows for a change at one level to effect change at another level. Since causality in this scheme is a two-way street, this position is not reductive in a simplistic or straightforward way. Organic stimulation can effect a structural reorganization of the unconscious as well as consciousness, and, conversely, a structural reorganization of consciousness and the unconsciousness can result in organic stimulation.

In spite of this complex account of causality, critics of Lévi-Strauss have repeatedly charged him and his followers with reductionism. Structuralism, poststructuralists, among others, insist, is nothing more than inverted and systematized Platonism. Though no longer transcendent, structuralist forms are still eternal. Having descended from the heavens, essential structures are now immanent in the mind and body. Furthermore, since Lévi-Strauss is persuaded that cultural symbols form systems, structuralism is actually a latter-day version of Hegelianism and, as such, could be understood as extending the repressive logocentrism characteristic of Western philosophy, society, and culture.

While agreeing with cultural constructionists' insistence that structuralism is but another rendition of neofoundationalism, poststructuralists do not simply propose an antifoundational position. Alternative critical strategies devised by poststructuralists reflect a recognition of the way in which cultural constructionists unwittingly perpetuate the very philosophical tradition they claim to oppose. As I have noted, cultural constructionism presupposes a notion of the thetic subject, which is most fully described and analyzed in Hegel's systematic philosophy. If ostensible nature is actually culture and all culture is a product of human activity, objectivity collapses into subjectivity. The omnipotent God dies but is reborn in the sovereign subject, who creates the world in its own image. In this way, cultural constructionism remains bound by, and committed to, the ontotheological tradition.

There is, however, another reason that poststructuralists are not content with merely countering structuralism by proposing antifoundational arguments. Like Kierkegaard, who, in resisting Hegelianism, realized that "to do the opposite is also a form of imitation," poststructuralists know that to oppose structuralism is to provide further evidence of its truth. If the structure of structure is binary opposition, then opponents inevitably affirm structuralism in their denial of it. Structuralism must be criticized in the same way that Kierkegaard attacked Hegel—indirectly. Instead of opposing from without, it is necessary to criticize *as if* from within by showing the impossibility of structuralism *on its own terms*. Though the contexts vary and emphases differ, the common thread running through poststructuralists' critiques of structuralism is the effort to demonstrate that every structure necessarily entails as a condition of its own possibility that which is also a condition of its own impossibility. As if to mime transcendental analysis, the poststructuralist deconstruction of structuralism articulates "quasi-transcendental" structures, which undercut that which they nonetheless ground. Structures, which seem to be complete, are inevitably constituted by processes of exclusion, which render them unavoidably incomplete. Contrary to the principles of both Aristotelian and dialectical logic, every structure "contains" that which it cannot contain as an "exterior" that is "interior." This "outside," which is "inside," faults structures in a way that leaves them open to both the irreducibility of altarity and the incalculability of the aleatory.

Shadowing Theory

One of the most intriguing but least examined formulations of this poststructural critique of structuralism is suggested by Derrida in a parenthetical reference offered in the course of his extended analysis of Mallarmé in *Dissemination*. Derrida notes in passing that the deconstructive notion (or "nonnotion") of undecidability bears a certain resemblance to Gödel's famous incompleteness theorem. In a 1931 essay entitled "On Formally Undecidable Propositions of Principia Mathematica and Related Systems," Gödel demonstrated the inherent limitations of any formal system. While the logical support for Gödel's incompleteness theorem is extremely complex, his basic conclusion is relatively straightforward: if a system is consistent, it is necessarily incomplete; more precisely, a system's consistency cannot be proven in terms of the system itself. In other words, "metalogical statements concerning the completeness and consistency of systems any more complex than logical systems of the first order cannot be demonstrated within these systems."[24] In strictly formal terms, "every consistent recursively axiomatizable extension of S [i.e., the set of axioms composing a system] is subject to the

Gödel-Rosser Theorem, and therefore has an undecidable sentence."
Gödel's theorem, Ernest Nagel and James Newman explain,

> presented mathematicians with the astounding and melancholy conclusion
> that the axiomatic method has certain inherent limitations, which rule out
> the possibility that even the ordinary arithmetic of the integers can ever
> be fully axiomatized. What is more, he proved that it is impossible to
> establish the internal logical consistency of deductive systems—elementary
> arithmetic, for example—unless one adopts principles of reasoning so
> complex that their internal consistency is as open to doubt as that of the
> systems themselves. In light of these conclusions, no final systematization
> of many important areas of mathematics is attainable, and no absolutely
> impeccable guarantee can be given that many significant branches of
> mathematical thought are entirely free from internal contradiction.[25]

Ever since its initial formulation, thinkers in a variety of fields have
been quick to appropriate Gödel's theorem for their own purposes. While
Derrida does not elaborate his insight, he does point to a certain similarity
between Gödel's demonstration of the necessary incompleteness of systems and his own claim that structures are inevitably rendered incomplete by that which also makes them possible. The term Derrida uses
for this quasi-transcendental is the same as the term Gödel uses for the
nonsystematizable condition of systems: "undecidable": "An undecidable
proposition, as Gödel demonstrated in 1931, is a proposition which, given
a system of axioms governing a multiplicity, is neither an analytic nor
deductive consequence of those axioms, nor in contradiction with them,
neither true nor false with respect to those axioms. *Teritum datur,* without
synthesis." Such undecidability, Derrida insists, is not the function of
equivocality or polysemy but "the formal or syntactical *praxis* that com-
poses and decomposes" "the lexical richness, the semantic infiniteness of
a word or concept." Irreducibly liminal, undecidability designates the
precise operation that simultaneously brings together and holds apart the
binary, dialectical, or digital oppositions constitutive of every system and
all structures. As such, this function "is the 'between,' whether it names
fusion or separation, that thus carries all the force of the operation."[26]
Unencompassable within any structure and incomprehensible within any
system, the operation of the "undecidable between" is nothing other than
the condition of the possibility and the impossibility of structures and
systems. When read in this way, Gödel's theorem seems to imply something like the nonfoundational foundation for which we have been
searching.

This apparent detour through the poststructuralist critique of structuralism seems to have led us away from the problem of the relationship between the mind and the brain, but this is not the case. To the contrary, the poststructuralist critique of structuralism provides resources for rethinking the interplay between the mind and the brain in a way that builds upon Lévi-Strauss's insights but does not necessarily lead to the reductionism and foundationalism resulting from his lingering logocentrism. What is required is a poststructuralist critique of Lévi-Strauss's effort to ground conscious and unconscious activity in the organic and physiological processes of the brain. This might be possible if something like Gödel's theorem is at work in neurological information processes. What if the operations underlying mental functions are riddled with undecidable lapses, which render thought both possible and impossible?

This unlikely prospect is opened up by the extraordinarily suggestive work of the Oxford mathematician Roger Penrose. In his highly influential *The Emperor's New Mind* and, more recently, *Shadows of Mind: A Search for the Missing Science of Consciousness,* Penrose is developing an analysis of the relationship between the mind and the brain with far-reaching implications for our understanding of nature and culture. While situating his argument within the hotly contested field of artificial intelligence, Penrose draws on insights from a remarkable range of disciplines to suggest nothing less than rethinking the mind-brain relation by way of a reconsideration of the neurophysiological conditions of information transfer. His argument depends on a creative use of the nonfoundational principles of quantum mechanics and of Gödel's incompleteness theorem to understand biochemical processes at work in the brain.

If structuralism has the last word in defining the mind-brain relation, the mind is, in effect, a calculating machine, which is hardwired and therefore preprogrammed. The binary structure of the mind as well as the brain would, then, be as seamless as it is immutable. So understood, the mind-brain would be the functional equivalent of a computer. The binary opposition that structuralists discover everywhere can be readily translated into 0/1 code to create digital programs. Though approaching the problem from the opposite direction (i.e., from machine to mind rather than from mind to machine), this is the same view of mental operations that informs theorists who adhere to what Penrose describes as "strong Artificial Intelligence." From this perspective, "all thinking is computation; in particular, feelings of conscious awareness are invoked merely by carrying out appropriate computations."[27] If all mental activity is inescapably computational, then everything passing through the mind can be coded and decoded. Apparent enigmas and mysteries are merely codes waiting to be cracked. In this scheme, nothing remains incalculable. If thinking—be it conscious or unconscious—is computing, there seems to be no reason that mental activity cannot be perfectly simulated by computers. And this, in fact, is the conclusion drawn by those who espouse strong artificial intelligence. "According to the aspirations of *artificial intelligence,*" Penrose explains, "one strives to imitate intelligent behavior, at whatever level, by some kind of computational means" (19). The stronger the claim for the computational characteristics of mental operations, the more likely the insistence that the procedures for calculation both exhibit a "top-down" organization and are executed in a consistently sequential manner by "serially" connected machines. Recent research, however, casts doubts on the claim that such a serial top-down architecture represents the way the mind operates.

Penrose, as well as a growing number of scientists, mathematicians, and philosophers, is convinced that the assumptions that have guided most artificial intelligence research are seriously flawed. The development of inexpensive high-speed microprocessors makes it possible to experiment with alternative simulations of mental activity. It now appears that the mind neither is centrally organized nor functions serially. Synthesizing and summarizing the revolutionary conclusions currently being proposed by computer scientists and neuroscientists, Daniel Dennett writes:

> There is no single, definitive "stream of consciousness," because there is no central Headquarters, no Cartesian Theater where "it all comes together" for the perusal of a Central Meaner. Instead of such a single stream (however wide), there are multiple channels in which specialist circuits try, in parallel pandemoniums, to do their various things, creating Multiple Drafts as they go. Most of these fragmentary drafts of "narrative" play short-lived roles in the modulation of current activity but some get promoted to further functional roles, in swift succession, by the activity of a virtual machine in the brain. The seriality of this machine (its "von Neumannesque" character) is not a "hard-wired" design feature, but rather the upshot of a succession of coalitions of these specialists. . . . The result is not bedlam only because the trends that are imposed on all this activity are themselves the product of design. Some of this design is innate, and is shared with other animals. But it is augmented, and sometimes even overwhelmed in importance, by microhabitats of thought that are developed in the individual, partly idiosyncratic results of self-exploration and partly the predesigned gifts of culture. Thousands of memes, mostly borne by language, but also by wordless "images" and other data struc-

tures, take up residence in an individual brain, shaping its tendencies and thereby turning it into a mind.[28]

The mind, in other words, is neither hardwired in a way that inevitably imposes immutable structures nor a tabula rasa passively awaiting impressions. Rather, the structure of the brain is noncentralized, multidimensional, and malleable. Organized performance *emerges* from ostensibly chaotic behavior through something like a phase shift or quantum leap. While partly preprogrammed, the matrices of perception and conception are also culturally constituted and thus historically emergent and constantly changing.

It should be clear that the architectural structure and computational model informing this reading of mental activity differs from strong versions of artificial intelligence in at least three significant ways. Mental operations are not centralized but radically decentered. Since the mind does not seem to perform by sequentially following recursive algorithmic procedures, mental activity more closely approximates the parallel distributed processing, which characterizes the operation of neural networks. "A serial machine," Penrose explains, "is one that does its computations one after the other, in a step-by-step action, whereas a parallel one does many independent computations simultaneously, the results of these different computations being brought together only when appropriately many of them have been completed" (19–20). This shift from serial to parallel distributed processing carries two further consequences. In the absence of centralized control or foundational algorithms, computational processes are not governed by a single preestablished program. Though fully interconnected, neural networks are neither linear nor unified. Instead of pre-scribed codes, the rules at work in nonlinear networks *emerge* from the interaction of local networks. Finally, the architecture of this alternative computational model is bottom-up instead of top-down. While top-down design deploys fixed computational procedures, in bottom-up organization

> such clearly defined rules of operation and knowledge store are not specified in advance, but instead there is a procedure laid down for the way that the system is to "learn" and to improve its performance according to its "experience." Thus, with a bottom-up system, these rules of operation are subject to continual modification. One must allow that the system is to be run many times, performing its actions upon a continuing input of data. On each run, an assessment is made—perhaps by the system itself— and it modifies its operations, in the light of this assessment, with a view to improving this quality of output. (18)

When understood as decentered, emergent, and structured from bottom up, mental activity is obviously considerably less determined and more flexible than proponents of artificial intelligence previously have believed. But flexibility is not yet undecidability and indeterminacy is not yet incalculability. In rejecting the strong artificial intelligence position, Penrose moves beyond Dennett by attempting to establish an undecidable factor in brain functions. He argues that "appropriate physical action of the brain evokes awareness, but this physical action cannot even be properly simulated computationally" (12). In support of this claim, he offers proof for the logico-mathematical necessity as well as the neurophysiological reality of certain aspects of the human mind, which seem to lie beyond all calculation. This incalculable factor, Penrose insists, transcends consciousness yet is not mystical.

In demonstrating the logico-mathematical necessity of a noncomputational factor in the computational procedures of the mind, Penrose, as I have noted, has recourse to Gödel's theorem. By "non-computational," Penrose means "something beyond any kind of effective simulation by means of any computer based on the logical principles that underlie all electronic or mechanical calculating devices" (48–49). Inasmuch as such machines operate according to digital principles, noncomputational factors would be irreducible to digital code and, by extension, unencompassable within binary structures and dialectical systems. To show that there is something like a noncomputational ingredient at work in mental activity, Penrose presents "a simplified form" of Gödel's theorem, which, he claims, requires "only very little mathematics." While the layperson might well find little comfort in such reassurances, it is not necessary to follow the details of Penrose's defense of the theorem to appreciate the importance of the implications he draws from it. When extended beyond the limits set by Gödel, the incompleteness theorem, Penrose avers, "would seem to provide a clear-cut case, demonstrating that human mathematical understanding cannot be reduced to (knowable) computational mechanisms, where such mechanisms can include any combination of top-down, bottom-up, or random procedures. We appear to be driven to the firm conclusion that there is something essential in human understanding that is not possible to simulate by any computational means" (201).

If Penrose's defense of noncomputational aspects of mental operations is to result in anything more than a *logical* possibility, he must explain where and how such activity actually occurs. To make the transition from the possible to the actual, he turns from logic and mathematics to quantum mechanics and neurophysiology. Following his suspicion that "there *is* something in the external physical world that is actually beyond computational simulation," Penrose argues that the neurological transmission of information upon which all mental activity depends involves the principles of both classical physics, which are digitizable and thus computational, and quantum mechanics, which resist digitization and thus remain indeterminate. Penrose locates "the subtle and mysterious features of quantum physics" at the interface or synapse between neurons in the brain.[29] Messages traveling along central neural axons are digitally coded in a way that conforms to classical physics and is expressible by electronic computers. But each axon branches into dendrites and ends in synapses, which must be bridged if messages are to arrive at their destination. The delivery of the message depends on chemicals known as neurotransmitters. Each neuron is encased in something like a cytoskeleton made up of microtubules, which secrete neurotransmitters. The effect of the impulse moving along the neuron is directly proportional to the strength of the synapse, and the strength of the synapse, in turn, is a function of the strength or weakness of the neurotransmitters produced by the neuron's microtubules. The crucial point for Penrose's argument is his insistence that the activities of the microtubules are not explainable in terms of classical physics but follow rules approximating the principles of quantum mechanics. If the synaptic connections and strengths can be treated in a classical way, all mental activity is, in principle, computational even if the present state of technology does not yet permit perfect simulation. If the production of neurotransmitters is regulated by the laws of quantum mechanics, however, then the synaptic clefts remain irreducibly indeterminate and some mental activity is, in principle, noncomputational regardless of the level of technological proficiency. Like Gödel, who discloses holes in every logical structure and mathematizable system, Penrose exposes an indeterminacy in the operation of the brain, which insinuates an inescapable factor of undecidability in all mental activity. Summarizing his intricate argument, Penrose writes:

> Our picture, then, is of some kind of global quantum state which coherently couples the activities taking place within the tubes, concerning microtubules collectively right across large areas of the brain. There is some influence that this state . . . exerts on the computations taking place along the microtubules—an influence which takes delicate and precise account of the putative, missing, non-computational OR [Objective Reduction] physics that I have been strongly arguing for. The "computational" activity

of conformational changes in the tubulins controls the way in which the tubes transport materials along their outside, and ultimately influences the synapse strengths at pre- and postsynaptic endings. In this way, a little of this coherent quantum organization *within* the microtubules is "tapped off" to influence changes in the synaptic connections of the neural computer of the moment. . . . On the view that I am tentatively putting forward, consciousness would be some manifestation of this quantum-entangled internal cytoskeletal state and of its involvement in the interplay . . . between quantum and classical levels of activity. The computer-like classically interconnected system of neurons would be continually influenced by this cytoskeletal activity, as the manifestation of whatever it is that we refer to as "free will." The role of neurons, in this picture, is more like a *magnifying device* in which the smaller-scale cytoskeletal action is transferred to something which can influence other organs of the body—such as muscles. Accordingly, the neuron level of description that provides the currently fashionable picture of the brain and mind is a mere *shadow* of the deeper cytoskeletal action—and it is at this deeper level that we must seek the physical basis of *mind!* (375–76)

Penrose is suggesting that the brain functions something like a postal system in which the arrival or nonarrival of messages is a function not only of calculable but also of incalculable factors. The destructured structure of synaptic clefts is the site of undecidable operations, which produce neurotransmitters necessary for the delivery of digital messages. Since the production of these chemicals does not conform to any knowable calculus, communication through neural networks is made possible by something that remains incalculable. The incalculable, however, is incommunicable. Thus, the circuits of exchange are never complete because something is always lacking from the messages that run through them. This lack creates unavoidable interference, which simultaneously permits and interrupts the flow of communication. In this way, neurotransmitters both facilitate whatever communication occurs and communicate a certain lapse in all communication processes. At the most rudimentary stage of biomental activity, the condition of the possibility of communication is also the condition of the impossibility of communication. As Derrida constantly reminds us, some messages never arrive at their destination or arrive by not arriving, thereby both breaching and bridging the circuits with and without which thought and communication are at once possible and impossible. Far from accidents or mistakes, lapses in the delivery system make arrival possible and nonarrival unavoidable.

There is always something shadowy about the relation between mind and brain. Is mind a shadow of the more rudimentary brain? Or is the brain a shadow cast by the light of mind? When Penrose insists that "the currently fashionable picture of the brain and mind [i.e., the picture of the brain and mind as nothing but computational machines] is a mere *shadow* of the deeper cytoskeletal action—and it is at this deeper level that we must seek the physical basis of *mind,*" he seems to be espousing yet another neofoundationalism, which reduces the mental to the physical. While there can be little doubt that this is the conclusion toward which Penrose is drawn, his argument can be read differently. The "deeper level" to which he leads us is unlike any depth neuroscientists have known in the past. In his description of the "physical basis of mind," Penrose revises the characteristics of physicality and redefines the critical term "basis."

It follows from the arguments of Penrose and others that the physical is not as physical as it previously has seemed to be. If conclusions reached by researches in fields as disparate as computer science, information theory, genetic and evolutionary biology, neuroscience, and biochemistry are to be believed, materiality and immateriality are not simply opposites but are interfaces of information processes, which, though all-pervasive, are neither all-comprehensive nor completely comprehensible. The ramifications of this insight have not yet been registered by most people working in the humanities and social sciences. When the relation between the material and the immaterial is revised in terms of information processes, it becomes necessary to refigure oppositions ranging from mind/body to culture/nature. Such a rethinking of opposites does not necessarily result in a reduction of difference to identity through a neofoundational metaphysics of information. If Penrose is right, the "basis" of both brain and mind is a nonfoundational foundation, which simultaneously grounds and ungrounds nature and culture. Rather than seamless systems and faultless structures, infoprocesses informing everything that appears to be "natural" and "cultural" are incomplete nets and open-ended webs, which are riddled by operations that are irreducibly incalculable and hence undecidable.

The strange notion of a nonfoundational foundation makes it possible to move beyond the theoretical standoff between neofoundationalists and antifoundationalists. If nature is not merely natural and culture is not only cultural—if nature as well as culture is informational—if circuits of information transfer inevitably include lapses, then the "basis" upon which everything rests is a nonfoundational foundation, which creates an opening for nonreductive explanations.

With the emergence of this theoretical prospect, something ends and something begins. The liminal domain of such ending and beginning always remains shadowy. Shadows, it seems, cast their spell at twilight— that strange, enigmatic time between day and night, that strange, enigmatic place between light and dark. Does the interplay of day and night create twilight? Do light and dark join to cast shadows? Or is twilight the difference that constitutes day day and night night? Are shadows the "between" that makes light and dark possible? Only a shadowy theory—a theory that comes to light in the twilight of the idols, a theory that rises, like the owl of Minerva, with the falling of twilight—only a theory whose shadow can never be dispelled might be able to begin to address the urgent theoretical and practical questions we face.

Five

Terminal Condition

LSD is a way of mining the invisible electronic world; it releases a person from acquired verbal and visual habits and reactions, and gives the potential of instant and total involvement, both all-at-onceness and all-at-oneness, which are the basic needs of people translated by electric extensions of their central nervous systems out of the old rational, sequential value system. The attraction to hallucinogenic drugs is a means of achieving empathy with our penetrating electric environment, an environment that in itself is a drugless inner trip.

MARSHALL MCLUHAN

Cyberspace. A consensual hallucination experienced daily by billions of legitimate operations, in every nation, by children being taught mathematical concepts. . . . Lines of light ranged in the nonspace of the mind, clusters of data. Like city lights, receding.

WILLIAM GIBSON

Much more than the philosophic theory of the unity of matter, it was probably the old conception of the Earth-Mother, bearer of embryo-ores, which crystallized faith in artificial transmutation (that is, operated in a laboratory). It was the encounter with the symbolism, myths and techniques of the miners, smelters and smiths that probably gave rise to the first alchemical operations.

MIRCEA ELIADE

Electronics . . . all-at-onceness . . . all-at-oneness . . . drugs . . . crystals . . . cyberspace . . . hallucination . . . lights . . . light . . . Earth Mother . . . mining . . . miners . . . smelters . . . alchemical operations: scattered points that seem utterly disconnected and unrelated. What thread, what fiber links them without necessarily drawing them together? If there were such a line, it would not always be above ground but would often be something like an underground or underwater cable; nor would it always be obvious, for it frequently would be occult. Never a thread, this line is sometimes metal—usually copper (whose therapeutic powers have long been acknowledged) and always heavy, heavy metal. More recently, this line for which we always seem to be searching has become light, unbearably light—a mere fiber or even an immaterial link (up and down) with extraterrestrial bodies. Within this net that is becoming ever more light, our condition gradually becomes terminal. The end, it seems, is approaching without yet arriving from the ever-not-so-distant future. We are counting down or up to the end and the beginning of a new millennium. As in the past, at least in the past we know or think we can know, the transition from one to another millennium appears to be a time of endings as well as beginnings, deaths as well as rebirths. The darker the old era seems, the brighter the New Age appears. Always inscribed within some economy of redemption, millenarianism promises a new world in which all things are transformed. When read religiously, and it is difficult to imagine a millenarianism that is not implicitly or explicitly religious, the New Age will be the end of time and dawn of eternity. The end of time is, in effect, the collapse of space. Along the margin that draws together and holds apart the epochs between which we are suspended, every place is terminal space. In this terminal space of endtime, the dreams of ontotheology and theoesthetics, many believe, come true. Presence becomes totally present in a kingdom that is completely realized here and now. This is a story that is as old as history itself, and yet, it might not be old enough, for it remains all too historical.

A century ending with a strange return of millenarianism in multiple guises began with apocalyptic dreams that have repeatedly run wild. Throughout modernity, diverse representatives of the avant-garde have been united by a certain millenarianism that usually borders on the apocalyptic. Though the vision of the New Age varies, the expectation of a cataclysmic reversal or radically transformative revolution remains remarkably constant. Whether change is understood as outward or inward, sociopolitical or psychomystical, the birth of the new always seems to require the cleansing of impurities. With the death of God, the high priest of salvation becomes the artist who is the architect of New Jerusalem, which finally will be built.

The far-reaching implications of the transfer of power from priest to artist-architect are undeniably evident in Italian futurism, which emerged in the years immediately prior to the outbreak of World War I. Fully committed to the modernist project of industrialization, Filippo Marinetti calls for a break with the pastoral past and a rush into the urban future.

> When, oh when, he cries, will you rid yourselves of the lymphatic ideology
> of your deplorable Ruskin . . . with his morbid dreams of primitive rustic
> life, with his nostalgia for Homeric cheeses and legendary spinning-
> wheels, with his hatred for the machine, of steam and electricity, this
> mania for antique simplicity is like a man who in full maturity wants to
> sleep in his cot again and feed again at the breast of a decrepit old nurse
> in order to regain the thoughtless state of infancy.[1]

The machine, steam, and electricity—above all electricity—are the vehicles that will transport the futurist into the New Age. Electricity creates
the possibility of *speed,* which promises to break the chains that bind
humankind to time and space. In the famous manifesto, published in *Le
Figaro* on February 20, 1909, Marinetti confidently declares: "We stand
on the last promontory of the centuries! . . . Why should we look back,
when what we want is to break down the mysterious doors of the Impossible. Time and Space died yesterday. We already live in the absolute,
because we have created eternal, omnipresent speed."[2] This point is important enough for Marinetti to repeat it several years later in his infa-
mous *War, the World's Only Hygiene.* "We create the new aesthetic of
speed. We have almost abolished the concept of space and notably dimin-
ished the concept of time. We are thus preparing the ubiquity of multi-
plied man. We will arrive at the abolition of the year, the day, and the
hour."[3] The hallucinogenic effect of speed translates one from the world
of time and space into the omnipresence of the absolute.

It is important to note that Marinetti was not alone in his search for
an aesthetic of speed. Cubism's experiments with simultaneity and su-
prematism's probing of the fourth dimension can also be understood as
a quest for the experience of an all-at-onceness that is an all-at-oneness.
As Einstein had argued only a few years before these artistic innovations,
when we reach the speed of light, time itself is reversed. Nor was Marinetti the only one who believed that the dream of omnipresence could
be realized through electricity. For many early-twentieth-century artists
and nonartists, the Eiffel Tower, completed in 1889 for the Paris World's
Fair commemorating the centenary of the French Revolution, became
the symbol of the New Age. Mixing piety and irony to create a millenarianism that must be taken seriously, Apollinaire writes:

> At last you are tired of this old world.
> I shepherd Eiffel Tower, the flock of bridges bleats this morning
> You are through with living in Greek and Roman antiquity
> Here, even the automobiles seem to be ancient

Only religion has remained brand new, religion
Has remained simple as simple as the aerodrome hangars
It's God who dies Friday and rises again on Sunday
It's Christ who climbs in the sky better than any aviator
He holds the world's altitude record
Pupil Christ of the eye
Twentieth pupil of the centuries he knows what he's about
And the century, become a bird, climbs skyward like Jesus.[4]

At the end of the first decade of the century, the Eiffel Tower and its image underwent an important change that both is emblematic of the shift from the eighteenth to the nineteenth century and anticipates the transition from the mechanical age of industrial capitalism to the electronic age of postindustrial capitalism. In 1909, the year in which Marinetti published his Futurist Manifesto, the first regular broadcast system was installed on the Eiffel Tower. Though Robert Delaunay's paintings from this period present the tower as a synecdoche for the modernity, the significance of its electrification becomes evident only in Vicente Huidobro's 1917 work entitled *Eiffel Tower,* which was dedicated to Delaunay.

Eiffel Tower
Guitar of the sky

> Your wireless telegraphy
> Draws words to you
> As a rose-arbour draws bees

In the night the Seine
No longer flows

> Telescope or bugle
> Eiffel Tower

And a beehive of words
Or the night's inkwell

At the dawn's base
A spider with wire feet
Spins its web with clouds . . .

A bird calls
In the antennae
Of the wireless

> It is the wind
> The wind from Europe
> The electric wind[5]

The wire web at the feet of the tower grounds the wireless net created by the signal beamed around the world. For visionaries, the electric wind from Europe promised to unify the planet.

The history of the twentieth century gives ample evidence of the destructiveness of such futuristic visions. While there is no necessary relation between modernism and totalitarianism, we have discovered that a disturbing number of modernists were drawn to fascism. Speed not only creates "a new aesthetic" but is, as Paul Virilio argues, "the essence of war."[6] For Marinetti, war is the purifying ritual through which we must pass if we are to enter the New Age. In his incendiary Manifesto, he defiantly proclaims: "We will glorify war—the world's only hygiene— militarism, patriotism, the destructive gesture of freedom-bringers, beautiful ideas worth dying for, and scorn for women."[7] Marinetti's longing for war was soon satisfied. What started as faint sparks spread with electrifying speed to ignite a holocaust that quickly became all-consuming. According to those who fanned the flames of war, the heat generated in furnaces and ovens on and off the battlefield was supposed to burn away darkness, dirt, and disease and leave only light, propriety, and health. The color of this apocalyptic light was gold—gold that was pure as Margarete's flaxen locks.

It is a surprisingly short step from the futurists' apocalypticism to influential versions of the cybertopia many are projecting for the next century. Some of the most imaginative, compelling, and disturbing visions of possible futures opened by the current telecommunications revolution grow out of a curious mixture of vestiges of the '6os drug counterculture, New Age religion, and seemingly unbounded technophilia. Before fast-forwarding to the end of this century and beyond, it will be helpful to rewind from the beginning of this century, through the nineteenth century, to the ancient sources of modernism.

In a 1969 *Playboy* interview, Marshall McLuhan, whose reading of the mediascape remains surprisingly suggestive in spite of its obvious shortcomings, noted a startling series of relays whose connection is far from obvious.

> LSD is a way of mining the invisible electronic world; it releases a person from acquired verbal and visual habits and reactions, and gives the potential of instant and total involvement, both all-at-onceness and all-at-oneness, which are the basic needs of people translated by electric extensions of their central nervous systems out of the old rational, sequential value system. The attraction to hallucinogenic drugs is a means of achieving

empathy with our penetrating electric environment, an environment that in itself is a drugless inner trip.[8]

Though not immediately obvious, the fiber that links these disparate points is forged in the crucible of alchemy. Alchemy is, of course, a magico-religious practice devised to transform base metals into gold. Closely related to different strands of medieval Jewish and Christian mysticism and extremely important for the rise of modern science, alchemy originates in ancient rituals associated with mining and metallurgy.[9] Historian of religions Mircea Eliade argues that, throughout history in a broad range of cultures, the activities of mining are closely related to those religions devoted to the earth goddess. Within this framework, the earth is the generative *matrix* from which all arises and to which everything longs to return. Minerals are believed to be embryos that grow within the womb of mother earth. Gestation is a process of purification in which all minerals, given enough time, will eventually turn into gold. "It is indeed remarkable," Eliade observes, that

> traditions, as numerous as they are widespread, should bear witness to this belief in the finality of nature. If nothing impedes the process of gestation, all ores will, in time, become gold. "If there were no exterior obstacles to the execution of her designs," wrote a Western alchemist, "Nature would always complete what she wished to produce. . . . That is why we have to look upon the births of imperfect metals as we would on abortions and freaks that come about only because Nature has been, as it were, misdirected, or because she has encountered some fettering resistance or certain obstacles that prevent her from behaving in her accustomed way. . . . Hence although she wishes to produce only one metal, she finds herself constrained to create several. Gold and only gold is the child of her desires. Gold is her legitimate son because only gold is a genuine production of her efforts." (50)

Within this scheme, the labor of the miner assists the labor of the Mother. The miner is something like a gynecologist and obstetrician who attempts to prevent abortions, freaks, and bastards by facilitating the birth of the legitimate son. For the miner, the son is the gold that glimmers with the color of the sun. While probing the darkest depths of the Mother, the miner remains committed to a solar religion.

The role of the miner-gynecologist-obstetrician is to accelerate the labor process. In other words, the miner's contribution to nature is *speed,* whose agents are *heat* and *fire.* Within the religious economy of mining, it is not sufficient to extract the embryo or fetus from the womb. The

child, who is preferably a son, must be polished and refined by a process
of cleansing and purification. This need for purity and refinement gave
raise to the techniques and rituals of metallurgy. The metallurgist is the
"master of fire" who generates the heat necessary to speed up the transformation of the base into the pure. The process of purifying dark and
dirty traces of the base underground to form or rarefied products that
are light and clean is called *sublimation*. It is rarely noted that the metallurgist first developed the techniques of sublimation.

The process of sublimation takes place in ovens or furnaces, which
serve as a substitute womb or artificial uterus. Surrogate motherhood, it
seems, is not a recent invention. As a result of the association between
womb/uterus and furnace/oven, the site of metallurgical practice had to
be sanctified by either animal or human sacrifices. Describing a particularly illuminating example of this ritual practice, Eliade writes:

> Evidence that human sacrifices were made for metallurgical purposes is
> to be found in Africa. Among the Achewa of Nyasaland, the man who
> wishes to construct a furnace applies to a magician (*sing-anga*). The latter
> prepares 'medicines,' places them in a stripped maize cob and instructs a
> small boy how to throw it at a pregnant woman, causing her to miscarry.
> The magician then looks for the fetus and burns it, with other medicines,
> in a hole in the ground. The furnace is then built over the hole. The
> Atonga have a custom of throwing into the furnace a portion of the pla-
> centa to ensure the success of the smelting. (67–68)

As we have already discovered (chapter 3), traces of the ancient human
sacrifice can be found in the ashes that remain in twentieth-century ovens
constructed for no less sinister rituals of purification.

The smelting required for purification involves a dissolution of form
into *prima materia*. The process of transformation that the metallurgist
seeks to speed up presupposes that all substances are variations of an
original Ur-substance. By burning away polluting differences, fire returns the many materials to the one substance from which they all originate. The birth of the one, therefore, presupposes the death of the many.
The ritual sacrifice that sanctifies the womb-oven prefigures the sacrifice
enacted in the heat of the furnace. According to the cosmology of many
ancient metallurgical practices, smelting entails something like a *regressus
ad uterum* that returns matter to its original matrix. Mother, material,
and matter meet in *mater,* which is their common origin. This common
origin is more than material; it is also verbal. By digging deep enough,

one discovers a point where *mother, matrix, material,* and *matter* converge. All four words, Joseph Shipley explains, share a common stem: "'amma.' Baby talk, reduplicated form of *ma,* sound of suckling; *mamma. . . . amah:* wet-nurse, in India. Gk *meter:* mother. *metropolis:* mother city; first, see of a chief bishop of the Mother Church. *metropolitan. metronymic. metrorrhagia* (Gk *metron:* womb L and E *mater; alma mater; matriculate.* maternal, *maternity, matron. matroclinous. matrix:* first, the uterus. *material, matter.*"[10]

It begins to become apparent that the sublimation enacted by the metallurgist must be read in many ways. When psychoanalytically interpreted, the sublimation of base material into gold ritually enacts the sublimation of the desire for the mother. From this point of view, the subtext of mining and metallurgy is, in effect, incest. If earth is our Mother, then entering the earth is penetrating the mother. Reunion with the mother fulfills desire and harbors the prospect of negating the individual as such. If womb becomes tomb, eros and thanatos join in a time "before" culture when everything seemed to be one. This account of the rituals associated with mining suggests a variation on Freud's myth of origins. Instead of resulting from the originary violence inflicted by the sons upon the primal father, culture, which functions as a technique for sublimating primal desires, begins at the mouth of the mine. Civilization is never merely symbolic, for it always involves various technologies for cultivating so-called nature. The penetration of the earth prepares the soil for seeds, which eventually blossom in latter-day cultural systems and networks. Inasmuch as cultivation is inseparable from sublimation, technology simultaneously prohibits what it permits and permits what it prohibits. As an opening that is a closing and a closing that is an opening, technology is a matrix that supplements the matrix, which appears to be original. The fiber of this matrix must be left dangling for the moment, but will eventually return in a new light.

Alchemy extends and refines the techniques of metallurgy. No longer satisfied with speeding up nature by generating heat, the alchemist seeks a supplement to the supplement of fire. In alchemy, the religious prosthesis gives way to the chemical prosthesis. The philosophers' stone is the magical substance that is supposed to possess the power to transform base metals into gold. One of the most common forms of this "stone" was a fine white powder, which in some rituals served as an elixir. The word *elixir* actually derives from the Greek *xerion,* which "denotes a dry powder used for medicine and alchemical transmutation."[11] The alchemical elixir descends from yet more ancient hallucinogenic drugs, which once were thought to have curative and restorative powers and, in some cases, were even believed to be "chemical" agents of religious ecstasy.

The association of the philosophers' stone and elixirs with religious rituals points to a persistent motivation for alchemical practice. Far from being driven by so-called materialistic concerns, alchemy is, as Eliade insists, "a spiritual technique and a soteriology." The soteriological technique employed by the alchemist presupposes an isomorphism between the macrocosm and the microcosm. By refining base metals into gold, the alchemist seeks to purify both self and world. The goal of alchemy is to become as good as gold—pure gold. Gold is not just any substance but the most rarefied form of the *prima materia,* which is the true substance of all things. From this point of view, gold is, in effect, God. To become as good as gold is, therefore, to become God. In his *Opus Mago-Cabbalisticum,* Georg von Welling writes: "[O]ur intention is not directed towards teaching anyone how to make gold but towards something much higher, namely how Nature may be seen and recognized as coming from God and God from Nature."[12]

If gold is the purest form of nature, which, in turn, is God, then the alchemist's magic would seem to bestow the elixir of immortality. Over the years, the philosophers' stone has been transformed from its original white powder into acid, angel dust, ecstasy, and speed. When the dose is right and the charge sufficient, speed breaks the chains of space and time. "Like the good 'philosopher' or mystic that he was," Eliade concludes, the alchemist

> was afraid of time. He does not admit himself to be an essentially temporal being, he longed for the beatitude of paradise, aspired to eternity and pursued immortality, the *elixir vitae.* . . . Above all we must bear in mind that the alchemist became the master of time, when, with his various apparatus, he symbolically reiterated the primordial chaos and "death and resurrection." Every initiation was a victory over death, i.e., temporality; the initiated proclaimed himself "immortal"; he had forged for himself a post-mortem existence that he claimed to be indestructible.[13]

The alchemist, in other words, anticipates the futurist who, as I have noted, declares: "Time and Space died yesterday. We already live in the absolute, because we have created eternal, omnipresent speed."

Though alchemy starts with the metalurgist's effort to assist mother nature by speeding up her labor, the alchemist ends by becoming something like a god. The vision of the alchemist's creative power emerges in the fantasy of his ability to create an homunculus. As we shall see, the homunculus is the distant ancestor of contemporary alchemists' replicants, androids, terminators, and cyborgs. Since divine power is nowhere more evident than in the capacity to produce something like a human being, the aspiration to create a homunculus actually expresses the desire to become God. As humankind's Faustian striving repeatedly demonstrates, it is always possible for the creator to lose control of his creation. In certain Kabbalistic variations of the alchemical myth, the homunculus appears as the golem, who discloses unexpected consequences of human desire. In an 1808 edition of the romantic publication *Journal for Hermits,* Jakob Grimm records the following account of the golem:

> After saying certain prayers and observing certain fast days, the Polish Jews make the figure of a man from clay or mud, and when they pronounce the miraculous Shemhamphoras [the name of God] over him, he must come to life. He cannot speak, but he understands fairly well what is said or commanded. They call him golem and use him as a servant to do all sorts of housework. But he must never leave the house. On his forehead is written '*emeth* [truth]; every day he gains weight and becomes somewhat larger and stronger than all the others in the house, regardless of how little he was to begin with. For fear of him, they therefore erase the first letter, so that nothing remains but *meth* [he is dead], whereupon he collapses and turns to clay again. But one man's golem once grew so tall, and he heedlessly let him keep on growing so long that he could no longer reach his forehead. In terror he ordered the servant to take off his boots, thinking that when he bent down he could reach his forehead. So it happened, and the first letter was successfully erased, but the whole heap of clay fell on the Jew and crushed him.[14]

As the line of descent from the homunculus and the golem to Frankenstein and the Terminator suggests, today's cyborgs not only promise immortality but also threaten destruction.

This unexpected genealogy of the cyborg points to the fiber that links the final point in McLuhan's scattered circuit: mining . . . hallucinogenic drugs . . . electronics. When the golem is electrified, the matrix becomes the net, which now is known as "the matrix." The transition from the religious, to the chemical, to the electronic prosthesis extends the process of sublimation in which matter becomes increasingly rarefied or idealized and thus appears ever lighter until it becomes nothing but light. At this point, the thread we have been tracing becomes visible as a fiber optic. But these lines of communication are not yet complete; the way from the alchemical matrix to the electronic net passes through the grid of nineteenth-century speculative philosophy.

The abiding importance of alchemy and the so-called occult sciences for nineteenth-century romanticism and idealism is usually overlooked. Our consideration of the religious dimensions of alchemy implies that it is no accident that "mining and disciplines like geology and mineralogy exerted on the Romantic scientists an almost magical attraction; many of the Romantics (e.g., Novalis, Steffens, von Humboldt, Baader, and Schubert) studied at the famous Mining School at Freiberg."[15] Like their alchemical precursors, the romantics were searching for the philosophers' stone, which would allow them to enjoy the ecstasy of all-at-onceness and all-at-oneness. While for some, like Coleridge, Baudelaire, and De Quincey, the agent remained chemical, for others, like Schelling and Hegel, the drug became philosophical speculation. Hegel freely admits his interest in mysticism and occultism. When expressed in these terms, the goal of Hegel's religio-philosophical system is the unitive ecstasy in which eros and thanatos become One. The Hegelian logos is, in effect, the speculative translation of the generative matrix whose earlier guise was the Earth Mother. The relay that permits this translation is electricity.

Within Hegel's speculative vision, the absolute is an occult force that gradually reveals itself in nature and history. For Hegel, as for the alchemists, macrocosm and microcosm perfectly mirror each other. While everything exhibits an identical structure, the logos, which constitutes the identity of differences, is more clearly manifested in some things and events than in others. Once recognized, the absolute appears in all places at all times. In the natural realm, the absolute is nowhere more apparent than in the inextricably interrelated phenomena of electricity and light.

In his comprehensive philosophical system, Hegel develops a subtle revision of Schelling's philosophy of nature. Two years after leaving the Tübingen theological seminary, where he had shared a room with Hegel and Hölderlin, and one year before assuming a professorship in Jena, which was then the center of German romanticism, the young Schelling published *Ideas for a Philosophy of Nature*. This remarkable work set the course for later German idealism and, by extension, established the direction for much twentieth-century philosophy and art. Schelling devotes an entire chapter of his study of nature to the problem of electricity. "The system of nature," he argues,

> becomes obviously simpler if we assume that the cause of electrical phenomena—the force, the activity, or whatever we may call it—which seems thrown into conflict in electrical phenomena, is one originally quiescent

force, which in its unity with itself works perhaps merely mechanically, and first acquires a higher efficacy only when nature divides it within itself for special purposes. If that which causes electrical phenomena is originally *one* force or one matter . . . , then it is intelligible why opposite electricities fly towards each other—why divided forces strive to reunite.[16]

The reason for Schelling's fascination with electricity is clear: in this elusive phenomenon, he discerns the concrete expression of the absolute in the domain of nature. In Schelling's idealistic vision, the absolute is "the point of indifference" from which everything emerges and to which all seeks to return. In a manner reminiscent of Plato's myth of origins in the *Symposium,* electricity captures the erotic rhythms that constitute the life pulse of the cosmos.

Hegel's trenchant criticism of Schelling tends to obscure the abiding debt he owes to his erstwhile friend and roommate. From Hegel's perspective, Schelling's version of absolute idealism is, in every sense of the word, regressive. The *Indifferenzpunkt* for which Schelling searches collapses differences in an identity that can bear nothing other than itself. While preserving Schelling's desire for unity, Hegel insists that a return to an original oneness is impossible. If the division and fragmentation plaguing modern experience are to be overcome, it must be through a "progressive" dialectical process in which differences are preserved while opposition is overcome. In his reworking of Schelling's account of electricity, Hegel suggests the genealogy of his notion of the absolute.

Electricity, Hegel acknowledges, "appears as an occult agent, and resembles the occult qualities assumed by the scholastics."[17] The task of the philosopher is to render the occult perfectly transparent. In his most concise formulation of the philosophico-ontological significance of electricity, Hegel writes:

Electricity is infinite form differentiated within itself, and is the unity of these differentials; consequently the two bodies are inseparably bound together, like the north and south poles of a magnet. Magnetism is mere mechanical activity, however, and is therefore merely an opposition in the activity of movement. . . . In electricity, however, these fluctuating differentials are physical, for they are in the light. . . . Negative electricity is attracted by positive electricity, but repulsed by negative. In that the differentials unite themselves, they communicate themselves to each other; as soon as they have posited a unity, they fly apart again, and vice versa. . . . In the electrical process, each of the two distinct bodies has a differentiated determination that is only posited through the other, but in the face of which the further individuality remains free and distinct.[18]

While thoroughly committed to the metaphysics of light that runs throughout the ontotheological tradition, Hegel, in contrast to many others, insists that light does not simply destroy differences but is "the sublation of diremption." This notion of sublation (*Aufheben*) is Hegel's translation of alchemical sublimation. Through the process of sublation, opposition is negated by establishing the unity of differences. The difference between Hegel's unity *in the midst* of differences and Schelling's *Indifferenzpunkt* is reflected in their alternative interpretations of electricity. According to Hegel, the differential structure of electricity does not emerge from an initially undifferentiated identity. To the contrary, electricity is *originally* a unity of differences. Without the difference between positive and negative charges, there can be no electricity. Electricity, therefore, is nothing other than the interplay of differences, which are constituted in and through each other. In this way, electricity displays the infinite form, which is internally differentiated, and, as such, constitutes a differential unity. When philosophically comprehended, this form, which is the substance of all things, appears as spirit.

For Hegel, the philosophers' stone is philosophical knowledge. As the white powder that establishes the unity of differences, this knowledge is the golden light of the world. Speculative reason reveals the individual to be a particular incarnation of the divine Logos, which forms the generative matrix in which all things arise and pass away. To apprehend oneself as a moment in the life of the absolute is to overcome time and space by grasping their eternal essence. Repeating and extending ancient metallurgical and alchemical rituals, Hegel's version of the *imitatio christi* involves a birth within the divine matrix, which presupposes the death of the individual as such. In the concluding lines of *Phenomenology of Spirit,* the usually sober Hegel suggests the ecstatic dimension of his philosophical vision.

> The *goal,* Absolute Knowledge, or Spirit that knows itself as Spirit, has for its path the recollection of the spirits as they are in themselves and as they accomplish the organization of their kingdom. Their preservation, regarded from the side of their free existence appearing in the form of contingency, is history; but regarded from the side of their comprehended organization, it is the science of knowledge in the sphere of appearance: the two together comprehended history; they form the inwardizing and the Calvary of absolute Spirit, the actuality, truth, and certainty of his throne, without which he would be lifeless and alone. Only
>
> > from the chalice of this realm of spirits
> > foams forth for Him his own infinitude.[19]

The continuing fermentation of the grapes of this vine produces strange brews, which many people still find intoxicating.

Stop. Cut. Fast-forward.
Time: 21st Century
Space: Terminal

The twenty-first century is rapidly becoming wired for Hegelian *Geist*. Alchemy's occult forces and Hegel's electrifying spirit become actual in electronic tele-communications networks now encircling the globe. The matrix can be understood as the electronic embodiment of something like the Hegelian Logos, which, rumors to the contrary notwithstanding, is the mother of us all. Jack in . . . jack out . . . jack off. Matter . . . material . . . mother . . . matrix . . . sublation . . . sublimation. Everything . . . everyone is (always already) wired.

Pause. Rewind.
Not much. Just a few decades.
Time: End of the 20th century
Place: Cyberspace

In art and architecture as well as in life, everything is becoming immaterial. If grand narratives were still believable, it would be possible to imagine a philosopher arguing that the history of the twentieth century is the story of the progressive dematerialization of culture. As life increasingly imitates art and architecture, abstraction and formalism come to characterize experience itself until the world becomes a play of networks of exchange, which is more hyperreal rather than real. Within webs and networks of exchange, everything speeds up until there is a quantum leap into cyberspace.

Though cyberspace is a sci-fi projection of what our near future holds, it effectively captures important characteristics of present-day experience. Nearly three decades ago, McLuhan was already arguing that "in the mechanical age now receding, many actions could be taken without too much concern. Slow movement insured that the reactions were delayed for considerable periods of time. Today the action and the reaction occur almost at the same time. We actually live mythically and integrally, as it were, but we continue to think in the old, fragmented space and time patterns of the pre-electric age."[20] As the subtitle of his influential book, *Understanding Media: The Extensions of Man,* indicates, McLuhan saw electronic media as prosthetic extensions of the human organism. In the new world he imagined, computers become the brains, engines the legs, video cameras the eyes, telephones the ears, and wires the veins and arteries of the world organism. The lifeblood of this corporate body is electricity. The movement from the industrial to the electronic age repeats the shift from mechanical to organic metaphors for envisioning reality, which marks the emergence of nineteenth-century romanticism and idealism. In McLuhan's neoromanticism and neoidealism, organicism displaces mechanism to form a vision of a harmonious New Age in which all are one and one is all.

> Today, deep in the electric age, organic myth itself is a simple and automatic response capable of mathematical formulation and expression, without any of the imaginative perception of Blake about it. Had he encountered the electric age, Blake would not have met its challenge with a mere repetition of electric form. For myth is the instant vision of a complex process that ordinarily extends over a long period. Myth is contraction or implosion of any process, and the instant speed of electricity confers the mythic dimension on ordinary industrial and social action today. We *live* mythically but continue to think fragmentarily on single planes.[21]

Anticipating many of the insights usually attributed to Baudrillard and Virilio, McLuhan maintains that the implosion characteristic of experience in the electronic age is created by *speed*. When speed reaches a certain point, time and space collapse and distance seems to disappear.

Looking back on McLuhan's work, it is all too easy to dismiss his vision as a curious variation of the nostalgia that characterized so much of the 1960s counterculture. What makes the association between McLuhan's global village and Haight Ashbury as well as Woodstock so puzzling and yet so suggestive is that the '60s counterculture usually is depicted as technophobic. In tribal rituals that were unabashed reenactments of "primitive" rites, young people in the '60s sought to flee twentieth-century technology, which many people found unbearably repressive. By going back to "Mother" Earth from which everything emerges and to which all returns, personal and social renewal once again seemed possible. For many members of the '60s counterculture, this redemptive experience was impossible without the aid of certain pharmacological supplements. The stone of philosophers and white powder of the alchemist were transformed into the white powder of psychedelics, which held out the promise of religious ecstasy to latter-day initiates.

The distance between Haight Ashbury and Silicon Valley, however, is not as great as it initially appears. The '60s technophobia always har-bored a technophilia that promised to transform the chemico-religious prosthesis into the electronic prosthesis. After all, the vibrations that cre-ated the feelings of cosmic harmony were more often than not electroni-cally generated. When John Perry Barlow, who is the lyricist for the Grateful Dead, publishes his Internet address in what was for a typically brief time the slickest publication promoting electronic telecommunica-tions technology as the mind-altering agent that will bring the New Age (i.e., *Mondo 2000*), the circuit joining 1960s drug culture with 1980s–90s technoculture is complete. Stewart Brand, one-time member of Ken Kesey's Merry Pranksters, founder of the *Whole Earth Catalogue* and author of *The Medial Lab: Inventing the Future at M.I.T.,* makes the tell-ing point clearly and concisely: "This generation swallowed computers whole, just like dope."[22]

As its name suggests, the Berkeley-based *Mondo 2000* is an explicitly millenarian mega-zine. Mixing advanced telecommunications technology and imaginative software with designer drugs and mystico-eroticism, the contributors to *Mondo* create a blueprint for a cybertopia in which desires will be immediately fulfilled. Transferring his hopes from a psychedelic to a technological revolution, the late Timothy Leary preaches: "Turn On. Boot Up. Download." Editors Queen Mu and R. U. Sirius elaborate Leary's technofantasies, in an effort to explain the broader vision of the future that unfolds in the pages of *Mondo 2000:*

> We're talking Cyber-Chatauqua; bringing cyberculture to the people! Artificial awareness modules. Visual music. Vidscan magazines. Brain-boosting technologies. William Gibson's Cyberspace Matrix—fully real-ized!
>
> Our scouts are out there on the frontier sniffing the breeze and guess what? All the old war horses are dead. Eco-fundamentalism is out, con-spiracy theory is démodé, drugs are obsolete. There's a new whiff of apoca-lypticism across the land. A general sense that we are living at a very special juncture in the evolution of the species. . . .
>
> Yet the pagan innocence and idealism that was the sixties remains and continues to exert its fascination on today's kids. Look at old footage of *Woodstock* and you wonder: where have all those wide-eyed, ecstatic, organism-slurping kids gone? They're all across the land, dormant like deeply buried perennials. But their mutated nucleotides have given us a whole new generation of sharpies, mutants, and superbrights, and in them we must put our faith—and power.
>
> The cybernet is in place. If fusion *is* real, we'll find out about it fast. The kids are at the controls . . . We're talking about Total Possibilities.

> Radical assaults on the limits of biology, gravity and time. The end of
> Artificial Scarcity. The dawn of a new humanism. High-jacking technol-
> ogy for personal empowerment, fun and games. Flexing those synapses!
> Stoking those neuropeptides! Making Bliss States our normal waking con-
> sciousness. *Becoming* the Bionic Angel.[23]

It would be a mistake to allow the hype and irony of such declarations
to obscure what they teach about our present situation and the direction
in which we seem to be heading. Obvious excesses notwithstanding,
Mondo 2000 writers are attempting to build a bridge between the techno-
centric world of the late twentieth century and Gibson's twenty-first-
century cyberspace. From a certain perspective, of course, we already
inhabit cyberspace. Fiber-optic cables, satellite up-links and down-links,
telecommunications systems, Internet, Worldnet, and Reality Net combine to create a network of networks. In ways that are still only dimly
visible, this matrix is giving birth to new subjects by transforming the
very structures that constitute the time and space of our dwelling. Within
this net, we all become cyborgs.

The arrival of the cyborg is made possible by the gradual removal of
the barriers separating interiority and exteriority, as well as public and
private space. This complication of differences proceeds in two directions
at once: from outer to inner and, conversely, from inner to outer. On the
one hand, the body itself is progressively colonized by prosthetic devices.
Implants, transplants, artificial organs, artificial insemination, genetic en-
gineering, and synthetic drugs make it harder and harder to be sure
where the so-called human ends and the nonhuman begins. On the other
hand, artificial wombs, test-tube babies, artificial intelligence, and computer literacy "externalize" bodily and mental functions to such an extent
that the outer is not merely outer and the inner is not simply inner. No
longer purely human, we are not quite yet replicants. When Gibson and
his fellow cyberpunks extrapolate from the present to the near future,
they see a world where latter-day golems pose unimaginable threats and
unthinkable possibilities. When organisms can be cloned and minds preserved by being downloaded into the matrix, the dream of achieving
immortality might be realizable.

Though the technology is new, the dream is old—terribly old. Howard Rheingold, author of *Virtual Reality* and editor of *Whole Earth Re-
view,* describes the leading edge of telecommunications research as "the
science of presence." To underscore his point, Rheingold quotes Yama-
guchi's 1989 "Proposal for a Large Visual Field Display": "Effectiveness
of visual communication and remote operation can best be achieved if

the observer becomes totally involved in the displayed image through a feeling of 'being there.' The sensation of virtual existence or enhanced reality is activated by the capability of a precise pixel expression and a large visual field display."[24] The "feeling of 'being there,'" which enhances reality, is a fantasy that runs throughout the Western philosophical and religious traditions. Virtual technologies hold out the promise of making this vision a (virtual) reality.

This unexpected association between religious longings and postmodern technologies suggests ways in which what Guy Debord labels "the society of the spectacle" continues an ancient dream. With the inexorable expansion of various electronic technologies, all experience is mediated by tangled media networks until the hyperreality of contemporary culture renders reality virtual. For from a specific technology of limited use, virtuality is a cultural condition from which there is no escape. For critics, the virtualization of reality and realization of virtuality issue in a loss of the real, which is psychologically disorienting, socially disruptive, and culturally destructive. For others, however, virtual reality harbors a presence that is psychologically restorative, socially transformative, and culturally creative. Though still in its infancy, virtual reality, some technophiles believe, creates the possibility of "postsymbolic communication," which establishes presence-at-a-distance. Jaron Lanier, who invented the data glove and coined the term "virtual reality," describes the space of this new reality.

The images come from a powerful special computer which I like to call the Home Reality Engine. It will be sitting there in your room and will plug into the phone outlet. They have little headphone speakers very much like a Walkman, which allow you to hear the sounds of the virtual world. The glasses do one other thing too. They have sensors that can sense your facial expressions. That information is used to control the virtual version of your body, which both you and other people perceive as being you in Virtual Reality. . . . The gloves allow you to reach out and feel things that aren't really there. The inside of the glove has tactile stimulators so that when the Home Reality Engine can tell you your hand is touching a virtual object (even though there's no object there) you'll actually feel the object. The second function of the gloves is that they actually allow you to interact with objects. You can pick up an object and do things with it, just like you would with a real object. You can pick up a virtual baseball and throw it. So it allows you to do things to the world.[25]

But which world is this? Whose world is it? The answers are far from clear. As reality becomes virtual, outer and inner, subject and object, self and world become inextricably intertwined. For Lanier, the elixir that brings this ecstatic vision is digital. Expressing his most profound hope for the technology he fathered, Lanier boldly predicts that virtual reality "will bring back a sense of the shared mystical altered states of reality that is so important in basically every other civilization and culture prior to big patriarchal power. I hope that might lead to some sense of tolerance and understanding."[26]

Our consideration of metallurgical and alchemical myths and rituals suggests that such dreams of unity are far from innocent. In order to trace potentially darker aspects of virtual technologies, which Lanier overlooks, let us return to Freud's effort to rethink the origin of religion at the beginning of *Civilization and Its Discontents*. In the course of his reflections, Freud charts an astonishing course by arguing that human beings compensate for their inadequacies by fabricating chemical, artistic, religious, and technological or, more precisely, electronic "prostheses." He notes that his comments on religion are a "response to a call" from a friend who was responding to Freud's *Future of an Illusion*.

> I had sent him my small book that treats religion as an illusion, and he answered that he entirely agreed with my judgment upon religion, but that he was sorry I had not properly appreciated the true source of religious sentiments. . . . It is a feeling which he would like to call a sensation of "eternity," a feeling as of something limitless, unbounded—as it were, "oceanic."[27]

Describing this oceanic sense as "a feeling of an indissoluble bond of being at one with the external world as a whole," Freud traces its source to the original unity of the ego and the world. In the prelapsarian condition of plenitude, all desires are satisfied and every longing fulfilled; more precisely, neither desire nor need has yet emerged. The source of this archaic satisfaction is, of course, the mother. Once the maternal bond has been broken, life becomes a ceaseless *recherche du temps perdu*. While admitting that the oceanic feeling exists in some people, Freud denies that it is the *fons et origo* of religion. Trying to salvage his argument in *The Future of an Illusion,* he reasserts that religion originates in the infant's sense of helplessness and the longing for a protective father that it engenders. Having broached the issue of oceanic consciousness, however, he is forced to confess that his analysis might be incomplete: "The origin of the religious attitude can be traced back in clear outlines as far as the feeling of infantile helplessness. There may be something further behind that, but for the present it is wrapped in obscurity" (19). Though Freud never quite admits it, what lies behind the father is the mother. The loss of the mother, Freud suggests, creates desires that can never be fulfilled. In the absence of true satisfaction, a series of supplements inevitably emerges. The four "substitute satisfactions" Freud identifies represent gradual refinements of the method for sublimating base instincts into generally acceptable cultural currency.

If, as Marx insists, religion is an opiate, then opiates are, in a certain sense, religious. By incorporating "intoxicating drugs," Freud argues, people attempt to overcome the suffering caused by their incompletion and inadequacy.

> The crudest, but also the most effective among these methods of influence is the chemical one—intoxication. I do not think that anyone completely understands its mechanism, but it is a fact that there are foreign substances which, when present in the blood or tissues, directly cause us pleasurable sensations; and they also so alter the conditions governing our sensibility that we become incapable of receiving unpleasurable impulses. (25)

The artist refines the strategies of the pharmacist. Art is, in effect, a drug synthesized to relieve the symptoms of loss and deprivation. In art, Freud concludes, "satisfaction is obtained from illusions, which are recognized as such without the discrepancy between them and reality being allowed to interfere with enjoyment" (27). Psychoanalytic theory claims to show how thin the line separating the hallucinations of the addict and the fantasies of the artists from the delusions of the madman can be. To avoid falling into the prison house of solitary madness, individuals tend to join together to create shared fantasies. The result, according to Freud, is religion.

> A special importance attaches to the case in which this attempt to procure a certainty of happiness and a protection against suffering through a delusional remoulding of reality is made by a considerable number of people in common. The religions of mankind must be classed among the mass-delusions of this kind. No one, needless to say, who shares a delusion ever recognizes it as such. (28)

A shared delusion is nonetheless still a delusion. While effecting inward change, chemical, artistic, and religious fixes cannot bring about outward changes necessary for pleasure. This transformation of reality and its principles is what technology promises. To explain the modern, Freud once again returns to the "primitive."

Technology is not, of course, new. To trace its origin one must return to prehistoric times. In the beginning was light . . . fire . . . heat.

> If we go back far enough, we find that the first acts of civilization were the use of tools, the gaining of control over fire and the construction of dwellings. Among these, the control over fire stands out as a quite extraordinary and unexampled achievement, while the others opened paths which man has followed ever since, and the stimulus to which is easily guessed. With every tool man is perfecting his own organs, whether motor or sensory, or is removing the limits of their functioning. (37)

In this suggestive text, Freud seems to anticipate Eliade's claim that the founders of technology were "the masters of fire." Tools forged in the heat of fire function as "extensions of their [creators'] organs." But which organ is at stake in technology? Freud appends to his myth of the origin of technology a footnote in which he explains: "The legends that we possess leave no doubt about the originally phallic view taken of tongues of flame as they shoot upwards" (37). If fire is the trope for technology, the organ of technology appears to be the phallus. With the appearance of this organ, we return once again to the matrix.

In her remarkable work entitled *The Telephone Book,* Avital Ronell stresses that one of the names of the matrix in contemporary culture is Ma Bell. Drawing on Theodore A. L. DuMoncel's *The Telephone, the Microphone, and the Phonograph,* published in 1879, Ronell suggests an unexpected connection between Freud's account of the origin and function of religion and telephonic technology. DuMoncel's work is less interesting for the story it tells than for the images it contains. The figure of the telephone receiver that DuMoncel includes in his book makes it perfectly clear that teledildonics is more than a century old. Not only is the shape of the so-called receiver undeniably phallic, but the flow of communication is always one-way: from man to woman. More precisely, the flow is from the mouth or tongue of the man into the ear of the woman. Whether this ear is always "the ear of the other" remains unclear, for in some images the woman engages in auto-affection by stimulating herself. But who is this woman to whom man always seems to be talking?

In the sentence beginning the textual interruption where phallic significance of fire is explained, Freud lists the technological developments that have helped man correct his defects and hence overcome his inadequacies: motor power, ships and aircraft, spectacles, telescope, microscope, photographic camera, and gramophone disk. He concludes this

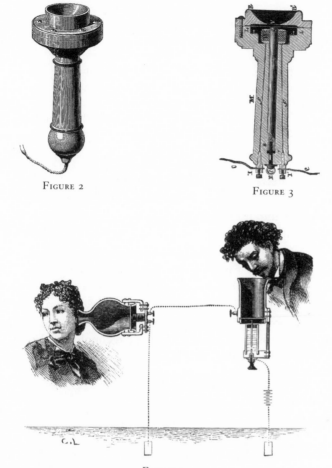

FIGURE 2

FIGURE 3

FIGURE 4

FIGURE 5

FIGURES 2–5 Theodore A. L. DuMoncel, *The Telephone, the Microphone, and the Phonograph*

catalogue with the instrument he believes most effectively represents the function of technology: the telephone.

> With the help of the telephone he can hear at distances which would be respected as unattainable even in a fairy tale. Writing was in its origin the voice of an absent person; and the dwelling-house was a substitute for the mother's womb, the first lodging, for which in all likelihood man still longs, and in which he was safe and felt at ease. (38)

The string of associations released in this brief passage is astonishing. The lines Freud connects suggest that the telephone, which is a synecdoche for technology, binds us back to our original "dwelling-house." As we know from his famous essay on the uncanny, this dwelling-house is the mother's genitals. Like the miner's tunnel and the alchemist's furnace, the telephone appears to be "a substitute for the mother's womb." Our deepest desire, our most profound longing, Freud insists, is to return to the womb-tomb of Mother Earth where eros and thanatos are one. If his call goes through, the telephone—and by extension technology— might make it possible to jack into the matrix.

"These things that, by his science and technology," Freud admits, "man has brought about on this earth . . . not only sound like a fairy tale, they are an actual fulfilment of every—or of almost every—fairy- tale wish."

> Long ago [man] formed an ideal conception of omnipotence and omni- science which he embodied in his gods. To these gods he attributed every- thing that seemed unattainable to his wishes, or that was forbidden to him. One may say, therefore, that these gods were cultural ideals. To-day he has come very close to the attainment of this ideal, he has almost be- come a god himself. . . . Man has, as it were, become a kind of prosthetic God. When he puts on all his auxiliary organs he is truly magnificent; but those organs have not grown on to him and they still give him much trouble at times. Nevertheless, he is entitled to console himself with the thought that this development will not come to an end precisely with the year 1930 A.D. Future ages will bring with them new and probably unimaginably great advances in this field of civilization and will increase man's likeness to God still more. (38–39)

From this point of view, to become one with the matrix would be to attain immortality by being transformed into the divine. In contemporary culture, the transformer is no longer religion or even the telephone but the electronic net in which we are already entangled. Freud hardly could have envisioned the radical changes that telecommunications would bring by the end of the century. The dream of this New Age, which many believe is dawning, is not only the achievement of omnipotence and omniscience but the realization of the omnipresence that immortality brings. To enjoy omnipresence is not to be nowhere but to be everywhere at once. The all-at-onceness of the net, Rheingold insists, "is a form of out-of-body-experience."[28] When carried far enough, sublimation creates a sense of the technical sublime in which even *jouissance* becomes immaterial. In the unspeakable moment of what Baudrillard describes as "the ecstasy of communication," the screen and I become one. As Paul Virilio explains: "Curiously, telecommunications sets in motion in civil society the properties of divinity: ubiquity (being present everywhere at every instant), instantaneousness, immediacy, omnivision, omnipresence. Every one of us is metamorphosed into a divine being here and there at the same time."[29] When everyone is everywhere, we have indeed entered a new age, which might just be the New Age. But what price must be paid for this terminal condition? What currency keeps it flowing? What spirit inspires this New Age?

Six

Christianity and the Capitalism of Spirit

Religion of Money

Few films have captured the spirit of an era more effectively than Oliver Stone's 1987 *Wall Street*. When Michael Douglas, playing a character reminiscent of Michael Milken, preaches "Greed is good, greed is right, greed works" to a meeting of eager stockholders, he forcefully summarizes the gospel of the 1980s. In the world of junk bonds and insider trading, what had long been regarded as sin becomes virtue and vice versa. Though Douglas will always be remembered for his paean to greed, Gordon Gekko presents a more suggestive analysis of the market frenzy of the 1980s later in the film. The scene is set when Bud Fox, his young protégé (played by Charlie Sheen), confronts Gekko about his plans to break up and sell off the airline for which Bud's father had long worked. In a desperate effort to become a player in the world of high rollers, Bud betrayed his blue-collar father by giving Gekko information he could use to manipulate the price of the airline's stock. Feeling guilty about his disloyalty to his father and rage at Gekko's duplicity, Bud charges into his boss's office and interrupts his meeting with Japanese businessmen. After a heated exchange, Gekko responds to Bud's challenge by presenting his interpretation of the world which he has, in no small measure, created.

> "It's all about bucks, kid; the rest is conversation. Hey, buddy, you're still going to be president, all right? And when the time comes, you're going to parachute out a rich man. With the money you're going to make, your dad's never going to have to have to work another day in his life."
>
> "So tell me, Gordon, when does it all end? How many yachts can you water ski behind? How much is enough?"
>
> "It's not a question of enough, pal. It's a zero-sum game. Somebody wins, somebody loses. Money itself isn't lost or made, it's simply transferred from one perception to another. Like magic. This painting here, I

bought it ten years ago for $60,000; I could sell it today for $600,000. The illusion has become real and the more real it becomes, the more desperately they want it. Capitalism at its finest."

"How much is enough, Gordon?"

"The richest 1% of this country owns half our country's wealth— $5,000,000,000,000. One third of that comes from hard work, two thirds from inheritance—interest on interest accumulating to widows' idiot sons, and what I do—stock and real estate speculation. It's bullshit. You got 90% of the American public out there with little or no net worth. I create nothing; I own. We make the rules, pal: the news, war, peace, famine, upheaval, the price of paper clips. We pick the rabbit out of the hat while everybody sits out there wondering how the hell we did it. Now you're not naive enough to think we're living in a democracy are you, buddy? It's the free market and you're part of it."

In this surprisingly astute analysis of the forces driving postindustrial capitalism, Gekko describes the complex interrelation between his financial activity and broader sociocultural processes. The most revealing moment in the film occurs when Gekko declares, "The illusion has become real." To complete Gekko's insight, however, it is necessary to add "and the real has become an illusion." In a world where illusions are real and the real is illusory, *creatio ex nihilo* becomes "I create nothing."

While the world of speculative capitalism usually is associated with the glitz and glamour of the 1980s, its roots can actually be traced to the early 1970s when fundamental changes in the world economy and financial institutions occurred. As Joel Kurtzman points out, "the new neural network of money made its debut rather abruptly on Sunday, August 15, 1971, although most people did not recognize its appearance for at least a decade."[1] Faced with the prospect of recession in the midst of his reelection campaign, Richard Nixon announced a ninety-day wage-and-price freeze. He also urged Congress to enact legislation that would make it illegal for unions to strike during the freeze and sought a 10% surtax on imported cars and an income tax reduction. Hidden in the midst of all of these actions was an initiative whose implications were far more radical and consequences considerably farther reaching than the policy changes that seemed so significant at the time. Nixon quietly announced that he had "closed the 'gold window.'" With the stroke of a pen, Nixon removed the very foundation of the postwar world economic system.

As World War II drew to a close, representatives from the United States and Europe met secretly to devise a plan to restore financial stability to global economic markets. Concerned about inflationary pressures, which had contributed to the social instability that led to the rise of the political right in Europe throughout the 1930s, and wary of promoting systems of centralized control, which would favor the spread of leftist socialist and communist regimes, the countries involved reached a compromise intended to preserve the free market system. On July 22, 1944, the Bretton Woods Agreement was signed. In addition to marking a shift in the center of economic power from Europe to the United States, this pact established economic accords that linked all of the world's major currencies to the dollar at fixed exchange rates and bound the dollar to gold at an official rate of $35 per ounce. The reinstitution of what was, in effect, a gold standard, guaranteed that the "money economy" and the "real economy" would expand and contract at roughly the same rate. When Nixon overturned this carefully crafted system, he initiated events whose consequences continue to transform our world today. "It was," as Kurtzman explains,

> a change of monumental proportions that not only redefined money but created the opportunity to dramatically speed up the rate at which transactions between companies and countries took place. It created enormous arbitrage possibilities and set the stage for the invention of a myriad of new financial products. It also initiated the process of decoupling the "money" economy from the "real" economy. As a result, two-plus decades later, the money economy, where transactions take place purely for financial or speculative gain, and the real economy, where the world's raw materials, goods, and services are produced and traded are badly out of balance. That was Nixon's economic legacy. (51)

The "process of decoupling the 'money' economy from the 'real' economy" transformed the way in which the value of currencies is established. No longer a function of the relationship to a fixed referent (i.e., gold), the value of the monetary sign now is determined by its relation to other monetary signs. During the year following the revocation of the gold standard, governments attempted to maintain economic stability by enforcing fixed rates of exchange. But these efforts proved futile and were quickly abandoned. In the absence of gold and without fixed exchange rates, currencies became floating signifiers whose value is determined by relations to other signifiers.

Nixon's economic legacy would not, however, have created Gordon Gekko's world without another important change in the constitution of currency: money had to become electronic. In 1973, Reuters, which is based in London, established the first electronic money-trading network. With over a century of experience in gathering and disseminating news and information, Reuters already had in place an electronic infrastructure that extended around the globe. A decade before the arrival of the personal computer, far-sighted executives at Reuters linked brokerage houses throughout the world with terminals and telephone lines, which transmitted currency prices as well as financial news influencing their fluctuation. As hardware and software rapidly became more sophisticated and more widely distributed, the implications of Reuters's innovation became increasingly obvious. Money had become information, which knows no boundaries. As we shall see, the transmutation of currency into electric current marks a further stage in the gradual dematerialization of money that has been going on for centuries.

As money becomes a floating signifier whose value is constantly shifting in global networks of exchange, economic and cultural processes become entangled in unprecedented ways. The dematerialization of money is, in effect, the aestheticization of the token of exchange. No longer a material substance, money becomes a "matter" of image. This is what Gekko implies but does not explain when, proudly pointing to one of the paintings decorating his office, he declares: "Money itself isn't lost or made, it's simply transferred from one perception to another. Like magic. This painting here, I bought it ten years ago for $60,000; I could sell it today for $600,000." As art is commodified and becomes money, money is aestheticized and becomes art. In a manner not unlike Reuters's wiring of financial networks, the extensive development of the New York gallery system in the late 1950s and 1960s created the infrastructure necessary for the explosion of speculation in the art market throughout the 1980s. With traders looking for ever higher rates of return, works of art offered investment opportunities that often appeared preferable to stocks, bonds, and other financial instruments.

While the significance of the similarities between changes occurring in financial and art markets should not be underestimated, it is no less important to recognize the way in which the transformation of the "substance" of money and the "content" of works of art have mirrored each other for the past several decades. As money was becoming a sign of other signs, art was becoming an image of other images. Resolutely rejecting the formalism and abstraction definitive of so-called advanced art in the twentieth century, postmodern artists and architects devised strategies of appropriation in which they borrow or steal images from other artists as well as from media and popular culture to create works that are defiantly nonoriginal: Sherri Levine photographs other photographs; David Salle repaints earlier paintings; Cindy Sherman strikes poses lifted from films; Robert Venturi rips off signs from the Las Vegas

Strip. When Jeff Koons decides he can make more money creating works of art, which reproduce reproductions, than he can trading junk bonds, which are nothing but figures of figures, it is no longer possible to be sure where the finances of art end and the art of finance begins.

It has, of course, become commonplace to associate postmodern art and architecture with late or postindustrial capitalism. This reading of contemporary cultural practices has been strongly influenced by Fredric Jameson's seminal 1982 essay "Postmodernism and Consumer Society." In an expanded version of his argument, developed in *Postmodernism, or The Cultural Logic of Late Capitalism,* Jameson, following Ernest Mandel, identifies three forms of capitalism, which he correlates with three technological revolutions: market capitalism ("machine production of steam-driven motors since 1848"); monopoly capitalism ("machine production of electric and combustion motors since the 90s of the 19th century"); and postindustrial or multinational capitalism ("machine production of electronic and nuclear-powered apparatuses since the 40s of the 20th century").[2] At the third stage of capitalism, the means of production and material conditions of life become completely imbricated with immaterial processes of reproduction ranging from financial and media networks to electronic and teletronic technologies. "Non-Marxists and Marxists alike," Jameson maintains,

> have come around to the general feeling that at some point following World War II a new kind of society began to emerge (variously described as postindustrial society, multinational capitalism, consumer society, media society and so forth). New types of consumption; planned obsolescence; an ever more rapid rhythm of fashion and styling changes; the penetration of advertising, television and the media generally to a hitherto unparalleled degree throughout society; the replacement of the old tension between city and country, center and provenance, by the suburb and by universal standardization; the growth of the great networks of superhighways and the arrival of automobile culture—these are some of the features which would seem to mark a radical break with that older prewar society in which high modernism was still an underground force.[3]

From Jameson's point of view, the shift from modernism to postmodernism is symptomatic of cultural processes of aestheticization, which relax the creative tensions between historical reality and imaginative ideality necessary for constructive political action and creative social change. "The transformation of reality into images," he argues, issues in a loss of any referent that might provide resources for resisting the spread of consumer capitalism. In order to break the hegemony of consumerism, it is necessary to crack the encompassing façade of simulacra by reconsidering "the fate of the referent." While the Gordon Gekkos of the world proclaim that "the illusion has become real," Jameson insists that the real is not illusory because illusions are merely imaginary. If illusions fabricated to promote consumerism and the market economy are to be overcome, "the real" must, in some way, be recovered. Jameson summarizes his conclusions about the relation of image and reality in an essay devoted to experimental video: "In the immediate instance that concerns us here, I have argued for the presence and existence of what seems to me a palpable referent—namely, death and historical fact, which are ultimately not textualizable and tear through the tissues of textual elaboration, of combination and free play ('the Real,' Lacan tells us, is 'what resists symbolization absolutely')."[4] By rereading Lacan's account of the role of the symbolic and the real in the machinations of the unconscious through the symbolic mediation and historical reality, Jameson attempts to uncover a referent that rends the fabric of images, which, he believes, is responsible for turning agents into passive consumers of fantasies promulgated by late capitalists who own the means of reproduction.

Jameson's critical assessment of the relation between postmodernism and consumer capitalism has exercised considerable influence on the rapidly growing field of cultural studies. Faced with sprawling media networks and proliferating electronic technology, critics frantically search for "materialities," which are supposed to "ground" cultural practices. Disguising political desires as descriptive analyses, representatives from what once was called the Left declare, "Postmodernism is over." One of the most thoughtful proponents of this position is David Harvey, who, in *The Condition of Postmodernity,* presents an interpretation of postmodernism that draws on a broad range of social analysis and economic data. In the concluding chapters of his study, entitled "The Crisis of Historical Materialism" and "Cracks in the Mirrors, Fusions at the Edges," Harvey makes the political presuppositions and interests of his critique perfectly clear. In words that could have been written by cultural conservatives or religious fundamentalists who currently dominate the political scene, Harvey charges that the most pernicious form of postmodernism—deconstruction—is ethically bankrupt and politically irresponsible.

> In their [i.e., deconstructionists'] suspicion of any narrative that aspires to coherence, and in their rush to deconstruct anything that even looks like meta-theory, they challenged all basic propositions. To the degree that all narrative accounts on offer contained hidden presuppositions and simplifications, they deserved critical scrutiny, if only to emerge the stronger for

it. But in challenging all consensual standards for truth and justice, of ethics, and meaning, and in pursuing the dissolution of all narratives and meta-theories into a diffuse universe, of language games, deconstruction-ism ended up in spite of the best intentions of its more radical practitioners, by reducing knowledge and meaning to a rubble of signifiers. It thereby produced a condition of nihilism.[5]

While the political Right attempts to counter purported nihilism by re-turning to basic values, Harvey and his colleagues struggle to revive the agenda of the Left by unearthing material infrastructures beneath the postmodern world of simulacra. Though usually overlooked, there is a striking symmetry between the Right and the Left. Not only do both find the vertiginous possibilities created by postmodernism profoundly unsettling, but they agree that the only way to overcome our current impasse is to recover a foundation that seems to be secure. Like his coun-terparts on the Right, Harvey intends his cultural diagnosis to serve a political end.

> [T]here is a renewal of historical materialism and of the Enlightenment project. Through the first we can begin to understand postmodernity as an historical-geographical condition. On that critical basis it becomes pos-sible to launch a counter-attack of narrative against the image, of ethics against aesthetics, of a project of Becoming rather than Being, and to search for unity within difference, albeit in a context where the power of the image and of aesthetics, the problems of time-space compression, and the significance of geopolitics and otherness are clearly understood. A re-newal of historical-geographical materialism can indeed promote adher-ence to a new version of the Enlightenment project. (359)

Firmly rooted in the tradition of dialectical thinking, Harvey insists that his critique does not have to be imposed from without but emerges within the conditions of postmodernity. Writing in the wake of the 1987 stock market crash, he argues that postindustrial capitalism has begun a process of self-negation that eventually will lead to its collapse.

> On 19 October 1987, someone peeked behind the reflecting mirrors of US economic policy and, frightened at what they saw there, plunged the world's stock markets into such a fearful crash that nearly a third of the paper value of assets worldwide was written off within a few days. . . . "The crash aftermath is the tale of two cultures—processing different information, operating on different time horizons, dreaming different dreams. . . . The financial community—living by the minute and trading by the computer—operates on one set of values," while "the rest of America—living by the decade, buying and holding—has a different

code" which might be called "the ethic of those who have their hands on shovels" . . .

Fictitious capital is even more hegemonic than before in its influence. It creates its own fantastic world of becoming paper wealth and assets. . . . Debts get rescheduled and rolled over at ever faster rates, with the aggregate effect of rescheduling the crisis-tendencies of capitalism into the twenty-first century. Yet cracks in the reflecting mirrors of economic performance abound. US banks write off billions of dollars of bad loans, governments default, international currency markets remain in perpetual turmoil. (357–58)

As the illusions of Wall Street fade, Harvey suggests, the way is cleared for a return to liberatory practices grounded securely in a dialectical materialism that resists the frivolity of aestheticization.

But a decade after the crash, Gordon Gekko's reading of the postmodern condition seems more persuasive than Harvey's account. What is most remarkable about the '87 crash is not how much but how little it changed the world. Between the height of the bull market in August 1987 and the meltdown in October, investors lost more than $1,000,000,000,000. Predictions to the contrary notwithstanding, the world did not plunge into another Great Depression; financial markets quickly recovered and life in the so-called real world seemed to continue without missing a beat. It is obvious that between 1929 and 1987 socioeconomic changes had been considerably more profound than most analysts realized.

The nature and scope of these changes begin to become apparent when we recognize the extent and the irreversibility of the processes of aestheticization or, more precisely, virtualization at work in contemporary society and culture. The line of analysis proposed by Jameson, Harvey, and those who follow their lead is theoretically deficient and practically misguided. Theoretically, it no longer makes sense to set up an opposition between material infrastructures and immaterial suprastructures. The globalization of the economy and the electrification of currency transforms the hierarchy of infrastructure/suprastructure into lateral extensions of information networks. While so-called material production does, of course, continue, the forces driving the economy are increasingly virtual. The theoretical challenge we now face is not to reduce suprastructure to infrastructure but to reread what once appeared to be surface and depth in terms of complicated surfaces where materiality and immateriality are thoroughly reconfigured. This theoretical shift harbors important practical consequences. If so-called materiality and immateriality are interfaces rather than opposites, then recasting one involves transforming the other. The "symbolic order" is not necessarily separate from or transcendent to the "real." In the virtual dimension, the symbolic becomes real in a world where reality is undeniably symbolic.

The Currency of God

A refiguring of the interplay between the symbolic and the real becomes possible when the *religious* preconditions and *theological* presuppositions of contemporary processes of virtualization are considered. Recent critics are undoubtedly right when they insist on a close connection between postmodernism and postindustrial capitalism. Unfortunately, however, simplistic understandings of religion resulting from certain political biases tend to obscure the significant relation between religion and economics. Religion, it seems, is often most effective when it is least obvious. Sociocultural processes that appear to be thoroughly secular harbor tacit traces of religion, which continue to influence cultural production and reproduction in ways that usually go undetected. In the present context, it is helpful to realize the ways in which the virtualization of reality, which is transforming, inter alia, the sphere of economics, grows out of and, in a certain sense, extends processes first articulated in the Christian doctrines of the Incarnation and the Trinity. While Max Weber effectively established the undeniable link between Protestantism and the spirit of capitalism, further light can be shed on our current cultural condition by examining the inextricable relation between capitalism and the structure of spirit as it is articulated in the Christian notion of the Trinity.

At a critical point in Shakespeare's *Timon of Athens,* a disillusioned Timon anticipates his dark destiny:

> Then, Timon, presently prepare thy grave.
> Lie where the light foam of the sea may beat
> Thy gravestone daily. Make thine epitaph,
> That death in me at others' lives may laugh.
> > *He looks on gold.*
> O thou sweet king-killer, and dear divorce
> 'Twixt natural son and sire; thou bright defiler
> Of Hymen's purest bed, thou valiant Mars;
> Thou ever young, fresh, loved, and delicate wooer,
> Whose blush doth thaw the consecrated snow

That lies on Dian's lap; thou visible god,
That sold'rest close impossibilities
And mak'st them kiss, that speak'st with every tongue
To every purpose; O thou touch of hearts:
Think thy slave men rebels and by thy virtue
Set them into confounding odds, that beasts
May have the world in empire."[6]

Money and God are bound in an alliance that always threatens to become less than holy. When Shakespeare describes money as a "visible god/ That sold'rest close impossibilities/ And mak'st them kiss," he puts a Christian spin on a relation between God and gold (or its equivalent), which can be traced to the earliest appearance of currency. Though origins inevitably remain obscure, primitive economies always seem to be surrounded by a magico-religious aura. Every economy is, in some sense, *sacrificial*. As people created networks for exchange, so they established economic bonds with their gods. Regardless of the currency, economies inevitably involve reciprocal relations of give-and-take. When the economy is sacred, devotees tend to offer the deity goods and services in return for divine favor. Though apparently all-powerful, gods are actually powerless apart from gifts from the faithful. Believers, in other words, create their gods as much as gods create their believers.

From East to West, ancient economic relations involve gift exchange, which is regulated by sacrificial rituals. In India, for example, the *Satapatha Brahmana* requires believers to pay priests who perform sacrifices with gold, cattle, clothing, or horses. Paper money was invented in China for use in ritual sacrifices. Four centuries before paper currency was used for commercial purposes, the Chinese offered pieces of paper decorated with images of the gods to deities, ghosts, and ancestors. "A small piece of tin foil was sometimes attached to the center of the paper in order to represent silver or, when dabbed with yellow tint, gold. Obviously this paper money had little real economic value, but this was in fact intentional, since it was believed that what was a mere imitation in this world would become, when transformed by the sacrificial fire, a genuine treasure in heaven. There it would be added to the Celestial Treasure for the benefit of the person making the offering."[7]

The relation between money and the gods is no less important in Western cultures. Indeed, the word *money* derives from the epithet for Jupiter's sister and wife—Juno Moneta. As the warning goddess, Juno Moneta was best known for three "monitory tales: (1) she advised the Romans to sacrifice a pregnant sow to Cybel, to avert an earthquake;

(2) she told them, when they feared for finances in the war against Pyrrhus, that money would never fail those whose cause was just; and (3) the geese that were crated for sacrifice in her temple at the city wall cackled and thus alerted the Romans to the intended surprise attack by the Gauls in 390 B.C.E. Roman coins were first minted in the Temple of Juno Moneta," thereby initiating the ancient practice of associating mints with temples. "The oldest altar to Juneo Moneta was located on Mons Albanus, where a bull sacrifice, the central ritual of the Latin confederacy, was annually held."[8]

Other etymological clues suggest a link between money and ritual sacrifice. The German word *Geld* (money), Horst Kurnitsky points out, "means more or less 'sacrifice' [*Opfer*]. Geld ist Geld, weil es gilt [Money is money, because it is valid.] But in the eighth century, this verb *gelten* [to be valid] meant 'to sacrifice.' "[9] The Greek word *drachma,* which is the name of a common coin, once was used to designate a handful of sacrificial meat (*oblos*). In Latin, *pecunia,* which is the root of the English *pecuniary,* derives from *pecus* (cattle). The association of money with sacrificial animals—especially with cattle and bulls—is particularly suggestive. The bull not only is a familiar figure on Wall Street but was commonly used in ancient sacrifices. In Rome, the Mithraic cult, which was a serious threat to early Christianity, centered on the sacrifice of the bull, and in Greece, the god Dionysus was traditionally represented as a bull, which was periodically ritually sacrificed.

As I have suggested, within a sacrificial economy, the current flows in two directions: from worshippers to god, and from god to worshippers. Ritual practices establish a system of exchange in which devotees offer sacrifices to secure protection and benefits from the gods. In the early stages of religious development, these offerings tended to be either human or animal sacrifices. In time, however, substitutions were introduced. At first, small figures of the sacrificial animals usually were made out of precious metals, and, later, coins bearing the images of animals were offered to the gods. As rituals were formalized, priests and other religious and political officials prescribed the terms of exchange.

A related aspect of ritual sacrifice, which is crucial for establishing and maintaining the economic relationship between god and believer, is the communal meal. Anthropologists have long recognized the important role that sharing and eating the flesh of the sacrificial animal plays in the constitution of religious communities. The animal is not only an offering *to* the god but also an embodiment *of* the deity. Sacrifice, therefore, involves the death, or more precisely the murder, of God. As Freud maintains in his myth of social origins in *Totem and Taboo,* participants in ritual sacrifice attempt to share guilt and identify with the god by consuming its body. From this perspective, all culture is originally consumer culture and every economy is a consumer economy.

In ancient Rome, it was not uncommon for shares of the sacrificial bull's flesh to serve as a legal means of payment. At this point, the practice of substitution once again tended to intervene. Tokens, which often took the form of coins made of precious metal with the imprint of the sacred animal, replaced animal flesh. Insofar as community is constituted by an act of "originary" violence, the god who dies on the sacrificial altar is reborn or, quite literally, becomes incarnate in the social body. The token of divine presence in the community is the coin of the realm, which bears the *imago dei.*

The Christian adaptation of these ancient ritual practices underscores the importance of Shakespeare's description of money as a "visible god/ That sold'rest close impossibilities/ And mak'st them kiss." As the visible presence of the invisible God, Jesus Christ is, in effect, the token of exchange, which establishes and maintains the relation between divinity and humanity. The person and work of Christ "sold'rest" together "impossibilities," like God/man, immaterial/material, spirit/matter, and universality/particularity, to create a salvific economy, which presupposes a ritual sacrifice.

A strange circuit joins the electronic money of Gordon Gekko and the earliest christological reflections of the Church Fathers. From the outset, Christian apologists sought to create analogies that would help to explain the seemingly paradoxical person of Christ. Tertullian was among the first to draw on the resources of classical philosophy to describe the unity of the person of Jesus. In his widely influential *Against Praxeas* he writes:

> If the Logos became flesh by a transfiguration of and change of substance, it follows at once that Jesus must be a substance [made up] of two substances—of flesh and spirit—a kind of mixture (*mixtura*) like electrum [made up] of gold and silver; and it begins to be neither gold, that is to say, spirit, nor silver, that is to say flesh—the one being changed into the other, and the third substance produced . . . a *tertium quid.*[10]

Electrum is the material out of which the earliest non-Chinese coins were made. Around the sixth century B.C.E., coins appeared for the first time in the Western world in Lydia and Ionia. In the rivers running through a region of what is now Turkey, the Lydians and Ionians panned for a light-yellow precious metal, which was a natural amalgam of gold and silver. "According to Greek legend, the rich deposits of the Pactolus river near Sardis, the Lydian capital, were the result of Midas's bathing in the torrents to wash away his dangerously embarrassing golden touch, which had even turned his food into gold. The Lydian metal was called 'electrum' because of its amber-like appearance."[11] The Greek word for amber is *elektron,* which refers to the electromagnetic field created when amber is rubbed.

While never expressed in precisely these terms, Christ is, for Tertullian, the currency of exchange between the divine and the human. The union of God and man in Christ is strictly analogous to the combination of gold and silver in electrum. Even though they remain separable, gold and silver combine to create electrum, whose defining characteristic is the capacity to generate and transmit electric current. In a similar manner, spirit and flesh, though remaining separable, fuse to create the God-Man whose distinguishing trait is the capacity to generate and transmit a *tertium quid.* Neither the Father nor the Son, "the third substance," which results from this combinatory process, is an occult force known as "Spirit."

The emergence of Spirit discloses the trinitarian nature of the Christian God. Over the centuries, the doctrine of the Trinity has been one of the most puzzling Christian notions. To many ordinary believers, the Trinity seems to be a product of theological excess, which unnecessarily complicates faith. While the controversies surrounding the Trinity have often been intricate and rancorous, this doctrine plays a crucial role in Christian belief. The notion of the Trinity represents an effort to mediate two apparently opposite claims: Jesus is God, and God is one. The problem Christians face is how to affirm the divinity of Christ without slipping into polytheism.

To maintain the divinity of Christ and the unity of God, theologians have traditionally distinguished the "immanent" and the "economic" Trinity. While the immanent Trinity refers to the relations among the Father, Son, and Spirit within the godhead, the economic Trinity specifies the relation between God and human beings in the process of salvation. According to the christological formulation established at the Council of Nicaea (325) and reconfirmed at the Council of Constantinople (381), the possibility of salvation presupposes the divinity of both the Son and the Holy Spirit. The actualization of this possibility takes place through an economic process, which involves an exchange of gifts between God and his followers. The transcendent God becomes incarnate in the person of the Son to redeem humankind.

The sins of the human race can be overcome only through the incarnation and sacrifice of God. Since human beings do not have the power of being at their disposal, they are indebted to God for their very existence. The proper religious attitude involves a confession of the creature's ongoing dependence upon the Creator. God gives life and in return expects faithful devotion. Within this network of exchange, the divine gift is acknowledged through countergifts or offerings. When people fail to appreciate the primordial debt incurred though the originary gift, they fall into a state of sin from which they cannot free themselves. Sin further compounds humankind's debt. Now the fallen sinner depends upon God not only for his or her creation but also for recreation or redemption. When the gift is doubled, debt becomes more profound. Totally dependent upon the Creator, human beings can offer only what they have always already received. While economic models and metaphors for the process of salvation run throughout the Christian tradition, Anselm of Canterbury develops one of the most influential christological formulations in his treatise *Cur Deus Homo?* Summarizing his argument for the rational necessity of the incarnation, he writes:

> The heart of the question is this: Why did God become man, to save man by his death, when it seems that he could have done this some other way? You have answered this by showing many necessary reasons, how it would have been right for the restoration of human nature to be left undone, and how it could not have been done unless man paid what was owing to God for sin. But the debt was so great that, while man alone owed it, only God could pay it, so that the same person must be both God and man. Thus it was necessary for God to make manhood into the unity of his person, so that he who in his own nature ought to pay and could not should be in a person who could. Then you showed that the Man who also was God was to be taken from a virgin, and by the person of the Son of God, and how he could be taken from the sinful mass without sin. Moreover, you have proved most straightforwardly that the life of this Man was so sublime, so precious, that it can suffice to pay what is owing for the sins of the world, and infinitely more.[12]

When understood in this way, Christ is something like a token of exchange, which restores the balance of payments between the divine and the human.

The Incarnation is a necessary but not sufficient condition for salvation. The redemptive power of Christ becomes effective in the lives of believers through the agency of the Holy Spirit. While Spirit can operate in any domain of life, the most common channel of its activity—especially in Catholicism—is the Eucharist. The Eucharist, as I have noted, is the Christian version of the ancient totem meal. By consuming the body and blood of Christ, human beings are reconciled to God. Spirit is no longer limited to intradivine relations but spreads to incorporate believers in the economy of salvation. Since the early years of Christianity, it has been common practice to produce communion wafers that resemble metal coins. "The wafer," Marc Shell explains,

> was expressly manufactured like coin: it was pressed between wafer irons and impressed with insignia like those of coins. . . . That the manufacturing process of making the Eucharist wafer from flour paste was often technically similar to making coins from metal ingots allowed thinkers like Nicholas of Cusa in fifteenth-century Germany to observe how the Eucharist wafer's symbolic representation of the body of Jesus—or its actually being that body—has a numismatically iconic character.[13]

The similarity between wafer and coin is underscored by the use of the term *species* to designate both coined money and the outward form of consecrated eucharistic elements. Indeed, the sign designating the dollar, $, was borrowed from the Christian numismatic sign IHS, which stands for *in hoc signo* (by the sign).[14] The Spirit of God represented in the eucharistic wafer is the currency of exchange, which establishes the identity of differences within the godhead and mediates the opposition between divinity and humanity throughout the history of salvation.

Speculative Investments

The far-reaching implications of the Christian doctrine of the Trinity did not become clear until Hegel developed his speculative philosophy. Far from a symptom of theological excess, the Trinity, Hegel insists, is not only central to Christian faith but is crucial for the course of history as a whole. In *The Philosophy of History,* he goes so far as to assert: "God is thus recognized as *Spirit* only when known as the Triune. This new principle is the axis on which the history of the world turns. This is *the goal* and the *starting point* of history."[15] Christianity is, for Hegel, the absolute religion in which truth is fully present but incompletely expressed. The doctrine of the Trinity provides a representation of the Absolute Idea, which constitutes the substance of all reality.

Within Hegel's system, the Trinity is implicitly the speculative Absolute Idea. As perfect mirror images of each other, Father and Son are joined through Spirit. "Father is the other of son, and son the other of father, and each *is* as this other of the other; and at the same time, the one determination only is, in relation to the other; their being is a *single* subsistence."[16] The "single subsistence," which constitutes the being of the Father and Son, is the *tertium quid* that Tertullian identifies with electrum. Unlike his more conservative predecessors, Hegel does not view God as transcendent to the created order but regards the divine as immanent in the processes of nature and history. The self-reflexivity of Spirit revealed in the Trinity discloses the universal structure of reality. In Hegel's speculative system, Spirit is the medium in and through which differences are reconciled without being negated: "The Idea is just this act of distinguishing or differentiation, which at the same time gives no difference and does not hold to this difference as permanent. God beholds Himself in what is differentiated; and when, in His Other, He is united only with Himself, He is in close union only with Himself, He beholds *Himself* in His other."[17] In contrast to those who insist that the doctrine of the Trinity is irrational, Hegel maintains that it is thoroughly logical. Indeed, the entire Hegelian system is based on the logical structure of the Trinity.

The heart of Hegel's notoriously complex *Logic* is his consideration of the "Determinations of Reflection" at the beginning of the second book. Contrary to common sense, Hegel argues, "a consideration of everything that is shows that *in its own self* everything is in its selfsameness different from itself and self-contradictory, and that in its difference, in its contradiction, it is self-identical, and is in its own self this movement of transition of one of these categories into the other, and for this reason, that each is in its own self the opposite of itself."[18] Within this scheme, identity and difference are not merely opposites; rather, each contains the other within itself as a condition of *its own* actuality. Identity becomes itself in and through difference, and difference becomes itself in and through identity. In Hegel's words: "Identity is the reflection-into-self that is identity only as internal repulsion, and is this repulsion as reflection-into-self, repulsion, which immediately takes itself back into itself. Thus it is identity as difference that is identical with itself" (413). The self-relation that forms identity is necessarily mediated by opposition to otherness. Consequently, in the act of affirming itself, identity negates itself and becomes its opposite, difference. *"Identity is difference,"* for *"identity is* different from difference" (413).

Conversely, difference *as* difference, so-called pure or absolute difference, is indistinguishable from identity. Difference constitutes itself by opposition to its opposite, identity. Since Hegel has argued that identity is inherently difference, he claims that in relating itself to its apparent opposite, difference really relates to itself. Relation to other turns out to be self-relation. In the act of affirming itself, difference likewise negates itself and becomes its opposite, identity. "Difference," Hegel concludes, "in itself is self-related difference; as such it is the negativity of itself, the difference not of an other, but *of itself from itself;* it is not itself but its other. But that which is different from difference is identity. Difference is, therefore, itself and identity. Both together constitute difference; it is the whole, and its moment" (417).

Identity, in itself difference, and difference, in itself identity, join in contradiction, which Hegel defines as the identity of identity and difference. Inasmuch as identity and difference necessarily include their opposites within themselves, they are inherently self-contradictory.

> Each has an indifferent self-subsistence of its own through the fact that it has within itself the relation to its other moment; it is thus the whole, self-contained opposition. As this whole, each is mediated with itself *by its other* and *contains* it. But further, it is mediated with itself by the *non-being of its other;* hence it is a unity existing on its own account and it *excludes* the other from itself. . . . It is thus contradiction. (431)

Though not immediately obvious, Hegel's intricate analysis of the union of identity and difference in contradiction is a speculative rendering of the Christian doctrines of the Incarnation and the Trinity. Just as the Father becomes the Father in and through the Son, and vice versa, so identity becomes itself in and through difference and vice versa. Since Christ, according to orthodox Christology, is fully God and fully man, the Son is *in himself* the Father and the Father is *in himself* the Son. The unity of Father and Son creates the contradiction definitive of Spirit.

Spirit, as I have suggested, is rational; more precisely, spirit *is* reason. In order to translate religious image into philosophical concept, it is necessary to demonstrate the universal validity of the truth disclosed in the particular person of Jesus. When philosophically comprehended, the Christian doctrine of God reveals the structure of the Absolute. As the self-reflexive principle, which is the ground of being, the Absolute is the universal medium in and through which identities and differences are created and sustained. If one moves beyond the Aristotelian principle of noncontradiction, it becomes possible to discern the syllogistic structure of the Hegelian Absolute.

I—U—P
[Individuality—Universality—Particularity]

> The middle term of this syllogism is indeed the unity of the extremes, but a unity in which abstraction is made from their determinateness; it is the *indeterminate* universal. But since this universal is at the same time distinguished as *abstract* from the extremes as *determinate,* it is itself still a *determinate* relatively to them, and the whole is a syllogism whose relation to its Concept has now to be considered. The middle term, as the universal, is the subsuming term or predicate to *both* its extremes, and does not occur once as subsumed or as subject. Insofar, therefore, as it is supposed to correspond, as *species* of syllogism, to the syllogism, it can do so only on the condition that when one relation I—U already possesses the proper relationship, the other relation U—P also possesses it. (678)

The species of the syllogism is the currency that forms the medium for every type of exchange.

While the species of the syllogism is the rational articulation of the eucharistic species, our analysis of speculative logic seems to have led us far from the question of money. But the relationship between God and the Absolute, on the one hand, and, on the other, currency is closer than it initially appears. In order to understand the way in which Hegel's speculative system prepares the way for later accounts of money and financial networks, it is necessary to underscore four aspects of his argument. (1) The Hegelian Absolute functions as something like what Aristotle, in his account of money, describes as "the universal equivalent," which creates the possibility for exchange by providing a common measure that establishes the identity of differences. (2) Though Hegel remains committed to an onto-logic, which presupposes the isomorphism of subject and object, his dialectical logic implies a shift from a referential to a relational interpretation of meaning and value. Translating speculative logic into semiotic terms, meaning is not secured by the reference of a signifier to a signified but emerges from the diacritical play of signs. (3) The structure of the Absolute Idea implies a notion of speculation that involves not only rational reflection but also rational economic relations. Within a reasonable economy, investment is never made without the expectation of a profitable return. The dialectical structure of the Idea is an insurance policy against excessive spending and irrational expenditures. (4) Materiality and immateriality are not merely opposites but are coimplicated in such a way that each entails the other. Since the foundation of nature as well as history is the divine Logos, immaterial structures are constitutive of ostensibly material realities.

While apparently far removed from the world of Gordon Gekko's speculative ventures, Hegel's speculative philosophy actually anticipates the aestheticization of money, which characterizes postindustrial capitalism. In the late twentieth century, something approximating the Hegelian Absolute appears in global networks of exchange where money is virtually immaterial. When read through Hegel's logical analysis of Spirit, it becomes clear that money is God in more than a trivial sense.

Immaterial Materialities

"Money," Marx declares, "is the god among commodities." This God is simultaneously immanent in and transcendent to worldly processes, which appear to be thoroughly secular. Elsewhere Marx clarifies his cryptic identification of God and money when he writes, "Money is the incarnation of exchange value."[19] Since capital is "the most developed form of money," God eventually appears as capital and capital is ultimately revealed to be divine. According to conventional wisdom, Marx develops his dialectical materialism by turning Hegel on his head and reinterpreting speculative logic in terms of concrete processes of production. While this reading of Marx is not incorrect, it tends to obscure the extent of his debt to Hegel. Since Marx formulates his analysis of capital by appropriating Hegel's interpretation of the Spirit, capital functions in Marxist economics like God, Spirit, and the Absolute function in Hegelian philosophy.

As the incarnation of exchange value, money always involves a certain excess. Exchange becomes possible when a surplus that exceeds use value accumulates. For example, members of a certain community might produce more cows than they can use but not have enough horses to plow their fields. A neighboring community might have more horses than they need but not have enough cows. The obvious solution to this dilemma is for the groups to trade their cows and horses. On the most rudimentary level, economic relations involve the exchange of actual items for which there is either need or desire. As social communities become more complex, such one-for-one exchange becomes less common. A village might produce more cows than it can use but not want the horses its neighbors are trying to trade. To move beyond such a barter economy, it is necessary to develop a measure that can establish the relative worth of different commodities. This measure, medium, or *tertium quid* is Aristotle's "universal equivalent." By providing a common standard of value, the universal equivalent establishes the unity of differences, which makes exchange possible.

For commodities to circulate, exchange value must be embodied or incarnate in a particular commodity, which is not itself an object of exchange. The universal equivalent, therefore, should not have any use value but must remain superfluous, excessive, and, in a certain sense, useless. Money, whether in the form of precious metals, scraps of paper, or bits of light, meets these requirements.

> Commodities, first of all, enter into the process of exchange just as they are. The process then differentiates them into commodities and money, and thus produces an external opposition corresponding to the internal opposition inherent in them, as being at once use-values and values. Commodities as use-values now stand opposed to money as exchange-value. On the other hand, both opposing sides are commodities, unities of use-value and value. But this unity of differences manifests itself at two opposite poles, at each pole in an opposite way. Being poles they are necessarily opposite as they are connected. On the one side of the equation we have an ordinary commodity, which is in reality a use-value. Its value is expressed only ideally in its price, by which it is equated to its opponent, the gold, as to the real embodiment of its value. On the other hand, the gold, in its metallic reality, ranks as the embodiment of value, as money. Gold, as gold, is exchange-value itself.[20]

As the mediating third, which secures the unity of differences, money is the "metamorphosed shape of all commodities." Through a magic approaching alchemy, different things are, in effect, transformed into gold, which assures the "equation of the heterogeneous."[21] Marx expresses the structural relation between money and commodities with the following formula:

$$\text{Commodity—Money—Commodity}$$
$$\text{C—M—C}$$

This equation summarizes the two moments of exchange: sale, in which commodity is transformed into money (C—M); and purchase, in which money is transformed into commodity (M—C). The currency of exchange allows opposites to flow into each other.

Though never explicitly acknowledged, Marx's argument rests upon a deployment of Hegel's speculative logic to formulate the logic of money and, by extension, of capital. The logic of capital conforms to the syllogistic structure of Hegel's Absolute Idea. Just as universal Spirit unites individuality and particularity (I—U—P), so the universal machinations of money and capital mediate particular commodities (C—M—C). Money is the condition of the possibility of exchange, which is both immanent in and transcendent to the world of commodities. Systems of exchange presuppose something that is not subject to exchange and, therefore, remains "outside" the economic system. This "exteriority," which, paradoxically, is "inside" every system of exchange, is, like God, "omnipresent." Invoking biblical terms to describe money, Marx writes: "If money appears as the general commodity in all places, so also does it in all times. It maintains itself as wealth at all times. Its specific durability. It is the treasure which neither rusts nor moths eat up. All commodities are only transitory money; money is the permanent commodity. Money is the omnipresent commodity."[22] Far from static, the permanence of money is its ceaseless circulation.

As money assumes its final form in capital, the self-reflexivity of the exchange process becomes clear. When exchange value no longer is anchored in use value, "growing wealthy is an end in itself." "Exchange value posits itself as exchange value only by realizing itself; i.e. increasing its value. *Money* (as returned to itself from circulation), *as capital, has lost its rigidity, and from a tangible thing has become a process.*"[23] Marx's argument again turns on his reading of Hegel. As we have seen in our consideration of Hegel's speculative logic, everything becomes itself in and through its own other. Just as the Father who in himself is also the Son, and the Son, who in himself is also the Father, are united through Spirit, so every particular entity includes its other within itself as a condition of its own actuality. This structure of identity-in-difference and difference-in-identity is "the universal process" through which everything arises and passes away. Expressed in terms of the speculative syllogism, the universal is the particular and the particular is the universal. Marx translates Hegel's speculative universal into the universal equivalent and interprets specific commodities as particularities, which are essentially concrete universals.

> The transition from simple exchange value and its circulation to capital can also be expressed in this way: Within circulation, exchange value appears double: once as commodity, again as money. If it is in one aspect, it is not in the other. This holds for every particular commodity. But the wholeness of circulation, regarded in itself, lies in the fact that the same exchange value, exchange value as subject, posits itself once as commodity,

another time as money, and that it is just this movement of positing itself in this dual character and of preserving itself in each of them as its opposite, in the commodity as money and in money as commodity. This in itself is present in simple circulation, but is not posited in it. Exchange value posited as the unity of commodity and money is *capital*, and this positing itself appears as the circulation of capital.[24]

Since the commodity is both itself and a concrete instantiation of capital, capital, which posits itself as other in the commodity, relates itself to itself in and through its own other. The self-referentiality of capital is a further extension of the self-reflexivity of the Absolute Idea.

Capital closes the circle of money's self-becoming. Investment is always calculated to yield the most profitable return. In this autotelic process, the purpose of the economy is nothing other than its own self-perpetuation.

> In the circulation of capital, the point of departure is posited as the terminal point and the terminal point is posited as the point of departure. The capitalist himself is the point of departure and of return. He exchanges money for the conditions of production, produces, realizes the product, i.e. transforms it into money, and then begins the process anew. The circulation of money, regarded for itself, necessarily becomes extinguished in money as a static thing. The circulation of capital constantly ignites itself anew, divides into its different moments, and is a *perpetuum mobile*.[25]

The economy, like speculative philosophy, "exhibits itself as a *circle* returning upon itself, the end being wound back into the beginning, the simple ground, by the mediation; this circle is moreover a *circle of circles,* for each individual member as ensouled by the method is reflected into itself, so that in returning into the beginning it is at the same time the beginning of a new member."[26] Perpetually in motion, the circle of circles is the divine pulse of an economy that knows no bounds.

Marx recognizes the incipient idealism of his analysis of capital when he acknowledges money "as the medium of circulation becomes coin, mere vanishing moment, mere *symbol* of the value it exchanges." "After money is posited really as commodity, the commodity will be posited ideally as money."[27] This change initiates a process of separation between coin and value, or, in different terms, image and thing, or signifier and signified. The disjunction of appearance and "reality" releases a chain of substitutions through which the expenditure of surplus is repeatedly displaced.

The fact that the currency of coins itself effects a separation between their nominal and their real weight, creating a distinction between them as mere pieces of metal on the one hand, and as coins with a definite function on the other—this fact implies that the latent possibility of replacing metallic coins by tokens of some other material, by symbols serving the same purposes as coins. . . . Silver and copper tokens take the place of gold in those regions of circulation where coins pass from hand to hand most rapidly, and are subject to the maximum amount of wear and tear. . . . The weight of the metal in the silver and copper tokens is arbitrarily fixed by the law. When in currency, they wear away even more rapidly than gold coins. Hence their functions are totally independent of their weight, and consequently of all value. The function of gold as coin becomes completely independent of the metallic value of that gold. Therefore things that are relatively without value, such as paper notes, can serve as coins in its place. This purely symbolic character is to a certain extent masked in metal tokens. In paper money it stands out plainly.[28]

The process that Marx charts can be described as the *dematerialization of the token of exchange.* As currency develops, the medium of exchange shifts from the thing itself (for example, a cow or a horse) to gold, to gold coins, to silver and copper coins, to paper, and eventually to information coded in blips of light on video terminals. This dematerialization or idealization is an aestheticization in which the thing becomes a symbol or image. The threat Marx sees in the separation of signifier and signified is the possibility of confusing "semblance" with "reality." "The only difference, therefore, between coin and bullion, is one of shape, and gold can at any time pass from one form to the other. But no sooner does coin leave the mint than it immediately finds itself on the high-road to the melting pot. During their currency, coins wear away, some more, others less. Name and substance, nominal weight and real weight, begin their process of separation."[29] Paradoxically, the disappearance of the image from the face of the coin creates the possibility for the image to return as the "thing itself." If the image is the thing itself, the flow of capital is the circulation of images. The symbolic constitution of capital subverts the opposition between the ideality of suprastructures and the materiality of infrastructures. When the token of exchange dematerializes, we approach Gordon Gekko's world where "the illusion has become real."

While Marx acknowledges processes of idealization at work in the circulation of currency, he resists working out the implications of the aestheticization of capital. Undoubtedly part of the reason for this reluctance is his realization that the symbolic status of currency poses problems for the distinction between immaterial suprastructure and material infrastructure, which undergirds his entire analysis. It was left for Georg Simmel to explore the territory Marx had opened. In his remarkable book *The Philosophy of Money,* Simmel attempts "to construct a new storey beneath historical materialism such that the explanatory value of the incorporation of economic life into the causes of intellectual culture is preserved, while these economic forms themselves are recognized as the result of more profound valuations and currents of psychological or even metaphysical preconditions."[30] By reconsidering historical materialism in terms of symbolic networks of exchange, Simmel effectively bridges the idealistic economies of the nineteenth century and the virtual economies of the twenty-first century.

For Simmel, as for Marx, money functions in a manner strictly parallel to the operation of Hegel's Absolute. As we have seen, within Hegel's speculative logic, meaning and value are relational rather than referential. Simmel bases his account of money on this new theory of value. "The philosophical significance of money," he argues, "is that it represents within the practical world the most certain image and the clearest embodiment of the formula of all being, according to which things receive their meaning through each other, and have their being determined by their mutual relations" (128–29). While Marx occasionally draws analogies between money and God, Simmel consistently stresses what can only be described as spiritual and metaphysical dimensions of money. At one point he goes so far as to assert that money "is, as it were, an *actus purus;* it lives in continuous self-alienation from any given point and thus forms the counterpart and direct negation of all being in itself" (511). By negating all being-in-itself, this *actus purus* establishes a network of constitutive relations in which being is always being-for-another. When understood in this way, the significance of money extends far beyond the domain of economics. Money, according to Simmel, "is the historical symbol for the relative character of existence" (510).

While Marx recognizes that "coin is also only a *symbol* whose material is irrelevant," his commitment to materialism prevents him from developing the implications of his own insight. Simmel, by contrast, never accepts dialectical materialism and therefore realizes that money can facilitate exchange only when it is symbolic and thus in some sense ideal.

> The significance of money is only to express the value relations between other objects. It succeeds in this with the aid of man's developed intelligence, which is able to equate the relations between things even though the things themselves are not identical or similar. This ability only gradually evolves from the more primitive capacity to judge and express the

identity or similarity of two objects directly. . . . This ideal significance
of money as a standard and expression of the value of goods has remained
completely unchanged, whereas its character as an intermediary, as a
means to store and transport values, has changed in some degree and is
still in the process of changing. Money passes from the form of directness
and substantiality in which it first carried out these functions to its ideal
form; that is, exercises its effects merely as an idea, which is embodied
in a representative symbol. (147, 148)

When money functions "merely as an idea, which is embodied in a representative symbol," the process of dematerializing currency reaches closure.

One of Simmel's most important contributions is his recognition of
the aesthetic dimensions of money. By underscoring the interrelation of
dematerialization and aestheticization, he points to an aspect of Hegel's
system that becomes important in later interpretations of currency.
Hegel, as I have noted, argues that philosophy provides the rational articulation of the truth revealed in religious images. But religion is not the
only domain of culture in which truth appears. Prior to religion and
philosophy, truth is manifest in artistic images. Art, religion, and philosophy, according to Hegel, differ in form but not in content. Just as the
Christian doctrine of the Trinity prefigures the self-reflexive structure
of the Absolute Idea, so the work of art anticipates the Trinity.

Hegel draws his analysis of art from Kant's critical philosophy.[31] Indeed, Hegel's entire system can be understood as an extended elaboration
of the account of beauty that Kant presents in the *Critique of Judgment*.
The beautiful is, in Kant's well-known definition, "purposiveness without purpose." Kant identifies two primary examples of such purposeless
purpose—one natural, the other cultural: the living organism and the
work of art. To argue that the living organism is characterized by purposiveness without purpose is to insist that the end, purpose, or goal of
the organism is nothing other than the organism itself. In contrast to
mechanical relations in which means and end are external to each other,
in the living organism means and end are internally related in such a
way that they are mutually constitutive. This reciprocity engenders a
harmonious accord that insures the vitality of the organism. The internal
relation of means and end creates the "inner teleology" constitutive of
the organism. When inner teleology is translated from the natural into
the cultural domain, it appears as a beautiful work of art in which parts
and whole are internally related. The source of pleasure in a beautiful

artwork is the harmony it displays. Simmel's argument rests on his claim that the principles constitutive of art are also at work in money.

> The possible conformity of such relations to a norm produces an aesthetic cosmos, a precise order, an ideal homogeneity in relation to value, from the individual works which are initially quite heterogeneous. This is not only true for the world of art. Out of the material of our isolated valuations there develops a pattern of graded significance. Disharmony is experienced only as a result of the desire for a consistent order and an inner relation of values. We owe this essential feature of our world view to our ability to balance against each other not only two things, but also the relations of these two to two others, and so unite them by judging them equal or similar. Money, as a product of this fundamental power or form of our mind, is not only its most extreme example, but is, as it were, its pure embodiment. (146–47)

With the recognition of the aesthetic dimensions of money, we are brought to the threshold of virtual culture in which signs are real and reality is always already a sign of a sign.

The Death of Go(l)d

Going off the gold standard is the economic equivalent of the death of God. God functions in religious systems like gold functions in economic systems. God, like gold, is a sign constructed to deny its status as sign. The function of God and gold is to safeguard the meaning and value of signs by providing a secure referent. When this referent is abandoned, signs are left to float freely. Meaning and value no longer are determined by reference to a transcendental signified but now emerge through the diacritical interplay of freely floating signifiers. In economic terms, the value of any particular currency is a function of its relation to other currencies circulating in global financial networks. The shift from a referential to a relational determination of value marks a fundamental economic change that Baudrillard labels "the structural revolution of value." The unlinking of the monetary sign from its material referent creates "spectacular capital," which is liquid or, more precisely light. Money, he explains,

> becomes speculative. From the gold-standard, which had already ceased to be the representative equivalent of a real production but still retains

traces of this in a certain equilibrium (little inflation, the convertibility of money into gold, etc.) to hot money and generalized flotation, money is transformed from a referential sign into its structural form—the "float-ing" signifier's own logic, not in Lévi-Strauss's sense, where it has not yet discovered its signified, but in the sense that it is well rid of every signified (every "real" equivalent) as a brake to its proliferation and its unlimited play.[32]

If the play of signs is not arrested by any residual exteriority, money ceases to be the medium through which commodities circulate and be-comes "circulation itself." This circulation is an end in itself, which, like speculative philosophy, is a "circle of circles."

During the last quarter of the twentieth century, this circulation has become both global and electronic. In the ether nets of worldwide webs, currency is coded information. The universal equivalent is no longer a dialectical idea but a binary code that permits absolute convertibility of differences into identity and identity into differences. As currency be-comes electronic, capital is virtualized. Virtualization extends and ampli-fies the processes of dematerialization and aestheticization through which the "real" disappears. The binary code operating in electronic financial networks reflects the dialectical idea prefigured in the beautiful work of art and the trinitarian God. Not only are speculative philosophy and the speculative economy a play of mirrors, but the isomorphic self-reflexivity of one is the mirror image of the other. The reversibility of the code at work in what once appeared to be infrastructure and suprastructure makes it impossible to determine which is ground and which is grounded. The networks in which "reality" is constituted are neither profound nor superficial but are complex symbolic systems, which remain open-ended and indeterminate.

Important practical consequences follow from this conclusion. As we have seen, some of the most influential critics of postindustrial capitalism insist that if illusions fabricated to promote consumerism and the market economy are to be overcome, "the real" must, in some way, be recovered. Only if there is an "extratextual" referent, they argue, can cultural criti-cism and political action be effective. But this line of analysis is, I have argued, theoretically mistaken and practically misguided. Marx's latter-day followers could profit from a careful reconsideration of his grudging acknowledgment of the inescapable ideality of capital. "Reality" is always already encoded and, thus, can never be definitively distinguished from appearance or even illusion. Moreover, so-called materiality is so thor-oughly imbricated in immaterial structures and processes that we cannot be sure where the material ends and the immaterial begins. It is simply impossible to establish the qualitative difference between symbolic suprastructures and material infrastructures. What once appeared to be clearly defined opposites now seem to be complex interfaces.

While it is generally acknowledged that postindustrialism is inseparable from an information economy, there is little agreement about how this latest transmutation of economic systems is to be understood. The information economy has two primary characteristics: information becomes currency, and currency becomes information. Though the token of exchange has become immaterial, the consequences of its circulation are no less real. What once was known as reality now is constituted in complex information networks. Accordingly, to transform the "real," it is necessary to reconfigure the "ideal." The psychological, social, political, and economic struggles we face do not involve a conflict between the symbolic and the real but entail a contest among competing symbolic systems and networks. In a world where all reality is becoming virtual reality, effective economic strategies and political action must be calculatedly artful.

Seven

The Virtual Kingdom

Bets Are Riding on Bible Theme Park in Gambling Capital

FIGURE 6   José Márquez, Las Vegas

LAS VEGAS, August 8—Walk with Jesus, watch the waters of the Red Sea part, stand in awe as Lazarus rises from the dead. A group of Hollywood investors thinks the public has had enough of Mickey Mouse theme parks and is ready for a more spiritual ride.

Welcome to "Holy Land"—a high-minded dream that seeks to become a full-blown reality and open its pearly gates just an hour's drive from the fleshpots and poker tables of America's gambling capital.

If the city of Mesquite, Nevada, approves the plans, the $1.1 billion religious theme park could be competing for the souls of Las Vegas gamblers.

"We are trying to reconstruct the Holy Bible," Daxx Edder, CEO of Quorum International Ltd., said. "The idea is it will be a historical document that you'll be able to walk through instead of read. All we need right now is the land. We've got the funds available," added Edder, who took the proposal to the Mesquite city council, which has asked for more details.

Mayor Ken Carter was keen: "If it is real, of course, I have some real optimism about the theme park as a very successful business venture for our area."

Carl Godfrey, a financial consultant hired by Quorum, said the 3,000-acre park will operate like Epcot Center. . . . Godfrey denied newspaper reports that the theme park would feature a 33-storey-high statue of Jesus that people could climb inside. "There will be some amusement rides of that nature but not what you would think (of) as coming from a large amusement park," he said. "We are thinking about creating the parting of the Red Sea and you would ride a tram past it like they do in Universal Studios theme park."

In addition to the parting of the Red Sea, he said, the park will feature virtual reality, holographic, theatrical, and statuary recreations of scenes from the Bible.[1]

"If it is real, of course . . ." This is the question—always *the* question. The question of the real is what Las Vegas is all about: What is real? Where is the real? Is anything real? Is everything real? Is nothing real?

Holy Land appears to have the blessing of at least certain church officials.

The Reverend Pat Leary, vicar general of the Roman Catholic diocese of Las Vegas, said he saw no problem with the park, as long as it is in good taste. "Jesus said, 'By their fruits ye shall know them,'" he said. "So if it helps people, if it brings them to a deeper understanding of faith or Christ, it's fine. However, I don't know that much about it. I hear it's a commercial endeavor. Sometimes such endeavors border on bad taste. Still, there's nothing intrinsically wrong or right about it," he added.

Godfrey also said he saw nothing wrong with using religion as the basis for a theme park. "How many movies and television shows have we seen about religious subjects? Everybody out there is making money off religion. The Catholic Church is the richest business in the world and the world's largest landowner," he said.

"We're not trying to embrace any one religion. All we're trying to do is to present it in the best light we can so people can experience these religions. If people had a chance to study and understand, I think it would make this world a better place to live."

The dream of Holy Land, it seems, is to "make this world a better place to live" (and, of course, to make a profit). This is an ancient dream that has long inspired the religious imagination. The longer one ponders the

FIGURE 7   José Márquez, Las Vegas

circuitous modern history of this dream, the less incongruous Holy Land becomes. Holy Land reveals a surprising truth about Las Vegas and, by so doing, sheds new light on our current sociocultural situation. Vegas is, among other things—many other things—*about* religion. In this city in the desert, where millions of people believe dreams come true, we discover what becomes of religion in the virtual culture that now is emerging. Las Vegas is where the death of God is staged as the spectacle of the Kingdom of God on earth.

This vision of Vegas admittedly seems as unlikely as Holy Land itself. Las Vegas, however, revels in the unlikely by promising to make the impossible possible. Eyes trained by the flickering lights of the Strip come to expect the unexpected. Far from an aberrant anomaly, Vegas forms the closure of a story that has been unfolding for more than two hundred years. To read Vegas through this story is to reread the story that is largely responsible for making us who we are and Western culture what it has become. This is a story about religion and art in which high becomes low and low becomes high through a process that is incarnational though not necessarily redemptive.

Artful Religion/Religious Art

The story begins at the end of a previous century. The 1790s, like the 1990s, was a period of extraordinary transition. As processes of modernization and industrialization spread, pressures for social, political, and economic reform mounted. Though the situation varied from country to country, the collapse of the French Revolution led to a widespread

FIGURE 8   New York, New York, Las Vegas

inward turn of the imagination, which directly and indirectly continues to shape our world. Summarizing an exceedingly complex course of events with admirable brevity and clarity, M. H. Abrams writes:

> To put the matter with the sharpness of drastic simplification: faith in an apocalypse by revelation had been replaced by faith in an apocalypse by revolution, and this now gave way to faith in an apocalypse by imagination or cognition. In the ruling two-term frame of Romantic thought, the mind of man confronts old heaven and earth and possesses within itself the

power, if it will but recognize and avail itself of the power, to transform
them into a new heaven and new earth, by means of a total revolution
of consciousness.[2]

Nowhere was this "apocalypse by imagination," which issued in "a total
revolution of consciousness," more patiently explored and creatively developed than in the small town of Jena in the duchy of Weimar.
Throughout the 1790s, a remarkable group of artists, writers, and philosophers gathered in Jena. Among those who were drawn to this cultural
cauldron were Herder, Goethe, the Schlegel brothers, Novalis, Tieck,
Fichte, Schiller, Hölderlin, Schelling, Schleiermacher, and Hegel. Out
of the creative tumult of these years comes a vision of "Weimar *Kultur*"
whose influence extends into this century in the search for a *Gesamtkunts-
werk,* which has inspired artistic endeavors as different as the *Festspiel*
of Bayreuth and the modern design of the Bauhaus. While Goethe's challenge to create a "poetic polity" loomed large in Jena, it was Kant's critical
philosophy that set the parameters within which Jena romantics interpreted their past and present, and projected a future that has become
our own. It is virtually impossible to understand adequately the significance of cultural developments in the twentieth century without an appreciation for the ways in which philosophers and poets appropriated
and elaborated Kant's insights.

The nineteenth century effectively begins with the publication of
Kant's *Critique of Judgment* in 1790. Intended to mediate the oppositions
and resolve the contradictions within and between the *Critique of Pure
Reason* (1781) and the *Critique of Practical Reason* (1788), the Third Critique marks a seismic shift in the intellectual landscape. The transition
from the eighteenth to the nineteenth century can be understood in terms
of a change from mechanistic to organic images and metaphors for con-
ceiving the world as well as human thought and experience. Kant develops his analysis of the difference between mechanism and organism by
recasting the ancient distinction between efficient and final causality in
terms of the problem of teleology or purposiveness. In mechanisms, cause
and effect, and, by extension, means and end, are *externally* related.
Drawing on the deistic image of God as a transcendent clockmaker, Kant
illustrates his understanding of mechanism with the example of a watch.
In a watch, he explains, "one part is certainly present for the sake of
another, but it does not owe its presence to the agency of that other. For
this reason, also, the producing cause of the watch and its form is [*sic*]
not contained in the nature of this material but lies outside the watch
in a being that can act according to ideas of a whole which its causality

makes possible."[3] The cause of the watch, in other words, is imposed from without by a watchmaker who remains external to his creation. Furthermore, the different parts of the watch are not integrally related but held together by an external design. In contrast to a machine, an organism is a *"self-organized being."* Rather than imposed from without, order in the organism *emerges* from within through a complex interplay of parts, which, in the final analysis, constitutes the activity of the whole. According to the principle of *"intrinsic finality,"* *"an organized natural product is one in which every part is reciprocally both end and means."* "The parts of the thing," Kant continues,

> combine of themselves into the unity of a whole by being reciprocally cause and effect of their form. For this is the only way in which it is possible that the idea of the whole may conversely, or reciprocally, determine in its turn the form and combination of all the parts, not as cause . . . but as the epistemological basis upon which the systematic unity of the form and combination of all the manifold contained in the given matter becomes cognizable for the person estimating it.[4]

Since means and end are reciprocally related, the parts of the organism do not point beyond themselves to an external telos but constitute their own end or purpose. In this way, the organism displays "inner teleology" or "purposiveness without purpose" (*Zweckmäßigkeit ohne Zweck*).

With the notion of "purposiveness without purpose," Kant identifies what he believes to be an "analogy" between nature and culture. The beautiful work of art, like the living organism, is its own end or purpose. Pointing to nothing beyond itself, the value of the work of art is *intrinsic.* This analogy between the living organism and the work of art must be qualified in three important ways. First, Kant establishes an analogy between the organism and art object rather than its production. Inasmuch as he regards artistic creation as similar to watchmaking, the production of the work of art still entails mechanical relations. Kant implies but does not articulate a reciprocity of whole and part, or form and content, which must arise from within. Accordingly, he seems to be struggling to imagine something like a work of art that has no creator or is self-creative. Second, from a certain point of view, the intrinsic value of the work of art is indistinguishable from its uselessness. The externality of cause and effect, which characterizes mechanism, entails a notion of utility in which the value of the means can be assessed in terms of the end. If an object is purposeless, it seems to be good for nothing. Paradoxically, it is precisely this purposelessness that is the purpose of art. Art is useful only if it is useless, and thus, when it becomes useful, it is useless. Third, the notion of "purposiveness without purpose" is a "regulative idea" or heuristic device that guides reflection and informs conduct but does not necessarily disclose anything about reality as such. The epistemological strictures articulated in the First Critique make it impossible for Kant to ascertain the truth of the ideas he conceives.

While thoroughly indebted to Kant's critical philosophy, even his most devoted followers insist that he does not carry his analysis far enough. Having glimpsed the reconciliation of the opposites rendering self and world, he fails to realize his vision. The challenge post-Kantian idealists face is to render his dream a reality. It should not be surprising that alternative efforts to address this challenge follow the basic structure of Kant's analysis. While some call for a practical realization of Kant's notion of beauty, others attempt to comprehend his aesthetic idea theoretically. This distinction between theory and practice, however, eventually erases itself in and through its development.

In *Letters on the Aesthetic Education of Man* (1795), Schiller develops the first sustained effort to translate Kant's aesthetic idea into reality by interpreting the distinction between mechanism and organism in terms of two forms of sociopolitical organization. Drawing on Adam Ferguson's account of the devastating impact of the division of labor necessary for industrialization, Schiller diagnoses the ills of modernity as isolation, alienation, and, most important, fragmentation. In his sixth letter, he describes a world in which life has become as routinized and mechanized as the machines that run it:

> Everlastingly chained to a single little fragment of the whole, man himself develops into nothing but a fragment; everlastingly in his ear the monotonous sound of the wheel that he turns, he never develops the harmony of his being, and instead of putting the stamp of his humanity upon his own nature, he becomes nothing more than the imprint of his occupation or of his specialized knowledge.[5]

Schiller situates his diagnosis within a narrative of loss and recovery that holds out the promise of a lasting cure. Like many of his fellow romantics, he was deeply influenced by Johann Joachim Winckelmann's interpretation of "aesthetic paganism." According to Winckelmann, ancient Greek life embodied an ideal order in which outer harmony reflected inner equilibrium. Using a term Nietzsche later employs for related purposes, Winckelmann labels this harmony "gaiety." "Balancing feeling and reason," Josef Chytry explains, gaiety, originally physiological, passes into the intellectual and spiritual capacities that are presupposed by the higher pursuit of beauty. When Nature and human being in this manner dwell together in beauty, the moment of "festival and play" occurs. This festive state allows the human being to dwell in his or her own beauty, both as a living artwork and as the highest manifestation of Nature's own character.[6]

Schiller reconceives Kant's aesthetic idea through Winckelmann's aesthetic paganism in such a way that the ancient past, where personal and social harmony were enjoyed by everyone, returns as an ideal future whose realization will overcome the isolation, alienation, and fragmentation plaguing the present. For Schiller, the reality of the work of art is not an aesthetic object but a sociopolitical community in which individuals are vital members of an organic whole. When completely actualized, the purpose of this community is nothing other than itself. This rereading of Kant's interpretation of the work of art marks a critical turning point in the history of Western aesthetics. *Letters on the Aesthetic Education of Man* initiates a displacement of religion by art that does not reach closure until the end of the twentieth century. The aesthetic utopia toward which we are supposed to be progressing is the worldly embodiment of what once was known as the Kingdom of God. The artist, who is leading us to this promised land, is a latter-day prophet whose religio-aesthetic pedagogy offers salvation to faithful followers. By reformulating religious mission as artistic practice, Schiller, in effect, defines what eventually becomes the task of the twentieth-century avant-garde.[7]

Recalling the ancient religious distinction between mysticism and militancy and anticipating competing strategies of many twentieth-century artists, Schiller argues that outward change presupposes inward transformation. "If principles I have laid down are correct, and if experience confirms my portrayal of the present age," he maintains, "then we must continue to regard every attempt at political reform as untimely, and every hope based upon it as chimerical, as long as the split within man is not healed, and his nature so restored to wholeness that it can itself become the artificer of the taste, and guarantee the reality of this political creation of reason" (45). This inner division, which reflects and is reflected by outer fragmentation, results from two opposing forces or drives: the "sense drive" (*Sinntrieb*) and the "form drive" (*Formtrieb*). Schiller elaborates this basic conflict through a series of binary oppositions: sensation/reason, feeling/thinking, passivity/activity, dependence/autonomy, necessity/freedom, change/identity, time/eternity, and becoming/being. If fragmentation is to be overcome and integration achieved, neither of these binaries can be completely repressed. Rather, *Sinntrieb* and *Formtrieb* must join in a mediating third that reconciles opposites without negating their differences. Schiller names this mediating third the *Spieltrieb*—the play drive, which, he explains, "is in duty bound to do justice to both drives equally: not simply to maintain the rational against the sensuous, but the sensuous against the rational too." Inasmuch as sense and reason are brought together in play, Schiller concludes, "man plays only when he is, in the full sense of the word, a man, and *he is only wholly man when he is playing*" (87, 80).

For play to have salvific effects, it must be expressed in art—or, more precisely, in fine art (*schöne Kunst*). Just as Kant attempts to reconcile theory and practice, reason and sensation, as well as obligation and inclination through aesthetic judgment, so Schiller seeks to heal the conflicts rending self and society through the beauty of art. Directly echoing Kant, Schiller contends that "beauty reflects all things as self-purposive." That which is beautiful is "not determined from outside" and thus represents what Schiller describes as "heautonomie."[8] Heautonomie mediates heteronomy and autonomy in such a way that determination by an other is at the same time self-determination. Since the heautonomie actualized in aesthetic play transforms external determination into self-determination, Schiller believes that "it is through beauty that we arrive at freedom" (27).

It should be clear that this account of the interrelation of art, play, and freedom reformulates Kant's notion of "purposiveness without purpose." Play, like the beautiful work of art, is purposeless or has no purpose other than itself. When activity is self-determined instead of determined by external circumstances, actors are free. But Schiller does not stop with the freedom of aesthetic play; the purposelessness of artful play actually has a purpose. As we have seen, inner freedom must be realized in the world. Art, therefore, not only brings self-transformation but also is the means by which society can be changed. In this way, art is "instrumental." This instrumentality, however, is strange, for the purpose of art is, in the final analysis, nothing other than art. Fine art, in other words, is the means to a more complete realization of art. Issuing a challenge to which the twentieth-century avant-garde indirectly responds, Schiller argues that the goal of aesthetic education is to *transform the world into a work of art*. Art becomes real in a social community where means and end are reciprocally related in such a way that individuals become themselves in and through a beautiful organic community and the community is vitalized by freely acting individuals. When this purpose is realized, the world and life in it become purposeless. As art becomes real and the real becomes artful, is and ought are reconciled until, at last, what is is what ought to be.

Schiller's *Letters on the Aesthetic Education of Man* is more a manifesto than a philosophical treatise. Having been inspired by Kant, Schiller takes to the streets armed with the resources of critical philosophy. In his eagerness to effect personal transformation and social reform, he overlooks other important challenges Kant issues. In the crucial passage in which he defines purposiveness without purpose, Kant points out that this guiding notion implies "the epistemological basis upon which the systematic unity of the form and combination of all the manifold contained in the given matter becomes cognizable for the person estimating it." While Kant never develops this insight and Schiller's practical preoccupations prevent him from engaging in sustained theoretical reflection, Hegel patiently elaborates the far-reaching implications of the "systematic unity" Kant suggests. Hegel's entire system can actually be understood as the extended outworking of Kant's interpretation of the beautiful work of art.

As we have seen, within Hegel's comprehensive system, truth reveals itself first in art, then in religion, and finally in philosophy. Philosophy brings to conceptual clarity and thus completion the vision initially formulated in artistic images and religious representations. In this way, philosophy differs from art and religion in form but not in content. Most important in this context, Hegel insists that Kant's aesthetic idea is isomorphic with the structure re-presented in the Christian doctrine of the Trinity. Just as means and end are reciprocally related in the beautiful object, so Father and Son are mutually constituted in and through Spirit. The philosopher reveals the vision of art and religion to be the truth of all reality. Beauty, for Hegel, is neither a regulative idea nor a utopian ideal but is incarnate here and now in nature and history. The difference between Kant and Schiller, on the one hand, and Hegel, on the other, is the difference between a deferred and a realized eschatology.

In an effort to demonstrate the reconciliation of the ideal and the real, Hegel presents a detailed analysis of Kant's notion of inner teleology or *Zweckmäßigkeit ohne Zweck*. In the pivotal chapter on teleology in his *Science of Logic,* Hegel simultaneously repeats and extends Kant's critical distinction between mechanism and organism.

> Now purposiveness shows itself in the first instance as a *higher being* in general, as an *intelligence* that *externally* determines the multiplicity of objects by *a unity that exists in and for itself,* so that the indifferent determi-

nateness of the objects becomes *essential through this relation.* In mechanism
they become so through the *mere form of necessity,* their *content* being indifferent; for they are supposed to remain external, and it is only understanding as such that is supposed to find satisfaction in cognizing its own con-
nective principle, abstract identity. In teleology, on the contrary, the
content becomes important, for teleology presupposes a notion, something
absolutely determined and therefore self-determining, and so has made a
distinction between the *relation* of the differences and their reciprocal de-
terminedness, that is the *form,* and the *unity that is reflected into itself, a
unity that is determined in and for itself* and therefore *a content.*[9]

In contrast to the externality of mechanical relations, this "unity that is
reflected into itself" and thus is "determined in and through itself" is
implicit in Kant's notion of self-organization. As we have seen, according
to the principle of inner teleology, order is not externally imposed but
emerges internally. By rendering this idea explicit, Hegel claims to have
laid bare the logic of all true thought and reality.

When philosophically articulated, the reciprocity of means and ends,
definitive of natural organism and beautiful works of art, displays the
reflexive structure of self-referentiality. Recalling the divine Trinity,
whose internal relations re-present the order of beauty, Hegel labels this
foundational structure spirit (*Geist*). "The spiritual alone is the *actual;* it
is essence, or that which has *being in itself;* it is that which *relates itself
to itself* and is *determinate,* it is *other-being* and *being-for-self,* and in this
determinateness, or in its self-externality, abides within itself; in other
words, it is *in and for itself.*"[10] The logos of reality articulated in Hegel's
Logic is the self-reflexive structure in which every identity and all differences are constituted through reciprocal relations. This idea, he is convinced, is neither an unrealized nor an unrealizable ideal but is actualized
or, theologically expressed, incarnate in everything that exists.

The good news of the Hegelian system is that the Kingdom is not
still to come but is present here and now. In preaching this gospel, Hegel
declares art to be a thing of the past, and God, in the words of Luther's
memorable hymn, to be dead. When philosophy arrives, art and religion
pass away. From Hegel's dialectical perspective, the end of art and the
death of God are necessary negations through which art and religion
are fully realized. When the world truly becomes a work of art, everyone
becomes an artist and art as such disappears. In a similar manner, the
death of God is not merely the negation of the divine but the disappearance of transcendence in an immanent process that finally reconciles the
secular and the sacred. In the kairotic moment of philosophical vision,

apocalyptic imagination becomes apocalyptic cognition, which comprehends heaven on earth "by means of a total revolution of consciousness."

From Prophets to Profits

Hegel had hardly put the finishing touches on his philosophical system when his grand synthesis began to unravel. While critics on the right like Hans Lassen Martensen appropriated his speculative philosophy to defend traditional Christianity, critics on the left like Feuerbach and Marx inverted Hegelian idealism to create a humanistic anthropology and dialectical materialism. The dissolution of Hegel's philosophical rendering of art took considerably longer but was no less significant. The course of much art in the twentieth century can be understood as a reversal of Hegel's dialectical analysis. Countering Hegel's translation of artistic images and representations into philosophical concepts, many leading modern and postmodern artists effectively transpose the Hegelian idea into artistic works and aesthetic practices. This is not to imply, of course, that artists deliberately deploy Hegel's philosophy to advance their own ends. However, the interpretation of the nature of the work of art and understanding of the responsibility of the artist governing much recent advanced art is consistent with the idea of art that Hegel derives from Kant and Schiller. By reversing Hegel's philosophico-historical dialectic and extending it into this century, familiar tendencies and patterns are recast in new ways. In order to delineate the coordinates that reframe twentieth-century artistic developments, it is necessary to return to Hegel's philosophical articulation of the beautiful work of art.

The idea that Hegel discerns in Kant's account of the living organism and beautiful artwork, we have discovered, is a self-referential structure. Developing the Kantian notion of inner teleology, the realized idea, which constitutes the logical and ontological structure of reality, is its own end and thus points to nothing beyond itself. Since all reference is finally self-reference, this idea is thoroughly reflexive. The idea, in other words, inevitably turns back on itself in such a way that it is always *about* itself. If the self-referential structure of the Hegelian idea is rendered artistically, it leads to two seemingly opposite conclusions. On the one hand, art becomes increasingly abstract until it dematerializes in conceptual works, and, on the other hand, art becomes increasingly concrete until it materializes through the embodiment of image in reality. When this reversal is itself eventually reversed, immateriality and materiality unexpectedly meet to create the virtual kingdom on display in Las Vegas.

Though Hegel believes that the logical idea he defines reveals the concrete structure of reality, it is possible to interpret his notion of self-reflexivity abstractly. In the early decades of this century, Hegel's self-referential idea returns under the guise of art that is about art. As we have seen, reflexivity implies a certain nonreferentiality. Since the Hegelian idea relates only to itself, it does not refer to anything other than itself. As a result of this nonreferentiality, the idea is implicitly nonrepresentational. By translating images and representations into concepts, Hegelian philosophy tries to erase the traces of figuration that plague less adequate forms of reflection. Within this dialectical scheme, thought advances through a process of disfiguration, which ends in abstraction.

Modern art's movement of abstraction repeats the trajectory Hegel plots. While Western suspicions about representation can be traced to Plato's criticism of mimesis in the *Republic,* in the early twentieth century, artists themselves began to accept this philosophical critique and attempted to turn it to their own advantage. Though the motivations, intentions, and strategies of abstract artists vary widely, they all share the conviction that advanced art must be nonrepresentational. Implicitly repeating the distinction between fine and applied art, or art and craft, abstract art came to designate high rather than low culture. When the high/low distinction is placed in a historical narrative, the movement from low to high marks the progress from the primitive to the modern, which characterizes the advance from figure to form. This progression can also be understood as the movement from naïve to critical art.

Art that is *about* art is critical art. "Critical" in this context carries at least two meanings. First, as we shall see in more detail in what follows, critical art develops perspectives from which judgments about art as well as nonartistic activities and processes can be proffered. Second, "critical" must be understood in terms of Kant's critical philosophy. For Kant, critique involves the activity in which thought turns back on itself to determine its own conditions and limits. Inasmuch as critical reflection is thought about thought, it is reflexive and thus self-referential. Art about art extends this Kantian enterprise by interrogating the conditions of its own possibility.

This understanding of critique lies at the heart of Clement Greenberg's highly influential art criticism. Greenberg's analyses not only shaped the understanding of and response to much modern art but also had a significant impact on the work leading artists produced. During the middle decades of this century, many artists read Greenberg's criticism as prescriptive rather than descriptive. Though his knowledge of Kant is limited, Greenberg claims to drive his interpretation of modernism from Kant's understanding of criticism. In his classic essay "Modernist Painting," he writes:

> I identify Modernism with the intensification, almost the exacerbation, of this self-critical tendency that began with the philosopher Kant. Because he was the first to criticize the means itself of criticism, I conceive of Kant as the first real Modernist.
>
> The essence of Modernism lies, as I see it, in the use of characteristic methods of a discipline to criticize the discipline itself, not in order to subvert it but in order to entrench it more firmly in its area of competence. Kant used logic to establish the limits of logic, and while he withdrew much from its old jurisdiction, logic was left all the more secure in what there remained to it.
>
> The self-criticism of Modernism grows out of, but is not the same thing as, the criticism of the Enlightenment. The Enlightenment criticized from the outside . . . ; Modernism criticizes from the inside, through the procedures themselves of that which is being criticized. It seems natural that this kind of criticism should have appeared first in philosophy, which is critical by definition, but as the 19th century wore on, it entered many other fields.[11]

Modern art, Greenberg is arguing, is *self*-critical. Turning away from the world and toward itself, art criticizes itself artistically. This insistence that modern art is by definition critical obscures or even erases the traditional difference between art and criticism.

As art becomes progressively self-critical, it gradually becomes clear that distinctions and discriminations must be made between and among different arts. Though all modern art might be critical, not all arts are critical in the same way; strategies of criticism vary from art to art and medium to medium. "What had to be exhibited," Greenberg argues, "was not only that which was unique and irreducible in art in general, but also that which was unique and irreducible in each particular art." The activity of criticism through which each art "narrows its area of competence" results in the purity of different arts. Thus would each art, Greenberg insists, "be rendered 'pure,' and its 'purity' find the guarantee of its standards of quality as well as of its independence. Purity meant self-definition, and the enterprise of self-criticism in the arts became one of self-definition with a vengeance" (86). When read in this way, the movement from primitive to modern, figure to form, low to high, and

[handwritten margin note: art criticizes itself artistically]

popular to elite involves a process of purification. The art that most intrigues Greenberg is painting. When painting subjects itself to critical analysis, its distinguishing characteristic appears to be its flatness: "It was the stressing of the ineluctable flatness of the surface that remained, however, more fundamental than anything else to the processes by which pictorial art criticized and defined itself under Modernism. For flatness alone was unique and exclusive to pictorial art" (87). Though Greenberg briefly suggests the way in which flatness emerges in modern art, the reason he privileges this quality of painting remains unclear until its relation to the reflexivity of criticism is recognized. The flatness of the painted surface mirrors the self-referentiality of critical reflection. Referring only to itself, the flat surface of the painting is resolutely nonrepresentational. What modernist painting "has abandoned in principle," Greenberg insists, "is the representation of the kind of space that recognizable objects can inhabit" (87). When art is no longer about anything other than itself, it becomes autonomous. This autonomy of the work of art is reminiscent of something approaching religious transcendence.

An undeniable spirituality informs both Greenberg's criticism and much of the art it inspires. The "kingdom of the abstract" is undeniably an otherworldly kingdom in which works of art become icons for devoted followers who seek a better world. This spiritual vision manifests itself most explicitly in Greenberg's relentless attack on kitsch. In contrast to the elevated ideals of "high" art, "low" art is "contaminated" by the machinations of market forces. Invoking the metaphor of the machine so carefully crafted by Kant and Hegel, Greenberg argues that "the work of art in the age of mechanical reproduction" has been completely debased.

> To fill the demand of the new market, a new commodity was devised: ersatz culture, kitsch, destined for those who, insensible to the values of genuine culture, are hungry nevertheless for the diversion that only culture of some sort can provide.
>
> Kitsch, using for raw material the debased and academicized simulacra of genuine culture, welcomes and cultivates this insensibility. It is the source of its profits. Kitsch is mechanical and operates by formulas. Kitsch is vicarious experience and faked sensations. Kitsch changes according to style, but remains always the same. Kitsch is the epitome of all that is spurious in the life of our times. Kitsch pretends to demand nothing of its customers except their money—not even their time.[12]

Though not immediately evident, the notion of uselessness implicit in Kant's account of purposiveness without purpose lies behind Greenberg's attack on kitsch. The utility of art within economic networks of exchange makes it "false." "True" art, by contrast, cannot be commodified and thus is, at least economically, useless. "Because it can be turned out mechanically," Greenberg concludes, "kitsch has become an integral part of our productive system in a way in which true culture never could be, except accidentally."[13]

As we have already discovered, however, uselessness has its uses. Only insofar as high art transcends mundane economies can it provide a perspective from which this world can be criticized. Once again we discover the way in which art displaces religion. Just as the transcendent Kingdom of God once posed an alternative to the fallen kingdom of man, so the kingdom of the abstract now reveals the ills of the modern world. If a critical tension between transcendence and immanence is maintained, abstract art can remain politically engaged in social criticism. But as the history of religions makes painfully clear, transcendence all too often leads to world denial rather than worldly reform. Art, like God, can become so abstract that it loses all relevance for the world it is supposed to transform. While the world is going to hell, the elect remain caught up in reflection on themselves and the precious autonomy of their work.[14]

In an effort to make a persuasive case for what he regards as the progressiveness of abstraction, Greenberg disregards much of what is most interesting and revolutionary in modern art. He virtually ignores major movements like dada, surrealism, futurism, and Russian constructivism, as well as influential artists like Duchamp, Schwitters, and Rodchenko. Even in what he does consider, Greenberg's vision is always highly selective. While he takes cubism, for example, seriously, he approaches it primarily in terms of its formal innovations. As a result, he expresses little appreciation for the abiding contribution of cubist collage. At one point, Greenberg goes so far as to assert, "The alternative to Picasso is not Michelangelo, but kitsch."[15] There is, however, plenty of kitsch in cubist art. Freely mixing the mechanically reproduced and the handmade original, Picasso, as well as others, incorporates newspapers, playbills, and industrial products like oilcloth and chair caning in his collages. Though obviously drawn to the practice of abstraction, Picasso remains obsessed with life beyond the work of art. The vitality of modern boulevards, brothels, and cafés breathes life into many of his most important works.

As one ponders what Greenberg's criticism leaves out, it gradually becomes clear that he tends to ignore works that suggest a reconciliation between art and the modern world. When Duchamp transforms a me-

FIGURE 9   Pablo Picasso, *Still Life with Chair Caning,* 1912

chanically produced urinal into a work of art by the seemingly simple gesture of signature, he not only asks "What is art?" but also "What is not art?" and "Who is or is not an artist?" The gap separating art and world can be bridged from two apparently opposite directions. Simultaneously repeating and extending Picasso's collage practice, works of art can incorporate fragments of the so-called real world in a way that transforms reality into image. What begins with cubist collage continues, inter alia, in Rauschenberg's assemblages, Johns's sculptures, and Warhol's silk screens.[16] As creative production gives way to appropriative reproduction, found objects and images obscure the line separating art from nonart. Alternatively, art can be embodied in the world through artistic practices that are explicitly political. Throughout this century, artists committed to a variety of social and political agendas have taken up Schiller's challenge by struggling to transform the world into a work of art. As the real becomes image, images become real, thereby creating a world that figures reality in new ways.

The tension between transcendence and immanence running throughout the Western religious tradition also defines competing artistic alterna-

FIGURE 10   Jasper Johns, *Painted Bronze II,* 1960

tives. When art becomes so abstract that it is irrelevant, it provokes efforts
to develop socially useful art; conversely, when art becomes so worldly
that everything seems to be art, strategies to create critical distance begin
to emerge. The history of art in this century can be understood as the
dialectical interplay of these two contrasting tendencies. This is not to
suggest that the imperatives toward transcendence and immanence can
always be clearly separated. To the contrary, their dialectical tension is
often found within seemingly unified movements and can be detected
even in the work of individual artists.

The interplay between transcendence and immanence is directly mirrored in the tension between inward transformation and outward change.
Over a century after Schiller's reformulation of the religious distinction
between mysticism and militancy into an aesthetic education that pro-
motes personal change as a propaedeutic to political reform, his program
was implemented in one of the most influential modernist institutions—
the Bauhaus. Addressing students of the Staatliche Bauhaus in 1919, the

founding director, Walter Gropius, indirectly takes up Schiller's challenge.

> We find ourselves in a colossal catastrophe of world history, in a transformation of the whole of life and the whole of inner man. This is perhaps fortunate for the artistic man, provided he is strong enough to bear the consequences, for what we need is the courage to accept inner experience, then suddenly a new path will open for the artist. . . . No large spiritual organizations, but small, secret, self-contained societies, lodges. Conspiracies will form which will want to watch over and artistically shape a secret, a nucleus of belief, until from the individual groups a universally great, enduring, spiritual-religious idea will rise again, which finally must find its crystalline expression in a great *Gesamtkunstwerk*. And this great total work of art, this cathedral of the future will then shine with its abundance of light into the smallest objects of everyday life . . . . We will not live to see the day, but we are, and this I firmly believe, the precursors and first instruments of such a new, universal idea.[17]

The ideal of the *Gesamtkunstwerk,* as we have seen, was first formulated by Wagner at Bayreuth, which, like the original Bauhaus, is located near Jena. For Wagner, the total artwork both integrates different arts and reconciles art and world. This harmonic dream runs directly counter to Greenberg's effort to separate different arts and to secure the opposition between art and the "fallen" world. Though expressed in utopian terms, circumstances in war-torn Europe lent an urgency to efforts to realize Gropius's vision. While Gropius is convinced that social reform presupposes inner change, he realizes that in a world in desperate need of rebuilding, art for art's sake has no place. The only art that matters is art that is useful, practical, instrumental—in short, functional.[18]

Rejecting the traditional distinction between fine and applied arts, Gropius organized work at the Bauhaus according to principles that had long guided the work of craftsmen. In addition to painting and sculpture studios, the Bauhaus included workshops for weaving, graphic and furniture design, metalwork, and, perhaps most important, architecture. In 1925, Gropius defined the purpose of instruction as "the training of artistically talented people to become creative designers in the fields of crafts, industry, and architecture."[19] As this comment indicates, the emphasis on the importance of craft work does not represent a turn away from modern industrialism. In contrast to predecessors like Gottfried Semper and William Morris, for whom the handiwork of the craftsman was supposed to overcome the dehumanizing effects of modern industry, artists working at the Bauhaus sought to humanize machines without dehumanizing human beings. In a manifesto issued on the occasion of the first Bauhaus exhibition in Weimar in 1923, the painter, sculptor, and stage designer, Oskar Schlemmer, declares:

> Reason and science, "man's greatest powers," are the regents, and the engineer is the sedate executor of unlimited possibilities. Mathematics, structure, and mechanization are the elements, and power and money are the dictators of these phenomena of steel, concrete, glass, and electricity. Velocity of rigid matter, dematerialization of matter, organization of inorganic matter, all these produce the miracle of abstraction. Based on the laws of nature, these are the achievements of mind in the conquest of nature, based on the power of capital, the work of man against man. The speed and supertension of commercialism make expediency and utility the measure of all effectiveness, and calculation seizes the transcendent world: art becomes a logarithm. It, long bereft of its name, lives a life after death, in the monument of the cube and in the colored square. Religion is the precise process of thinking, and God is dead. . . . Thus we become the bearers of responsibility and the conscience of the world. An idealism of activity that embraces, penetrates, and unites art, science, and technology and that influences research, study, and work, will construct the "art-edifice" of Man, which is but an allegory of the cosmic system.[20]

Reversing the relation between machine and organism defined by Kant and elaborated by Hegel, Schlemmer envisions a synthesis between art and technology that creates a world in which God is dead—or, perhaps more accurately, a world in which capital eventually becomes God.[21]

One of the most important contributions of the Bauhaus was its fostering of collaborations between artist-designers and the engineers of mass production and financiers of modern industrialism. As the years passed, the Bauhaus became a research and development studio where prototypes for industrial products were designed and developed. In the following section, we will consider the lasting impact of this alliance of artist, industrialist, and capitalist on the art and commerce of this century.

It would be a mistake to conclude that this new relation between modernism and modernization was limited to the European scene. Though the sociopolitical context is obviously very different, artistic developments surrounding the 1917 Russian Revolution bear a striking resemblance to what was occurring at roughly the same time in Europe. In some cases, similar innovations emerged independently, while other changes were mediated by artists who traveled between Europe and Russia. Kandinsky and Moholy-Nagy, for example, made significant contributions to the transformation of Russian art and society and played important roles in the Bauhaus. In the complexity and diversity of Russian art during the opening decades of this century, one movement stands out as particularly important in this context: constructivism. Christina Lodder begins her comprehensive and informative study by confidently asserting that "Russian Constructivism posited an entirely new relationship between [*sic*] the artist, his work, and society. This radical reassessment of artistic activity was a direct response to the experience of the Russian Revolution of 1917 and of the ensuing Civil War."[22] Though the developments in Russia are undeniably distinctive, our examination of the artistic and philosophical responses to the French Revolution casts doubt on Lodder's claim for the originality of the constructivist program.

"Constructivism" is an inclusive term used to designate different and sometimes conflicting artistic positions. By the 1920s, Russian constructivism stood in direct opposition to what had come to be known as European or international constructivism. This distinction between two different strands of constructivism, however, tends to dissolve as soon as it is formulated. Major Russian artists like Malevich, Tatlin, Rodchenko, and Popova share enough with their European counterparts to be labeled international constructivists. The issue dividing the two camps of constructivism is once again the problem of the purpose or purposelessness of art. Just as the social exigencies of postwar Europe occasioned a rethinking of the function of art, so the social and political turmoil in postrevolutionary Russia fueled heated debates about the utility or inutility of art. Committed to the principles of nonrepresentation and nonexpression, international constructivists seemed to continue a tradition of art for art's sake that no longer made sense to many Russian artists and critics. Against the imperative of "pure art," constructivists posed the challenge of developing "production art," which unites studio and factory in a revolutionary practice that effectively extends Schiller's aesthetic education.

In September 1921, Moscow's Institute for Artistic Culture (INKhUK) mounted a controversial exhibition, entitled "5 × 5 = 25," which marks a decisive turning point in the emergence of a distinctively Russian version of constructivism. Rodchenko, whose abstract formalism had long made him suspect for many Russian artists, displayed monochromatic paintings done in the three primary colors. The exhibition also included works by Alexandra Exter, Liubov Popova, Varvara Stepanova, and Alexander Vesnin.[23] Even as the show was opening, Rodchenko realized that this work signaled an end rather than a beginning. As if to echo Nietzsche's proclamation of the death of God, Rodchenko declares: "Art is dead! . . . Art is as dangerous as religion as an escapist activity."

. . . Let us cease our speculative activity and take over the healthy bases of art—color, line, materials and forms—into the field of reality, of practical construction."[24] But just as the death of God is not a simple negation but a complex process in which the divine becomes incarnate when the profane is grasped as sacred, so art ends not because it disappears but because it appears everywhere. Art dies when everyone becomes an artist and the world is finally transformed into a work of art.

For Rodchenko, the move from "speculative activity" to "practical construction" entails a commitment to create socially useful products. As "pure art" becomes "production art," Rodchenko turns his attention to graphic design—advertising posters, books, and magazines—furniture design, information centers (i.e., kiosks), interior design, theater sets, and eventually film. The course of Rodchenko's career both illustrates and illuminates broader social and artistic currents circulating in Russia dur-

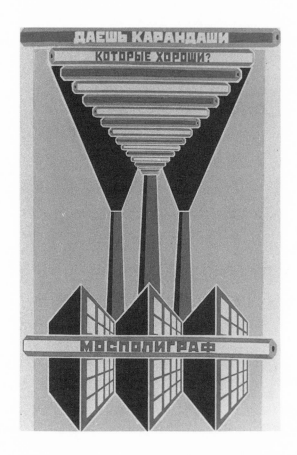

FIGURE 11
Aleksandr Rodchenko,
Shouldn't We Produce Pencils We Can Use?
1923

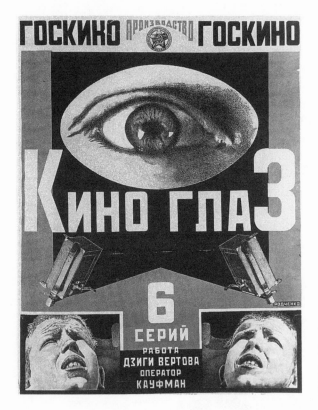

ing the decisive decade of the 1920s. The movement from studio and
gallery to street and factory spread as the effort to implement the communist vision accelerated. In the catalogue accompanying the 1922 exhibition
entitled *The Constructivists: K. K. Medunetskii, V. A. Strenberg, G. A.
Strenberg,* the featured artists state "unequivocally that all artists should
now 'go into the factory, where the real body of life is made,' and asserted
that 'this route is called Constructivism.'" These artists, Lodder explains,

> wrote of Constructivism as "the highest springboard for the leap into uni-
> versal human culture" and juxtaposed it to art and aestheticism which
> they considered corrupting: "The Constructivists declare art to and its
> priests to be outlaws." In a rather vague form this declaration gave expres-
> sion to the most basic principles that were developed by Constructivism:
> the call for the artist to go into the factory; the recognition that the factory
> is the real creative force in the world; the impediment that conventional
> concepts of art and practicing artists represent to such a link between art
> and life, and therefore the call for their banishment; and the identification

with a new political and social order. The artists' declaration that "Constructivism will lead humanity to master a maximum of cultural values with the minimum expenditure of energy" shows that Constructivism was seen to represent the culture of the future.[25]

Behind this constructivist agenda lies the persistent avant-garde determination to transform the world into a work of art. However, in the century separating the Jena romantics and the Russian constructivists, a significant change occurred. Whereas Schiller and his associates see modern industrialism as the cause of personal alienation and social fragmentation, leading twentieth-century avant-garde artists see modern industry as the means to the realization of their utopian ideals. "Russian Modernism," Hubertus Gassner correctly points out, "abandoned all opposition to the modernization of life effected by industrialization and mass production, and began to assume the functions of oil and engine in the machinery of progress. The stated goal was no longer just the reconciliation of consciousness and machine but the total alignment of human psycho-physical being to machine mechanisms and motions."[26] What inspired this attempt to integrate modernism and modernization was the conviction that social equality, economic justice, and political freedom could be realized only when artistic vision became practically effective by directing the forces of mass production and mass media.

This revolutionary struggle foundered in the midst of growing economic difficulties and increasing political repression. Art, intended to be socially productive, became little more than political propaganda for a regime whose inadequacies and failures eventually led to its collapse. The dream of transforming the world into a work of art, however, does not die with the failure of the Russian experiment. Through a dialectical reversal that is both intriguing and unexpected, the synthesis of art and technology that once inspired Soviet communism reappears in postwar America as consumer capitalism, whose capital now appears to be Las Vegas.

From the Factory to the Strip

In a 1963 interview with G. R. Swenson, Andy Warhol provocatively announced: "I think everybody should be a machine. I think everybody should be like everybody."[27] Though the distance separating the factories of communist Russia from the Factory of Andy Warhol Enterprises

FIGURE 13   Andy Warhol, *Window Display, Bonwit Teller,* 1961

seems to be more than geographical, there are surprising similarities between the practices of some members of the Russian avant-garde and
the strategies Warhol devised. In many ways, Warhol's activity in his
Factory inverts the relation between art and industry in 1920s Russia.
While Rodchenko, for example, takes his artistic skills into the factory
to produce advertising and packaging for everything from beer, candy,
and biscuits to pacifiers, cigarettes, and galoshes, Warhol brings ads for
everything from shoes, telephones, and televisions to soup cans, scrubbing
pads, and cars into his Factory to be transformed into works of art. Like
many leading artists of his generation, Warhol began his career as a commercial artist who did drawings for newspapers and magazine ads, and
designed display windows for department stores. Having become adept
at using his skills in fine arts to promote consumer products, Warhol
reverses his tactics and uses consumer products—or more precisely, their
images—to create art. In this process, he collapses the distinction between
high art and popular culture that Greenberg struggles to maintain.[28]

Warhol actually revels in the kitsch Greenberg abhors. Far from a
technique to be avoided, mechanical reproduction becomes the preferred
procedure for turning out series after series of formulaic works. Warhol
goes so far as to declare, "I think somebody should be able to do all my
paintings for me." Exploring the limits of this possibility, workers in
his Factory use techniques that mime industrial processes of production.

FIGURE 14
Andy Warhol, *À la Recherche du Shoe Perdu*, 1951

Instead of a lonely genius, the artist in Andy Warhol Enterprises was more like a supervisor who oversees workers on an assembly line, or a film editor who repackages found footage. As Campbell's Soup cans and Brillo boxes roll off the assembly line and screened images quickly flash by like flickering faces and scenes on a television screen, the identity of the artist becomes as obscure as the difference between art and non-art.

In Warhol's Factory, art becomes business—big business. The work of art in the age of mechanical reproduction holds up a mirror in which the world sees itself reflected. The business of art is the inverted image of a consumer culture in which the consummate art is the art of the deal. Explaining his "philosophy" in 1975, Warhol writes:

FIGURE 15
Andy Warhol, *Tele-phone,* 1961

Business art is the step that comes after Art. I started as a commercial artist, and I want to finish as a business artist. After I did the thing called "art" or whatever it's called, I went into business art. I wanted to be an Art Businessman or a Business Artist. Being good in business is the most fascinating kind of art. During the hippie era people put down the idea of business—they'd say, "Money is bad," and "Working is bad," but making money is art and working is art and good business is the best art.[29]

Far from a useless object that exceeds productive networks of exchange, the work of art is a valuable commodity. Warhol's art makes money—both as product and as process. "I don't understand anything except GREEN BILLS," he declares (129). At one point Warhol goes so far as to suggest that his silk-screened sheets of money should be replaced with "the real thing": "I like money on the wall. Say you were going to buy a $200,000 painting. I think you should take that money, tie it up, and hang it on the wall. Then when someone visited you the first thing they

FIGURE 16   Andy Warhol, *Front and Back Dollar Bills,* 1962

would see is the money on the wall" (134). This characteristically ironic remark expresses an important insight: not only has art been commodified but money has been aestheticized. As art becomes money, money becomes art. Money, in other words, is a matter or nonmatter of image.

In consumer capitalism, the token of exchange is not the thing itself but its image. Use value increasingly gives way to exchange value in an economy that consumes the thing itself. Like formally identical buildings distinguished only by applied ornament, mass-produced objects are differentiated by competing images. As products proliferate, the market expands by deploying images to create desire where there is no need. People buy and sell images: the shoe, the car, or the watch is not valuable because of the function it serves but because of the image it projects. This play of images, figured in the work of an erstwhile window designer, makes it virtually impossible to distinguish showroom from gallery.

In the world of simulacra created and sustained by complex networks of exchange, differences become indifferent until it seems as if nothing is special. Warhol's economy of consumption realizes Kierkegaard's nightmare of a society in which decisive distinctions are "leveled" and everything and everybody become more or less the same. For Warhol, this leveling process holds the promise of realizing the equality of which his avant-garde predecessors dreamed. What Europe imagines, America realizes.

> What's great about this country is that America started the tradition where the richest consumers buy essentially the same things as the poorest. You can be watching TV and see Coca-Cola, and you can know that the President drinks Coke, Liz Taylor drinks Coke, and just think, you can drink Coke, too. A Coke is a Coke and no amount of money can get you a better Coke than the one the bum on the corner is drinking. All the Cokes are the same and all the Cokes are good. Liz Taylor knows it, the President knows it, the bum knows it, and you know it.
>
> In Europe the royalty and the aristocracy used to eat a lot better than the peasants—they weren't eating the same thing at all. It was either partridge or porridge, and each class stuck to its own food. But when Queen Elizabeth came here and President Eisenhower bought her a hot dog I'm sure he felt confident that she couldn't have had delivered to Buckingham Palace a better hot dog than the one he bought her for maybe twenty cents at the ballpark. Because there *is* no better hot dog than a ballpark hot dog. Not for a dollar, not for ten dollars, not for a hundred thousand dollars could she get a better hot dog. She could get one for twenty cents and so could anybody else. (100–101)

Deliberately ignoring new hierarchies created by consumer capitalism, Warhol envisions a world in which commodities create social equality. This social leveling harbors important cultural implications. The distinction between high and low implodes, leaving extraordinary ordinary and, conversely, making the ordinary extraordinary. Just as there are no better or worse Cokes or hot dogs, so there are no better or worse paintings. "You see," Warhol explains, "I think every painting should be the same size and the same color so they're all interchangeable and nobody thinks that they have a better or a worse painting. And if the one 'master painting' is good, they're all good. Besides, even when the subject is different, people always paint the same painting. In the absence of master artists and masterpieces, art is 'just another job'" (178). When art becomes an ordinary job, it is possible to see ordinary workers as artists.

Within Warhol's specular economy, the work of art remains incomplete until it turns back on the artist to close the reflexive arc outlined by Kant and extended by Schiller and Hegel. In the final analysis, War-

FIGURE 17
Andy Warhol, *Self-Portrait,* 1979

Figure 18   New York, New York, Las Vegas

hol's art is *about* himself; his *Gesamtkunstwerk* is nothing other than "Andy." Extending the work from canvas to skin, "Andy" becomes his own production. To create "Andy," Warhol must become nothing.

> I'm sure I'm going to look into the mirror and see nothing. People are always calling me a mirror and if a mirror looks into a mirror, what is there to see? . . .
> Some critic called me the Nothingness Himself and that didn't help my sense of existence any. Then I realized that existence itself is nothing and I felt better. But I'm still obsessed with the idea of looking into the mirror and seeing no one, nothing. (7)

Emptying himself of himself, "Andy" reflects a world in which the image is real and the real is image. Warhol realized the far-reaching implications of information and media culture long before others were aware of their importance. By lining the Factory with reflective foil and taking up the electronic prostheses of tape recorder and video camera, Warhol screens a world in which nothing is hiding since everything is on display.

His relentless courting of celebrities exposes a society in which image constitutes reality. Shifting from mechanical to electronic means of reproduction, Warhol's work marks the transition from a manufacturing industrial economy to an information postindustrial economy. While he did not live to see the realization of the developments he anticipated, Warhol's prescient vision sheds considerable light on our current cultural

FIGURE 19   New York, New York, Las Vegas

conditions. If "Andy" were alive today, he would be the mayor of Las Vegas.

Stripping Reality

The course is never direct. The revolution that began in Paris and, after being redefined in Jena, spread to Weimar, Moscow, and New York, reaches a certain closure in today's Las Vegas. Vegas, I have suggested, is where the death of God is staged as the spectacle of the Kingdom of God on earth. As art displaces religion, the prophet becomes the artist, who develops an aesthetic education designed to transform the world into a work of art. The reflexivity of the work of art is reflected in a play of lights that seems to be as endless as it is purposeless. In contemporary media culture, the medium of the work of art changes first from

FIGURE 20   José Márquez, Las Vegas

FIGURE 21   José Márquez, Las Vegas

paint to neon, and then from neon to pixels. The lights of the Strip illuminate a world in which reality itself seems to be morphing before our eyes. As image is embodied in reality and reality becomes a "matter" of image, art is realized in a world that is effectively transformed into a work of art. When high becomes low, and low becomes high, foundations seem to crumble and everything becomes unbearably lite. In light of this darkness, there appears to be nothing beyond this city—absolutely nothing and nothing absolute.

From one point of view, Holy Land is a bitter parody of the Holy Land. There is, indeed, something apocalyptic about "virtual reality, holographic, theatrical, and statuary recreations of scenes from the Bible." Yet, from another point of view, it is possible to rewind the tape of history and replay it in a way that makes this oasis in the desert the Promised Land toward which we have always been heading. If this end seems disappointing, perhaps it is because we have not learned the lessons Las Vegas teaches. In the hot sands of Vegas's silicon lights, the transcendence of the real vanishes, leaving nothing in its wake. In the dark light of this nothingness, it appears that what is is what ought to be. When this word of acceptance is actively embraced, the Holy Land ceases to be a distant dream and the Kingdom becomes virtually real.

Eight

Apprehension

To enter the gallery is to be immersed in emptiness. Far from space waiting to be filled, this emptiness is a void, which seems to "fill" everything and everyone. In the midst of the bare white walls, between the pale gray floor and recessive ceiling, nothing appears. This emptiness—this nothingness provokes a certain apprehension. What *is* this emptiness? What *is* this nothingness? What *is* the apprehension they provoke?

When emptiness not only surrounds but also invades in a way that allows nothing to appear, light becomes darkness. In its transparency, the light bathing the gallery is as obscure as the darkness of a theater to which eyes must adjust. As vision becomes possible, forms emerge from the darkness of light. Conversely, as forms emerge from the darkness of light, vision becomes possible. The invisible forms that slowly become visible are not really forms, however, but are lines or, more precisely, outlines drawn in pale shades of red, blue, gold, brown, and black yarn. The softness of the colors and the material is offset by the tautness of the threads. Subtly taunting, these lines are on the verge—always on the verge—of snapping. This creates the tension and the suspense of the work of art. Forever strung out between the opposites they articulate, outlines inscribe the emptiness of forms by tracing the form of emptiness. The shapes are geometric: squares, rectangles, and triangles. Nothing is crooked; nothing is curved. As if retracing Kandinsky's painterly trajectory, these diaphanous forms are (impossibly) simultaneously at rest and in motion. "The geometric line is an invisible thing. It is the track made by moving the point; that is, its product. It is created by movement—specifically through the destruction of the intense self-contained repose of the point. Here, the leap out of the static into the dynamic occurs."[1] From point to line to plane, the tales this yarn spins are volumes other than books. Rarely has so much been made of so little. In the emptiness of the gallery, everything, it seems, hangs by a thread.

It is difficult to know how to describe, much less classify, the art of

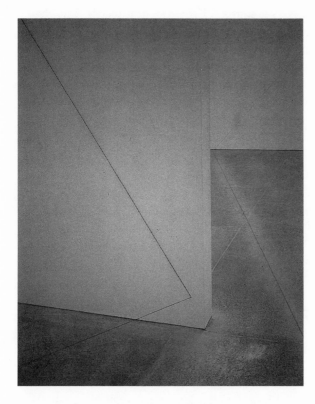

FIGURE 22
Fred Sandback,
Sculpture

Fred Sandback. Reflecting on two decades of work in 1986, Sandback observed: "The first sculpture I made with a piece of string and a little wire was the outline of a rectangular solid . . . lying on the floor. It was a casual act, but it seemed to open up a lot of possibilities for me."[2] If Sandback's work is sculpture, it is unlike any previous sculpture. Not only are his works made of virtually nothing, but they are, in an important sense, *about* nothing.

Sandback came of age as an artist when the influence of minimalism was at its height. While a student at Yale, he studied with Robert Morris and Donald Judd. As Rosalind Krauss notes in her survey of modern sculpture, "the very term minimalism" points to "a reduction of art to the point of emptiness." The emptiness that preoccupied minimalists not only was a matter of the materials used but also involved the question of the meaning of the work of art. "Contrary to the procedures of Gabo or Moore," Krauss proceeds to explain, "minimalist sculptors, in both their choice of materials and their method of assembling them, were intent to deny the interiority of the sculpted form—or at least to repudiate the interior of forms as a source of their significance."[3] The denial of the interiority of sculpted form was a direct response to and criticism of abstract expressionists for whom the work of art was the outward embodiment of the creative artist's inward intention. By emptying the work of art of its inner purpose, minimalists attempted to inscribe meaning in "a public, rather than a private space."[4] With the shift from the private to the public sphere, meaning changes from a hidden product waiting to be discovered to a manifest process always on the verge of realization.

The objects produced by minimalist sculptors, however, were not always effective realizations of the ideas and ideals to which they were committed. The use of rigid geometries and industrial materials often resulted in objects that appear closed and impenetrable. Though no longer placed on a pedestal, art had not yet become sufficiently mundane. Sandback expands the tenets of minimalism by opening the work of art to an emptiness that borders (on) nothingness: "I wanted to make something without an interior, at least in the sense of a conventional sculpture, which has an interior; I didn't want a volume enclosed by a surface. . . . I have moved from a more contained, enclosed situation to one in which the sculpture turns outward, exists more on an equal footing with an observer in a pedestrian space."[5] The "pedestrian space" of Sandback's art is utterly mundane and as such is completely open to exploration. One does not so much dwell *on* Sandback's art as dwell *in* it. Far from domestic space, the dwelling that art outlines is haunted by what Nietzsche and Freud describe as *das Heimliche*—the uncanny. To wander through this pedestrian space is to follow a *Holzwege* whose lines retrace something that approaches "the origin of the work of art."

The opening of the work of art extends from form to matter. In place of the industrial materials preferred by many minimalists, Sandback uses materials that are insubstantial. Insisting that he does not make "dematerialized art," Sandback explains: "There are big 'empty' spaces in between the lines. They're no less real or material than the lines themselves."[6] The lines between the empty spaces have been made of different materials over the years. While in early works Sandback used steel rods and wires as well as rubber cords, by 1973 he had settled on what was to become his signature medium—acrylic yarn. By shifting from steel and rubber to yarn, Sandback further emphasizes his movement away from the industrial presuppositions and implications of minimalism. Though synthetic rather than natural, acrylic yarn nonetheless connotes crafts and folk art, which have never been considered high culture.

Two additional points about Sandback's medium are important in this context. First, the insubstantiality of yarn underscores the fragility of his sculptures. There is, Sandback stresses, "an inherent transience to my work. My larger pieces only exist for a few days in a particular place, before being put away indefinitely. They are in principle always able to come into existence again at a future time, but will then be a part of a new situation. If I remake a piece in a new place, it's a different piece. If I remake a piece in the same place, it's still bound to be a different piece than before."[7] Rewinding from volume to plane to line to point, all that remains of the work of art is a ball of yarn. Never monumental, this sculpture is designed *not* to last. Second, unlike steel rods and wires or rubber cords, yarn is not a single fiber but a complex thread comprising twisted strands. The line inscribed by yarn is neither one nor many. As Lynne Cooke points out, yarn's "slightly fuzzy contours conjure a less crisp, less rigid line than that produced by metal, just as its matte surfaces absorb rather than reflect light."[8] The logic of Sandback's work is as fuzzy as the faint lines from which it is made.

Fuzzy logic eludes grids clearly articulated by either/or. Are "big 'empty' spaces in between the lines," or are the lines between big "empty" spaces? Neither one nor the other, the fuzzy lines of Sandback's sculptures stage a play between emptiness/form as well as void/volume in which all such questions remain undecidable. These lightly colored strands of yarn render the invisible visible by making spacing apprehensible. Lines trace planes, which, in turn, define volumes. But the volumes are empty—absolutely empty. Since the lines are about nothing, every thing is actually no thing. It is as if Sandback's sculptures retrace the outline of Heidegger's thing. Attempting to describe "the thing," Heidegger takes as an example a jug. "The jug," he explains, "is a thing as a vessel—it can hold something." But the holding that constitutes the thing is not so much the function of the jug as of the void the jug surrounds.

> The emptiness, the void, is what does the vessel's holding. The empty space, this nothing of the jug, is what the jug is as the holding vessel. . . . Sides and bottom, of which the jug consists and by which it stands, are not really what does the holding. But if the holding is done by the jug's void, then the potter, who forms the sides and bottom on his wheel, does not, strictly speaking, make the jug. He only shapes the clay. No—he shapes the void. For it, in it, and out of it, he forms the clay into the form. From start to finish, the potter takes hold of the impalpable void and brings it forth as the container in the shape of a containing vessel. The

jug's void determines all the handling in the process of making the vessel. The vessel's thingness does not lie at all in the material of which it consists, but in the void that holds.[9]

When Sandback's sculpture is read through Heidegger's account of the thing, the sculptor becomes the potter who makes something out of nothing by "shaping the void." But whether form brings forth void or void brings forth form remains obscure. What does seem clear is that the thingness of every thing is the no thing of the void.

The sides and bottom that form the void and void the form are as fragile as thin strands of yarn drawn taut in space that appears to be empty. Suspended between inside and outside, the thing sustains and is sustained by a tension that constantly approaches the breaking point. This tension—this suspense—generates the apprehension of the work of art. The apprehension created by Sandback's sculptures is not, however, merely a psychological condition. Something else is at work in his art. What *is* the work of art? What *does* art—this art as well as other art—do? What *can't* art do?

FIGURE 23
Fred Sandback,
untitled, 1977

Walking through the pedestrian space of Sandback's works, one begins to suspect that the work of art involves something like an endless process of framing. In one of his most provocative works, Sandback creates two planes, which almost meet, by running a thin strand of yarn from the ceiling, across the floor, and back up to the ceiling. The effect of this minimal gesture is remarkable. Not only do the lines make planes materialize out of nothing, but the yarn virtually materializes nothing. A peculiar feature of these works is the manner in which their vacant spaces make emptiness almost palpable. The sides of the thing are nothing, yet they seem to mark a limit that both forbids and invites transgression. It is nearly impossible *not* to step across the line, through the plane, and into the volume. The apprehension of the interplay of emptiness and form makes it difficult to be certain whether one is inside or outside the work of art.

While lines frame planes, which are nothing, planes, in turn, interact without intersecting to create volumes out of voids. Wandering through the gallery, static forms are set in motion. Lines shift, planes move, and volumes grow and shrink. When the gallery is empty, the planes appear to be mirrors whose reflections create a Borgesian labyrinth from which there is no exit. If other people are in the gallery, the outlines of empty forms create shifting frameworks, which have a cinematic effect. People moving through rooms seem to be flickering images projected on frames of film steadily rolling by. The longer one lingers *in* Sandback's sculptures, the more it begins to appear that the work of art is inseparable from the work of framing. Every artwork is a framework, and every framework is, in some sense, an artwork.

Threads frame emptiness, which frame threads in loops that seem infinite. The frame is less an object than a process. But "where does the frame take place," asks Derrida. "Does it take place. Where does it begin. Where does it end. What is its internal limit. Its external limit. And its surface between the two limits." In a manner not unlike On Kawara's timely dates, the frame appears by disappearing. "Neither work . . . nor outside the work, neither inside nor outside, neither above nor below," the frame "disconcerts all opposition but does not remain indeterminate and it *gives rise—gives place—to [donne lieu à]* the work." However, that which gives rise to the work by clearing space and giving place cannot itself be placed. The topos of the frame is nowhere, its place a no place of perpetual dis-placement. Paradoxically, as Derrida insists, "*There is* a frame, but the frame *does not exist* [*Il y a du cadre, mais le cadre* n'existe pas]."[10]

The nonexistence of the frame is an emptiness that is different from the emptiness that is the opposite of form, and a nothingness that is different from the nothingness that is the opposite of every thing. As the limit, border, margin, and fringe that lies between void and volume, the frame allows form to emerge from emptiness and things to materialize from nothing. By articulating forms that define things, frames create the possibility of apprehension. If artwork is framework, then the work of the work of art is, in effect, to create things. Art, however, is not limited to or by the objects it calls forth but can turn back on itself in such a way that it catches itself in the act of creation. Art that is about art moves beyond objects to render apprehension apprehensible. When apprehension is apprehended, it becomes clear that art creates not only things but also worlds. This is the work that occurs between the lines of Sandback's sculptures.

When understood in this way, Sandback's art is, in a certain sense, Nietzschean. "Only as an esthetic product," Nietzsche avers, "can the world be justified." God, according to an ancient metaphor revived by Nietzsche, is "the supreme artist" whose chef d'oeuvre is the world. Human creativity extends the divine work of art. Far from simply denying God, Nietzsche actually identifies God and human beings. The artist in the act of creation, he claims, "merges with the primal architect of the cosmos."[11]

While Nietzsche's remarks are suggestive, he never explains exactly how this identification of the divine and the human takes place. The task of developing Nietzsche's insight was left to the twentieth-century writer who gave his philosophical vision poetic voice. In his *Opus Posthumous,* Wallace Stevens writes in deliberately unpoetic terms:

Proposita: 1. God and the imagination are one. 2. The thing imagined is the imaginer.
 The second equals the thing imagined and the imaginer are one.
 Hence, I suppose, the imaginer is God.

If the point of contact between God and self is the imagination, then divine creativity is, in effect, displaced onto human creativity. Stevens's refinement of Nietzsche's view of art carries significant implications for the avant-garde's dream of transforming the world into a work of art. Neither art nor the theory that defines it is limited to a domain set apart. To the contrary, "the theory of poetry," Stevens maintains, "is the theory of life."[12] Within this philosophical aesthetic, God, self, and world intersect in the imaginative work of art.

But Nietzsche's understanding of the world as a work of art is considerably more complex than Stevens's formulation initially suggests. Though God and the imagination might be one, Nietzsche's God is always duplicitous. In his most sustained analysis of the genealogy of art, *The Birth of Tragedy,* Nietzsche argues that God is not one but at least two. The work of art emerges through the activity of Apollo and Dionysus. With Stevens as our guide, we can now recognize these gods as pseudonyms for the imagination.

Apollo, Nietzsche argues, is "the marvelous divine image of the *principium individuationis.*" As such, Apollo, in a manner not unlike the Roman god Terminus, enforces "the observance of limits" and "just boundaries." Dionysus, by contrast, is the god of "excess" and "indiscreet extravagance." Enacting and embodying "the shattering of the individual," the "Dionysiac vortex" issues in what Nietzsche somewhat surprisingly describes as the "fusion with the original Oneness." Though Apollo and Dionysus are obviously antithetical, they are not simply opposites but are interrelated in such a way that each presupposes and calls forth the other. While "Apollo found it impossible to live without Dionysos," "only so much of the Dionysiac substratum of the universe may enter an individual consciousness as can be dealt with by that Apollonian transfiguration; so that these two prime agencies must develop in strict proportion, conformable to the laws of eternal justice."[13] The result of the interplay of two contending yet cooperating gods is the world, which, as I have noted, is a work of art.

In order to appreciate the anthropological implications of Nietzsche's mythological musings, it is necessary to translate Apollo and Dionysus into principles of imaginative activity. Insofar as Apollo is the god of boundaries who defines the limits of individuality and Dionysus is the god of excess who voids the principle of individuality, their interrelation stages the interfacing of form and formlessness. Apollo gives form to the formlessness embodied in Dionysus.

> [T]he Dionysiac element, as against the Apollonian, proves itself to be the eternal and original power of art, since it calls into being the entire world of phenomena. Yet in the midst of that world a new transfiguring light is needed to catch and hold in life the stream of individual forms. If we could imagine an incarnation of dissonance—and what is man if not that?—that dissonance, in order to endure life, would need a marvelous illusion to cover it with a veil of beauty. This is the proper artistic intention of Apollo, in whose name are gathered together all those countless illusions of fair semblance which at any moment make life worth living and whet our appetite for the next moment.[14]

By his careful use of terms like "incarnation" and "transfiguration," Nietzsche discreetly underscores the way in which his theory of art rewrites theology as aesthetics. Art repeats the cosmogonic act of bringing darkness to light by creating forms out of the void. The intricate complexity of theology, anthropology, and cosmology makes it impossible to be sure where ontology ends and epistemology begins. Imaginative activity creates worlds by allowing appearances to appear. Things themselves are nothing apart from the work of the imagination.

From Nietzsche's perspective, the work of art is not a finished product but an ongoing process. Within this process, so-called objects and so-called subjects are isomorphic; the object reflects the subject and vice versa. In light of earlier observations about minimalism's criticism of abstract expressionism's reduction of art to the intentionality of the artist, it is important to stress that this relation between subject and object is *structural* rather than substantive.

These philosophical insights illuminate Sandback's sculptures in ways that are not immediately obvious. Through our analysis of the framing activity of yarn, we have discovered that Sandback's work displays the interaction between form and emptiness as well as volume and void. Nietzsche's imaginative rendering of Apollo and Dionysus suggests how the objects Sandback creates can be understood in terms of the structure of subjectivity, which exceeds every individual as such. Forever eluding form, this indeterminate excess is indistinguishable from nothing. Sandback's fragile lines, vacant planes, and hollow volumes repeatedly return to this question of nothingness.

Pondering Sandback's ephemeral works leads to consideration of ways in which emptiness and nothingness have been conceived in other artistic and spiritual traditions. Commenting on recurrent tendencies in Japanese and Chinese art, Torataro Shimomura writes:

> Eastern paintings do not aim at the expression of the real form of things; and even if they do portray the form of things, they do not portray the things themselves; by means of them they express the soul, but this soul is nothing other than the formless world. On the surface of the canvas the blank spaces dominate. These blank spaces are wholly different from the *backgrounds* of Western paintings. Instead the blank spaces are expressed by the form of the things portrayed.[15]

Can this relationship between the work of art and the soul or the "formless world" help us to understand the art object and the structure of subjectivity, which we have identified in Sandback's sculptures?

Cross-cultural analysis is always fraught with difficulties. In this case, however, important work done by members of the Kyoto school of philosophy facilitates the task of comparison. As Yoshinori Takeuchi points out, the founder of the Kyoto school, Nishida Kitaro (1870–1945), sought "to build a system permeated with the spirit of Buddhist meditation by fully employing Western thinking."[16] The method of thinking that Nishida and his most influential student, Keiji Nishitani, found most productive was post-Kantian German philosophy. By drawing on thinkers from Kant and Hegel to Nietzsche and Heidegger, Nishida and Nishitani open lines of communication between certain ancient Buddhist traditions and modern Continental philosophy. The dialogue Nishida and Nishitani initiate is especially helpful in understanding certain aspects of contemporary minimalist art.

In his late work *Nothingness and the Religious Worldview,* Nishida interprets Kant and post-Kantian philosophy through the tenets of Buddhism and vice versa. Describing the self in terms designed to recall Hegel's dialectic, Nishida argues:

> The self . . . possesses itself through its own self-negation. It has its existence in a bottomless self-negation that is inconceivable either in the direction of the grammatical subject or in the direction of the predicate. Its nothingness is grounded in the contradictory identity of the creative world, which is self-transforming through the dialectic of its own negation and affirmation. At the ground of the self, therefore, there must be that which, in its own absolute nothingness, is self-determining, and which, in its own absolute nothingness, is being. I believe this is the meaning of the ancient Buddhist saying, "Because there is No Place in which it abides, this Mind arises."[17]

In this rich text, Nishida maintains that subjectivity is haunted by an "absolute nothingness," which is best understood as the "No Place" where "Mind arises." Elsewhere he draws on the insights of Kant to describe the homologous relation between objectivity and subjectivity.

> The phenomenal world is spatial in the form "from many to one" (the one negating the many), and yet it is temporal in the form "from one to many" (the many negating the one). This is the self-contradictory structure of the conscious act. The natural world is schematized, to use Kant's word, by having these transforming perspectives as centers. The self-origination of these centers may be regarded as the acts of imagination in the dimension of consciousness; in the dimension of practical reason, the schemata are the laws that appear as self-determinations of the predicate. From my

standpoint, the *Ding-an-sich* is nothing other than the transforming matrix in which the self finds itself.[18]

In Kant's epistemology, knowledge arises through a synthesis of a priori forms of intuition and categories of understanding, on the one hand, and, on the other, the sensible manifold of intuition. Since awareness is always already processed, we can never know the world as such or, in Kant's terms, we can never apprehend the *Ding-an-sich*. In other words, we know only appearances or phenomena and never noumenal reality. Forever beckoning from just beyond our reach, the thing-in-itself remains completely indeterminate or utterly formless and, thus, is indistinguishable from nothing.

What is not immediately apparent in this line of analysis is that the very distinction between appearance and the *Ding-an-sich* or phenomena and noumena is drawn by consciousness itself. This is Nishida's point when he argues that, far from remaining independent of the subject, "the *Ding-an-sich* is nothing other than the transforming matrix" of the self, which simultaneously inhabits and exceeds the conscious ego. Nishida's devoted follower Shin'ichi Hisamatsu names the self that transcends the self the "Formless Self."

> I have expressed this Self as the Fundamental Subject that is Absolutely Nothing. Here the word "nothing" should be understood in the sense of Formless. Nothingness, as it is ordinarily spoken of in the West, seems to be derived from the concept of negation. Also in Japan, in philosophy and other fields, the word is commonly used in the sense of negation. As to the Nothingness of Dr. Kitaro Nishida, my most respected teacher, it is, according to my understanding, no mere negation, but the "No" of the Self of "No Form."

"The Fundamental Subject that is *Absolutely Nothing*," Hisamatsu maintains,

> is also the Fundamental Subject that is *Actively Nothing*. . . . The form that constitutes the activity of the Formless Self, however, is the form of No Form. For this kind of formless form, Zen has the term "wondrous being." This term signifies that, unlike ordinary being, this is at once being and nonbeing. Here, being never remains static, but is constantly one with the Formlessness. So that the Formless Self is characterized as the True Void.[19]

As Nishitani explains, the Formless Self that is the True Void is "absolutely nonobjectifiable."[20]

With these insights in mind, let us return to Nietzsche by way of Kant and, conversely, to Kant by way of Nietzsche. Insofar as the structure of the object reflects the structure of the subject, the distinction between appearance and the *Ding-an-sich* mirrors the contrast between the conscious subject and the "Formless Self that is Absolutely Nothing." Hisamatsu's "Fundamental Subject," which "has no form" yet "comes—through activity—to have form," is structurally the same as Nietzsche's "True Subject" whose activity results from the interplay of Dionysian formlessness and Apollonian form. "[T]he distinction between subjective and objective, which even Schopenhauer still uses as a sort of measuring stick to distinguish the arts," Nietzsche argues, "has no value whatever in esthetics; the reason being that the subject—the striving individual bent on furthering his egoistic purposes—can be thought of only as an enemy to art, never as its source. But to the extent that the subject is an artist he is already delivered from individual will and has become a medium through which the True Subject celebrates His redemption in illusion."[21] This True Subject, which has no form but engenders all forms, is nothing other than the imagination. Expressed in terms derived from Nishida and his followers, the No Place where form emerges from emptiness is the imagination, which, as the True Void, is Actively Nothing. To draw the threads of this analysis together, it is necessary to return to the work of the frame.

The frame, we have discovered, "gives rise to the work." As the limit, border, margin, and fringe that lies between void and volume, the frame allows form to emerge from emptiness and things to materialize out of nothing. The work of the frame, however, is two-edged: framing delimits. Framing, in other words, simultaneously inscribes the limit, edge, or border and traces the fading of the limit in the unlimited. As the agency through which framing occurs, the imagination is the liminal faculty that makes apprehension possible and renders the subject of apprehension apprehensive.

In the First Critique, Kant not only describes the activity of the imagination in terms of bringing form to matter by unifying the sensible manifold but also defines the imagination as something like a frame. The imagination is the *Mitte* or *Mittelglied* between sensibility and understanding. Accordingly, Derrida explains,

> the imagination, being the intermediate between sensibility and understanding, is capable of *two operations*. And we rediscover here the two borders, the two faces of the trait, of the limit or of the edge [*taille*]. Imagination is the edge because it has two edges. The edge always has two edges: it de-limits. It has the edge of what it delimits and the edge

of what it de-limits, of what it limits and of what is liberated in it of its limits. Two operations of the imagination, then, which are both *prehensions*. Apprehension (*apprehensio, Auffasung*) can go to the infinite *without difficulty*. The other operation, comprehension (*comprehensio, Zusammenfassung*) cannot follow, it is finite, subjected to the *intuitus derivatus* and to the sensory.[22]

Ceaselessly oscillating between fusion and diffusion, the imagination creates the possibility of comprehension while exposing one to the apprehension of the incomprehensible.

It is important to realize in this context that the imagination is not merely mimetic or reproductive but also creative or productive. The imagination, in other words, "is not the placing-in-form of something else but the forming itself, for itself, without object." Nor is the imagination simply the work *of* the subject; rather, the imagination, like Apollo and Dionysus, works *through* the subject: "The 'imagination' does not signify the subject who makes an image of something but rather the image imaging itself, not as a figure of something else but as form forming itself, unity happening upon manifoldness, coming out of a manifoldness, in the manifold of sensibility, simply as unity without object and without subject—and thus without end."[23] In the First Critique, Kant attempts to account for the activity of the imagination in terms of what he describes as the "schematization" of the categories. By mediating sensation and understanding, the schemata deployed by the imagination issue in something like an "originary figure *of figuration itself.*" By the time of the Third Critique, Kant associates the activity of schematization with the work of art. Jean-Luc Nancy concisely summarizes Kant's point.

> Kant calls the free *Bild* that precedes all images, all representations, and all figurations (one is tempted to say the nonfigurative *Bild*), a *schema* in the first *Critique*. He says in the third *Critique* that aesthetic judgment is nothing other than the reflexive play of the imagination when it "schematizes without concepts": that is, when the world that forms itself, that manifests itself, is not a universe of objects but merely a schema (*skema,* "form," or "figure"), merely, a *Bild* that makes a "world" on its own, because it forms itself, because it designs itself. The *schema* is the figure— but the imagination that figures without concepts figures nothing: the schematism of aesthetic judgment is transitive. It is merely the figure that figures itself.[24]

Since something "precedes all images, all representations, all figurations," there is something incalculable in the figuring of the imagination. Insofar as the imagination "figures nothing," it (impossibly) figures what cannot be figured. This figuring of the unfigurable is a disfiguring, which takes place through what Kant at one point in the First Critique confesses is "a blind but indispensable function of the soul."

> Synthesis in general . . . is the mere result of the power of imagination, a blind but indispensable function of the soul, without which we should have no knowledge whatsoever, but of which we are scarcely ever conscious. To bring this synthesis *to concepts* is a function that belongs to the understanding, and it is through this function of the understanding that we first obtain knowledge properly so called.[25]

If knowledge presupposes the activity of the imagination, which "is a blind but indispensable function of the soul," then blindness inevitably lies at the heart of all insight. This blindness brings us to the edge of the sublime.

Though written after the first two critiques, the Third Critique actually frames the *Critique of Pure Reason* and the *Critique of Practical Reason*. Forming the border both joining and separating his accounts of truth and goodness, the *Critique of Judgment* marks the space where Kant explores questions of beauty. In a manner that anticipates Nietzsche's interplay of Apollo and Dionysus, Kant insists that beauty cannot be understood apart from the sublime. If beauty is Apollonian, sublimity is Dionysian. Just as Apollo and Dionysus call each other forth, so there can be no beauty without sublimity and no sublimity without beauty.

> One can hardly speak of an *opposition* between the beautiful and the sublime. An opposition could only arise between two determinate objects, having their contours, their edges, their finitude. But if the difference between the beautiful and the sublime does not amount to an opposition, it is precisely because the presence of a limit is what gives form to the beautiful. The sublime is to be found, for its part, in an "object without form" and the "without-limit" is "represented" in it or on the occasion of it, and yet gives the totality of the without-limit to be *thought*.[26]

In terms previously invoked, while beauty is delimited, sublimity is delimited. Just as there can be no delimitation without de-limitation, so there can be no de-limitation without delimitation.

As the activity through which form is articulated from formlessness, the imagination is not merely representational but, more important, what might be called a presentational capacity, which, though active within, extends beyond the activity of the individual subject. Since the imagination is the condition of the possibility of presentation, it can be neither presented nor represented. Nor is the imagination never present. Neither present nor absent, the proximity of the imagination is always withdraw-ing. In and through this withdrawal, something unpresentable occurs in the midst of all presentation.[27] Nancy's analysis of the sublime illuminates Kant's elusive point.

> In the sublime—or perhaps more precisely at a certain extreme point to which the sublime leads us—it is no longer a matter of (re)presentation in general. It is a matter of something else, which takes place, happens, or occurs *in* presentation itself and in sum *through* it but which is not presentation: this motion through which, incessantly, the unlimited raises and razes itself, unlimits itself, along the limit that delimits and present itself. . . . In the sublime, then, presentation itself is at stake: neither some-thing to be presented or represented nor something that is nonpresentable (nor the nonpresentability of the thing in general), nor even the fact that it [*ça*] presents itself to a subject and through a subject (representation), but the fact *that* it presents itself and *as* it presents itself: it presents itself in the unlimitation, it presents itself always *at the limit*.[28]

Even with Nancy's helpful gloss, Kant's point can be easily misunder-stood. Instead of arguing that the imagination somehow presents the unpresentable or represents the unpresentable as such, Kant insists that imaginative activity inevitably entails a "presentation *without* presenta-tion," which actually presents nothing. The nothing that is not presented or is presented as a certain not-presenting is the "active nothingness" of the "formless self," rather than the indeterminate no thing that is the opposite of every determinate thing. Far from exterior to the subject, this nothingness haunts the subject as "a blind but indispensable function of the soul." Neither thing nor no thing, form nor emptiness, volume nor void, nothing "is"—but, of course, it "is not"—the infinite oscillation or alternation that allows appearances to appear. This movement, Kant explains, "especially in its inception, may be compared with a vibration, i.e. with a rapidly alternating repulsion and attraction produced by one and the same object. The point of excess for the imagination (toward which it is driven in the apprehension of intuition) is like an abyss in which it fears to lose itself."[29] This point of excess marks a strange abyss, which, though "inside" the subject, is an "exterior" that cannot be interiorized. As a result of this "outside" that is "inside," subjectivity is always excessive; it overflows itself in and through a limitation that is a de-limitation. Since the limit is the "No Place" where nothing becomes something and everything fades into emptiness, subjectivity (*sub,* under, + *jacere,* to throw) is always subjected to a nothingness it cannot compre-hend. This nothingness provokes the apprehension of the work of art.

When art works, apprehension must be understood in at least three ways. First, as we have seen, the work of art displays the activity of the imagination through which form emerges from formlessness. This formative process is the condition of the possibility of both apprehension and comprehension. Second, inasmuch as the subject always exceeds itself, the imagination not only grasps but is seized or apprehended by a nothingness it can never comprehend. Since this emptiness, void, or abyss is not outside but is a cryptic interiority to which consciousness is exposed, the incomprehensible is inescapable. Third, the apprehension of nothing makes the subject edgy or apprehensive. Kierkegaard identifies the experience Kant evokes when he describes the response to the sublime as a "rapidly alternating repulsion and attraction" as anxiety or dread. Dread, Kierkegaard maintains, "is *a sympathetic antipathy* and *an antipathetic sympathy.*" Exploring the apprehension that slumbers in ignorance, he writes: "In this state there is peace and repose, but there is simultaneously something else—something other that is not contention and strife, for there is nothing against which to strive. What, then, is it? Nothing. But what effect does nothing have? It begets dread."[30] Since dread arises from within rather than without—or more precisely from a without that is within—it is unavoidable. Yet much, indeed perhaps most, of life involves a sustained struggle to avoid the unavoidable by willing ignorance of that which we can never know.

When art works, it provokes the return of the repressed by rendering apprehension apprehensible. The art that really matters turns us toward that which turns away from us and from which we tend to turn away. This is what Sandback's empty sculptures do. They are effective because they are *about* nothing. When art is about nothing, it surrounds the nothingness that surrounds it. By de-limiting nothing, the work of art exposes us to the void in whose midst we are destined to dwell. In the seemingly tranquil spaces framed by fuzzy lines drawn by thin strands of yarn, nothing is apprehensible. For those who are patient enough to linger with the nothingness that inhabits the world as well as "our" selves, the lines of Sandback's empty forms retrace the lines of Stevens's abyssal poetry.

> For the listener, who listens in the snow,
> And, nothing himself, beholds
> Nothing that is not there and the nothing that is.[31]

Nine

Learning Curves

to fold
to bend
to twist
to differ
to open
to knot

RICHARD SERRA

to space
to time

Richard Serra's art is difficult—difficult to make, difficult to display, difficult to comprehend, difficult to accept. This difficulty tends to provoke resistance; many regard his work as assertive, aggressive, even coercive. This response, however, oversimplifies the difficulty of his art. For Serra, art is difficult because it is complex. More precisely, art is *about* complexity. The difficulty of complexity and complexity of difficulty make the work of art demanding. When art is not simple, it not only takes time but, more importantly, gives time (its due).

Serra's exploration of the art of complexity began when his work took an unexpected turn. After studying literature at the University of California at Berkeley and Santa Barbara and painting at Yale, Serra spent a year in Paris and a year in Florence, where his interest gradually shifted from painting to sculpture. In 1970, he lived for six weeks in Kyoto near the temple complexes at Myoshin-ji. During his time in Japan, Serra spent many long hours reflecting on the Zen gardens associated with various temples. This was Serra's first serious encounter with a non-Western culture, and it transformed his understanding of art. In a recent conversation, he recalled: "My stay in Kyoto completely changed my ideas

218

about sculpture."[1] At first glance, this claim is puzzling, for nothing seems farther from the delicate refinement of Zen gardens than the raw power of Serra's signature works. But as one considers this unlikely association more carefully, surprising connections begin to emerge. Though drawing on different cultural and artistic traditions, Zen masters and Serra are preoccupied with many of the same issues. Their works present thoughtful meditations on the intricate interplay of emptiness/form, void/volume, lightness/weight, balance/imbalance, continuity/discontinuity, transience/permanence and simplicity/complexity. In a 1992 interview with Lynne Cooke, Serra explains the significance of the gardens he discovered in Japan for the development of his work.

> The interior space of the temples is a dense, compressed volume, very simple and clear in terms of divisions and openings. I found the structure of the gardens more interesting than the temples. They are organized with a rigorous mode of placement. The primary characteristic of the garden is that the paths around and through them are curvilinear. The geometry of the site prompts walking in arcs. The articulation of discrete elements within the field and the sense of the field as a whole emerge only by constant walking and looking. Other gardens in Kyoto are laid out to be seen from a viewing porch. In some of them one element is hidden behind the other, and the entirety of the garden landscape is only revealed as one walks the length of the horizontal viewing platform of the temples. The layout of the gardens is based on the perceptual principles of time, meditation, and motion. This concept of space is essentially different from our western concept, which is based on central perspective and arranges all objects on a line emanating from the eye of the static viewer. In the Zen gardens, directions, continuity and paths work together to deny a fixed measure.[2]

As this remark suggests, different kinds of Zen gardens are created for different purposes.[3] Water gardens, dry gardens, and tea gardens vary in design as well as function. One of the distinctive differences in Japanese gardens is between those that are intended to be viewed from a distance, like a painting on a wall or a sculpture on a pedestal, and those that, in a manner reminiscent of Sandback's "pedestrian space," can be appreciated only by walking through them. Both types of garden can display either precise rectilinearity or evocative curvilinearity. Serra is fascinated by gardens that permit meditative wandering and is intrigued by the artistic possibilities of curvilinear shapes and forms.

> When I first started going to the gardens of Myoshin-ji, it became very apparent to me that you either walk horizontal to the view or you walk

through the interior of the garden. Walking through the garden is predicated on time in relation to movement, which implies continual apperceptive experience based on anticipation and memory. This is very different from what I had discovered when I was a student in Italy looking at Donatello or in Paris looking at Giacometti. You cannot find a correlative to the gardens in the western sculptural tradition.[4]

What Serra discovers in the gardens of Japan is a different sense of space. Unlike the perspectival space that has governed perception in the West since the Renaissance, space in the garden is inescapably temporal.

The primary characteristic of both the temples and stone gardens was that the ambulatory paths around and through them were circular. The geometry of the sites prompted walking in arcs. The articulation of discrete elements within the field and the sense of the field as a whole emerged only by constant looking. The necessity of peripatetic perception is characteristic of Myoshin-ji.[5]

Never merely visual, "peripatetic perception" involves the entire body in all of its spatial and temporal complexity. When roaming through the garden, it becomes clear that there is no space without time and no time without space because the fabric of experience is constituted by a complex interweaving of space-time.

The Japanese have developed a specific term to designate this distinctive understanding of space-time: MA. In an essay entitled "Space-Time in Japan," the architect Arata Isozaki explains:

While in the West the space-time concept gave rise to absolutely fixed images of a homogeneous and infinite continuum, as presented in Descartes, in Japan space and time were never fully separated but were conceived as correlative and omnipresent. . . . Space could not be perceived independently of the element of time. Likewise, time was not abstracted as a regulated homogeneous flow, but rather was believed to exist only in relation to movements or spaces. . . . Thus, space was perceived as identical with the events or phenomena occurring in it; that is, space was recognized only in its relation to time-flow.[6]

Rather than an a priori structure—be that structure objective (as in Newtonian physics) or subjective (as in Kantian philosophy)—space and time, as well as their experiential apprehension, are inseparable from bodily movement. Space-time, in other words, is a corporeal event, which is never fixed but always in transition. As the word *MA* suggests, the site of this transition is the interval.

MA [is] "the natural distance between two or more things existing in a continuity" or "the space delineated by posts and screens (rooms)" or "the natural pause or interval between two or more phenomena occurring continuously," gives rise to both spatial and temporal formulations. Thus the word MA does not describe the West's recognition of time and space as different serializations. Rather, in Japan, both time and space have been measured in terms of intervals. Today's usage of the word MA extends to almost all aspects of Japanese life—for MA is recognized as their foundation. Therefore architecture, fine arts, music, and drama are all known as "the art of MA."[7]

As an event that occurs in an interval, which is never present as such, space-time is actually a spacing that is a timing and a timing that is a spacing. MA insinuates time into space by exposing the space of time. The art of MA—and there is no other art—is the art of spacing-timing.

In recent years, a notion that approximates the spacing-timing expressed in the word *MA* has unexpectedly emerged in Western critical discourse. Derridean deconstruction is, in effect, an extended meditation on the far-reaching implications of the eventualities of spacing-timing. In his influential essay "Différence," Derrida stresses the intersection of space and time in the word *différer,* which is derived from the Latin verb *differre* and means both to differ and to defer or delay. Attempting to capture the oscillating rhythms of *différer* by insisting that his neologism *différance* implies both temporization (*temporisation*) and spacing (*espacement*), he writes:

> *Différer* in this sense is to temporize, to take recourse, consciously or unconsciously, in the temporal and temporizing meditation of a detour that suspends the accomplishment or fulfillment of "desire" or "will," and equally effects this suspension in a mode that annuls or tempers its own effect. . . . [T]his temporization is also temporalization and spacing, the becoming-time of space and the becoming-space of time, the "originary constitution" of time and space, as metaphysics or transcendental phenomenology would say, to use the language that here is criticized and displaced.
>
> The other sense of *différer* is the more common and identifiable one: to be not identical, to be other, discernible, etc. When dealing with *différen(ts)(ds)*, a word that can be written with a final *ts* or a final *ds*, as you will, whether it is a question of dissimilar otherness or of allergic and polemical otherness, an interval, a distance, *spacing*, must be produced between the elements['] other, and be produced with a certain perseverance in repetition.[8]

Neither spatial nor temporal, spacing-timing is the condition of the possibility or, in Derrida's terms, the "originary constitution" of space and time. So understood, spacing-timing is the complex "site" of the emergence of everything that is present. This "originary constitution" is, however, a strange "origin" because it is never present as such; nor, of course, is it simply absent. In a manner strictly analogous to MA, *différance* is the "interweaving" or "interlacing" of presence and absence in the interval that defines their difference. According to Heidegger, the work of art is to articulate this interval. This work, as we shall see, is inseparable from a certain tearing, rending, or cutting.

to sculpt
to draw

To sculpt, as the word implies, is inter alia to cut, carve, or chisel. Cutting opens by spacing. The space of the cut is the oscillating interval where differences are articulated. This articulation of differences, Heidegger maintains, is "the origin of the work of art." The work of art is not merely an object but, more important, a process or event through which differences are articulated and thereby worlds are formed and reformed. Stressing the eventuality of art, Heidegger opens his essay entitled "The Origin of the Work of Art" by asking, "Where and how does art occur?" "Art," he proceeds to argue, "breaks open an open place." The opening of art is a *Riss*—a break, crack, fissure, cleft, gap, or tear. The spacing and timing of this *Riss* create a play of differences that constitutes "the essential strife" of "world" (i.e., "the self-disclosing openness") and "earth," (i.e., "the essentially self-concealing").

> But as a world opens itself, the earth comes to rise up. It stands forth as that which bears all, as that which is sheltered in its own law and always self-secluding. World demands its decisiveness and its measure and lets beings extend into the open of their paths. Earth, bearing and jutting, strives to keep itself closed and to entrust everything to its law. The strife is not a tear [*Riss*] as the gaping crack [*Aufreissen*] of a pure cleft, but the strife is the intimacy with which opponents belong to each other. This tear pulls opponents together in the origin of their unity by virtue of their common ground. It is a basic design [*Grundriss*], an outline sketch [*Aufriss*], that draws the basic features of the rise of the lighting of beings. This tear does not let the opponents burst apart; it brings together the opposition of measure and boundary into their common outline [*Umriss*].⁹

Tearing alternates between two rhythms—one centrifugal, the other centripetal. By holding open this alternating difference, the origin of the work of art simultaneously joins and separates. This separation that joins and joining that separates is the cutting tear of pain.

> Pain tears or rends [*reisst*]. It is the tear or rift [*Riss*]. But it does not tear apart into dispersive fragments. Pain indeed tears asunder, it separates, yet in such a way that it at the same time draws everything together to itself. Its rending, as a separating that gathers, is at the same time that drawing [*Ziehen*], which, like the pre-drawing [*Vorriss*] and sketch [*Aufriss*] draws and joins together what is held apart in separation. Pain is the join(t)ing in the tearing/rending that divides and gathers. Pain is the join-ing or the articulation of the rift. This joining is the threshold. It delivers the between, the mean of the two that are separated in it. Pain articulates the rift of the difference. Pain is dif-ference [*Unter-schied*] itself.[10]

If art originates with rend(er)ing, then there can be no art without drawing.

Serra is obsessed with drawing; he is rarely without a sketchbook in which he draws and redraws incessantly. It is as if Serra thinks and speaks by drawing. The longer one ponders his drawing, the clearer it becomes that drawing is not only a means of expressing his ideas but a mode of experience more "primordial" than thinking. Drawing is noth-ing less than the "origin" of ideas. "To draw a line," Serra insists, "is to have an idea. A drawn line is the basis of construction. To draw is to innovate in multiplicity. The line gives to the work an inexplicable defi-nition. It defines and redefines structure. To cut is to draw a line, it is to separate, to make a distinction."[11] From this point of view, drawing obviously is not limited to the two dimensions of pencil and paper but can be a three-dimensional sculptural activity.

> I put down a ruler (or template) underneath five different materials, mak-ing a rectangle to the right and left of which I cut so that what was placed on top was divided into three parts. The line—a cut—was a way of making a division through diverse elements and separating the field. Cut as line reoccurs not only in all of the sculpture but later in the large black drawings. (54–55)

In this way, the act of drawing inscribes the spacing-timing that articu-lates the differences constitutive of every shape and form. Commenting on *Cutting Device: Base—Plate—Measure* (1969), Serra underscores the formative function of the cut: "the cut as line informs the material, the structure, and the process" (28). Implicitly extending Heidegger's *Riss* and Derrida's *différance,* the process of cutting creates the opening in and through which the work of art emerges. This opening is what the work of art is *about.*

Inasmuch as art is about a certain opening, cutting not only de-fines *l'oeuvre d'art* by outwardly differentiating the object from its surroundings but also rends the work as if from within. The work surrounds the opening as much as the opening surrounds the work. Never whole but always rent, the tear of art is the trace of its fragility. One of the most remarkable features of many of Serra's works is the complex interplay between stability and instability they establish. While working with the most stable materials, he nonetheless creates works that are extraordinarily unstable. Sculptures like *No. 1, 1-1-1-1, 5:30,* and *One Ton Prop (House of Cards)* (all 1969), are precariously balanced so as to appear on the verge of collapsing. These objects vividly display the way in which all entities are created and sustained by a play of forces as delicate as it is complex. Whatever stability objects have is the result of a momentary balance of forces, which simultaneously draw together what they hold apart and hold apart what they draw together. Serra is less interested in objects as such than in the fields of forces in which they emerge. In a 1977 interview with Lizzie Borden, bearing the suggestive title "About Drawing," he notes:

> Different shapes displace amounts of weights and volumes given the character of their mass. There's an intangible quality to a gravitational field. The degree to which I can articulate it through edge, boundary, centering, dislocation, mass and volume, is the degree to which I can point to an experience. To articulate a gravitational field is one way of constructing a place, but it has nothing to do with the logical process of putting something together. (56)

In contrast to classical sculpture, Serra opens the work of art to the opening that is its "origin." Having displaced sculpture from the pedestal, he proceeds to fissure it, leaving gaps that render the densest material virtually diaphanous.

Far from a sudden gesture, Serra's opening of the work of art is a gradual process that reflects an emerging critique of the autonomy of the traditional sculptural object as well as the self-referentiality of modernist artistic theory and practice. In the first moment of this critique, the self-contained object is torn asunder. While no longer formally discrete, the sculptural object remains a separate entity subject to the comprehensive gaze of the viewer. Artistic experience, therefore, remains primarily vi-

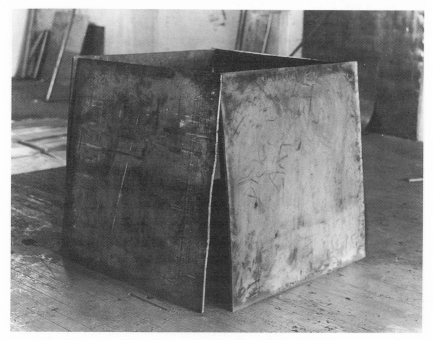

FIGURE 24 Richard Serra, *One Ton Prop (House of Cards)*, 1969

sual. Serra quickly becomes dissatisfied with these works because he is convinced that such "opticality" places needless limitations on the work of art: "I started building pieces very early (1968) that had to do with balance and weightlessness. Most of the pieces were closed. What disappointed me was that you couldn't enter into their physical space" (47). What is missing from these early works is precisely the space for the "peripatetic perception" that Serra had discovered in the Zen gardens of Kyoto. In order to create the space and time for experience that is more than visual, it is necessary to open the work of art in new ways.

As the opening expands, the works grow larger and larger. No longer autonomous objects to be viewed from a distance, Serra's sculptures become open fields that draw one into their midst. In *Circuit I* (1972) and *Circuit II* (1972–86), he begins to create what he had described in Japanese stone gardens as "ambulatory paths." In these works, four steel plates are situated in an empty room to form an X, which is open at the center. The size of the plates (8′ × 24′ × 1″ in the former and 10′ × 20′ × 2″ in the latter) makes it impossible to view the work as a whole. Apprehending this work takes time; it is necessary to enter and walk around in it. The space of the work cannot be experienced apart from the time of movement. When roaming through these broken circuits, senses other than vision are engaged. Unlike the ambulatory paths of the Zen gardens, the course Serra charts in these works remains rectilinear. Moreover, the work is confined to the space of the gallery.

Though long interested in the complex interplay between work and site, Serra did not build anything in the landscape until shortly after his return from Kyoto. The Pulitzers, he recalls, "gave me the opportunity to work on an enormous piece of land—probably about four or five acres. This was just after I came back from Kyoto and the impression of the temples and stone gardens was still fresh in my mind. This experience had a big impact on me and resulted in an enormous shift in my work."[12] The extent of the influence of the Zen gardens on Serra during this period is evident in both *Pulitzer Piece: Stepped Elevation* (St. Louis, 1970–71) and *Shift* (King City, Ontario, 1971–72). Freed from the limitations imposed by gallery walls, the openness of the site creates radically new possibilities for "peripatetic perception." Shortly after its completion, Serra described his purpose in *Shift*.

> The intent of the work is an awareness of physicality in time, space, and motion. Standing at the top of the eastern hill, one sees the first three elements in a Z-like linear configuration. The curvature of the land is only partially revealed from this point of view, because the configuration compresses the space.
>
> Until one walks into the space of the piece, one cannot see over the rise, as the hill descends into its second and third five-foot drop. This again is because the land's incline is inconsistent in its elevational fall. . . .
>
> The work establishes a measure: one's relation to it and to the land, to rise in relation to one's descending eye-level. . . . Insofar as the stepped elevations function as horizons cutting into and extending toward the real horizon, they suggest themselves as orthogonals within the terms of a perspective system of measurement. The machinery of renaissance space depends on measurements remaining fixed and immutable. These steps relate to a continually shifting horizon, and as measurements, they are totally transitive: elevating, lowering, extending, foreshortening, contracting, compressing, and turning. The line as a visual element, per step, becomes a transitive verb. (12–13)

As the work becomes transitive, it *shifts* from being a thing to being a process or from being a noun to being a verb. The "verbalization" of the work of art, which, for Serra, cannot be captured in language, presupposes the becoming-time of space and the becoming-space of time. The

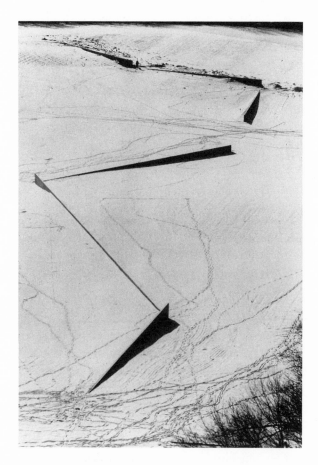

FIGURE 25
Richard Serra, *Shift,*
1971–72

site of this transition is, as Serra suggests, the "cut" of sculpture. The
opening and the work stand in a thoroughly paradoxical relationship:
the cut opens the work, which opens the cut.

As the opening expands (and contracts), it grows more complex. On
the one hand, the site becomes specific, while, on the other hand, the
locus of the work becomes endlessly mobile. *Shift* is about this shifting/
shifty site. Serra signals this shift when he notes: "The intent of the work
is an awareness of physicality in time, space, and motion." Elsewhere he
elaborates this important point at length.

From the top of the hill, looking back across the valley, images and
thoughts are remembered which were initiated by the consciousness of
having experienced them. This is the difference between abstract thought
and thought in experience. The time of this experience is cumulative—

slow in its evolution. One experiences a new kind of compression. The land is sensed as a volume rather than as a recessional plane, because from this point of view the valley has become abridged. For the first time, the alignment of the elevational steps is apparent. This alignment contracts the intervals of the space—not as drawing (or linear configuration) but as volume (as space contained).

The space between the two sets of walls—across the plane of approximately 120 feet—implies a center to the work. This center would coincide with both the measured center of the field and gravitational or topological center of the land mass. However, this is not the center of the work. The work does not concern itself with centering in that way. The expanse of the work allows one to perceive and locate a multiplicity of centers.

Similar elevations—elevations equal in height—in an open field, on a flat floor, shift both horizontally and vertically in relation to one's locomotion. Because of this, the center, or the question of centering, is dislocated from the physical center of the work and found in a moving center. (13)

This is a crucial text for any adequate understanding of Serra's contribution to the history of sculpture. His decentering of the work of art involves a thoroughgoing critique of linear perspective, which has informed art and determined perception since the Renaissance. An object that has no center is not an integrated whole but an open structure that never achieves closure. As the work is decentered, its site shifts. This is Serra's point when he stresses that "the expanse of the work allows one to perceive and locate a multiplicity of centers." These multiple centers, however, no longer are "in" the object; rather, "the center, or the question of centering, is dislocated from the physical center of the work and found in a moving center." The site of this moving center or these moving centers shifts from the object toward the subject. More precisely, the work of art becomes an event or process that occurs *between* the art object and the subject drawn into it. As Rosalind Krauss shrewdly observes:

By 1972 something fundamental had happened to Serra's conception of the cut. In that year he had made *Circuit* and *Twins,* in which cutting was no longer a force exerted on the patient body of the world outside the viewer, but was, somehow, what tied that world to the viewer, what shaped his perception, and, in so doing, could be shown to shape him. Intervening between the Base Plate Measure series and these later works, in 1969–1971, was *Strike,* a sculpture conceived as performing a cut on space itself and organizing it in relation to the viewer's body, so that the interdependence of body and space—coming apart and being put back together—is choreographed in relation to this work.[13]

As the opening of the work of art becomes more complex, it implicates the subject by altering the very conditions of experience. This change is neither sudden nor momentary but takes time, which is given by *l'oeuvre d'art*. Serra puts time to work in the space of art. The timing of this spacing and spacing of this timing mark the difference between "abstract thought" and "thought in experience." Serra's sculpture creates the occasion for thought in experience, which transforms the experience of thought.

The argument staged in Serra's work extends beyond a criticism of classical sculpture to a critical engagement with the most basic tenets of modernist architecture. Responding to Peter Eisenman's inquiry about the significance of modernist sculpture's "break away from figuration or . . . representation in terms of figuration," Serra observes: "The biggest break in the history of sculpture in the twentieth century occurred when the pedestal was removed. The historical concept of placing sculpture on a pedestal established a separation of the object from the behavioral space of the viewer" (141). The removal of the pedestal is necessary but not sufficient for overcoming the separation of object from the space of the viewer. The correlate of the autonomy of the work of art is the opticality of the experience of art. Insofar as modernist art remains committed to both the autonomy of the work of art and the principle of opticality, the gap between subject and object remains unbridgeable. Serra emphatically insists: "I'm not interested in looking at sculpture which is solely defined by its internal relations" (12). By rupturing the integrity of the sculptural work, Serra creates an opening for the reconfiguration of the subject-object relation and thereby recasts the experience of art. What distinguishes his sculpture from the work of artists like Irwin, Bell, Turrell, and Nauman, Serra maintains, is a shift away from a more or less exclusive preoccupation with opticality: "The way my work differs is that it's not opting for opticality as its content. It has more to do with a field force that's being generated, so that the space is discerned physically rather than optically" (40). Two closely related points in this telling comment deserve emphasis. First, if the work of art "has more to do with a field force that's being generated" than with a discrete, stable object, it can only be apprehended when what once was called "the viewer" is drawn into the play of forces constituting the work. Second, if the point of the work is not its opticality, perceptual experience must expand beyond the regime of the eye and its gaze to the entire body. Serra's mature sculpture, therefore, presupposes the primacy of bodily perception.

Serra's insistence that the work of art is not an integral object but a complex interplay between perceived object and perceiving subject is a direct response to the highly influential critique of minimalism advanced by Michael Fried in "Art and Objecthood." Yves-Alain Bois goes so far as to argue that "all of Serra's oeuvre is an implicit reply to Michael Fried's text."[14] Fried's argument is important in its own right as well as emblematic of the dominant version of modernism that Serra is intent on overthrowing. Responding to Robert Morris's claim that "the better new work takes relationships out of the work and makes them a function of space, light, and the viewer's field of vision," Fried charges minimalism with a pernicious theatricality, which destroys the integrity and autonomy of the work of art by identifying the space of the work with the experience of the spectator.

> It may seem paradoxical to claim both that literalist sensibility [with which Fried associates minimalism] aspires to an ideal of "something everyone can understand" (Smith) *and* that literalist art addresses itself to the beholder alone, but the paradox is only apparent. Someone has merely to enter the room in which a literalist work has been placed to *become* that beholder, that audience of one—almost as though the work in question has been *waiting for* him. And inasmuch as the literalist work *depends on* the beholder, it is *incomplete* without him, it *has* been waiting for him.[15]

In this remark, Fried indicates why he believes theatricality poses such a dangerous threat to art. The critical issue is *time.* If the work of art is not autonomous but depends on the "beholder" for its completion, it is always in a state of becoming and thus is irreducibly temporal. The purported autonomy and self-referentiality of the work are supposed to negate time by securing the ideality and transcendence of *l'oeuvre d'art.* When the object is taken off its pedestal and opened to perceptive subjects without whom it cannot do its work, art is set in motion. Since the work of art is forever incomplete, the time of its becoming is endless.

> Endlessness, being able to go on and on, even having to go on and on, is central both to the concept of interest and to that of objecthood. In fact, it seems to be the experience that most deeply excites literalist sensibility, and that literalist artists seek to objectify in their work. . . .
>
> Here finally I want to emphasize something that may already be clear: the experience in question *persists in time,* and the presentment of endlessness that, I have been claiming, is central to literalist art and theory is essentially a presentiment of endlessness, or indefinite, *duration.*[16]

Theatricality, in effect, secularizes the art object by knocking it off its pedestal and dragging it through the ever-changing world of quotidian experience. In his attack on theatricality, Fried struggles to resacralize art by immersing it in a moment that is an eternal present/presence.

> I want to claim that it is by virtue of their presentness and instanta-neousness that modernist painting and sculpture defeat theater. In fact, I am tempted far beyond my knowledge to suggest that, faced with the need to defeat theater, it is above all to the condition of painting and sculpture—the condition, that is, of existing in, indeed of secreting, or constituting, a continuous and perpetual *present*—that the other contemporary modernist arts, most notably poetry and music, aspire.[17]

Fried is convinced that this "perpetual present," though endless, is not haunted by the "endlessness" he sees in the "duration" of minimalist art. Indeed, the "eternal now," he believes, overcomes the relentless temporality of ceaseless duration. When opticality is not "contaminated" by theatricality, the viewer is lifted out of time and enjoys a foretaste of eternity. Far from disappearing, religious aspirations repeatedly return under the guise of art. Fried translates this spiritual tendency in twentieth-century art into the language of criticism. But time relegates the vision of Fried and the artists he champions to the past. The present for which they long is never present but has always already passed away and thus can only approach as a future that never arrives. The space of this infinite delay is the tear of spacing-timing, which, for those who still believe in the transcendent ideality of art, inflicts a wound that never heals.

Sculpture's fall from its pedestal is the artistic equivalent of the death of the transcendent God. When the autonomy of the work of art is exposed as a sham, atemporal ideality gives way to temporal materiality. As the work of art enters time, time enters the work of art; conversely, as time enters the work of art, the work of art enters time. No longer otherworldly, the "real" is incarnate in space-time. Incarnate art can only be apprehended carnally.

to body
to implicate

> The content of the drawing installations does not reside in the process of their making nor does it reside within the delineation of the field of a black canvas. The content resides in the viewer's experience of the space and place as it is redefined through the installation. For example, two

black canvases on walls opposite each other compress and redefine the
physical volume of the space and weight of the room. Your perception of
the room is mediated through the drawing in terms of weight, space,
place, and time. I am interested in the fact that, when you are in a space
that has been configured by a drawing, the sensation of time changes.[18]

Space, time, and the body are bound in a knot that cannot be undone:
space-time is unavoidably bodily, and the body is inescapably spatial-
temporal. This interpretation of the inherent corporeality of space and
time and the spatiality and temporality of the body represents a significant departure from the understanding of space and time that implicitly
or explicitly informs most twentieth-century aesthetic theory and artistic
practice. The decisive analysis of space and time for modern philosophy
and art is presented in the *Critique of Pure Reason,* where Kant thoroughly transforms the interpretation of space and time advanced in classical philosophy, developed in Western metaphysics, and deployed in modern science. Space and time, he argues, are not characteristics of objects
in the world but the conditions of the possibility of subjective experience.
Far from the blank slate or tabula rasa that Locke and his fellow empiricists describe, the mind has a definite structure that conditions all experience. At its most rudimentary level, the structure of the mind is constituted by the *forms* of intuition, which Kant identifies as space (external
intuition) and time (internal intuition), and twelve categories of understanding. The forms of intuition and categories of understanding are a
priori, that is, they are prior to and independent of experience and thus,
Kant insists, are universal. The structure of mind, in other words, is
hardwired or preprogrammed. Knowledge involves a process in which
the "raw" manifold of sensation is first processed by the forms of intuition
and then "cooked" by the categories of understanding. Though the *content* of experience and knowledge varies, the *form* remains the same for
all people in all places at all times. This argument, in effect, translates
the Platonic forms from the realm of ontology to the domain of epistemology. For Plato, the world is created through the agency of a demi-
urge, who brings together transcendent forms and mutable matter. In
Kant's critical philosophy, the mind takes over this demiurgic activity.
The world as we know it is created by the synthesis of the immutable
forms of intuition and categories of understanding and the endlessly mutable manifold of sensation. In this way, the creative subject effectively
displaces the creator God. Kant's appropriation of Plato's ontology for
epistemological purposes leads to a paradoxical view of time as nontem-
poral and space as nonspatial. As a priori conditions of experience, time

and space are unalterable and thus eternal. The immutability of space and time issues in the formal unity of experience for all rational subjects.

But what if the form and content of experience cannot be separated? What if *how* we experience is as mutable as *what* we experience? What if time is temporal and space is spatial? What if the primacy of perception transfigures the experience of thought? In 1962, the English translation of Merleau-Ponty's *Phenomenology of Perception* was published. Its impact on philosophy and art was immediate. For a generation searching for a way out of the dead end of empty abstraction and a conceptualism devoid of sensual experience, Merleau-Ponty's phenomenological investigation of perception and correlative reinterpretation of the bodily bias of thought provided rich resources for reflection. The value of this analysis for artists was enhanced by his knowledge of, and interest in, art. In *Phenomenology of Perception* as well as later studies like *The Visible and the Invisible* and *Sense and Non-Sense,* Merleau-Ponty draws on art to develop his argument, and subjects particular artists and works to thoughtful analysis. Serra was deeply impressed by Merleau-Ponty's insights. Though he studied *Phenomenology of Perception* while a student at Yale, it was not until he visited Japan that he really appreciated its importance for art: "I read Merleau-Ponty while I was still at Yale, but I did not really understand his work until I had been to Japan. I think that happens a lot of the time. You learn something, but it's not useful to you. Even though some seepage occurs, there has to be a catalyst to make you rethink the information. That's what happened for me with Merleau-Ponty in Japan. And I knew it at the time."[19] By the time Serra was formulating his mature view of sculpture, the body had already begun to insinuate itself into the work of many artists. From Pollock's gestural painting to a variety of performance strategies, artists incorporated the body in their work in numerous new ways. In most cases, the turn to the body represented an intuitive reaction rather than an analytic response to artistic tendencies that many viewed with increasing suspicion. Merleau-Ponty's thorough and rigorous account of perception prepared the way for a broad range of innovative artistic practices.

Art—especially so-called visual art—has, of course, always been associated with sensual experience. Indeed, the word *aesthetic* derives from the Greek *aisthetikos,* which means "pertaining to sense perception." It is precisely this relationship between art and the senses that has for centuries rendered art suspect. Art, many people believe, threatens to excite the senses, which can overwhelm reason. From Plato to Hegel and beyond, critics argue that the danger of art can be overcome only when reason controls the senses. Merleau-Ponty realizes that such control is impossible and admits that the struggle to achieve it inevitably leads to repression. Concluding his chapter entitled "Sense Experience," he argues: "It is in the experience of the thing that the reflective ideal of positing thought will have its basis. Hence reflection does not itself grasp its full significance unless it refers to the unreflective fund of experience which it presupposes, upon which it draws, and which constitutes for it a kind of original past, a past which has never been a present."[20] This "original past," "which has never been a present," is what subverts the possibility of the "continuous and perpetual *present*" for which Fried, as well as many artists, longs. While this "original past" can be neither conceived nor comprehended, it can, Merleau-Ponty insists, be experienced. This experience is "pre-objective" and thus "pre-conscious." That which is preobjective and prereflective is, however, also presubjective or, more precisely, is antecedent to the centered subject of consciousness and self-consciousness. Never crossing the threshold of consciousness, the "unreflective fund of experience" upon which reflection constantly draws derives from bodily perception.

> There is . . . another subject beneath me, for whom a world exists before I am here, and who marks out my place in it. This captive or natural spirit is my body, not that momentary body which is the instrument of my personal choices and which fastens upon this or that world, but the system of anonymous "functions," which draw every particular focus into a general project. Nor does this blind adherence to the world, this prejudice in favor of being, occur only at the beginning of my life. It endows every subsequent perception of space with its meaning, and it is resumed at every instant. Space and perception generally represent, at the core of the subject, the fact of his birth, the perpetual contribution of his bodily being, a communication with the world more ancient than thought.[21]

As this text suggests, the body is something like a topological knot that interlaces space and time.

Human experience, for Merleau-Ponty, is undeniably carnal. This carnality tears the subject in a way that faults self-consciousness. Never a self-contained entity, the body is a "gaping wound" that always remains "incomplete." The "openness" of the body is the "dehiscence or fission of [its] mass."[22] This faulty body is neither "subject nor object," neither "*in itself*" nor "*for itself*," neither *res extensa* nor *res cogito*.[23] Rather, the body is the mean between extremes—the *mi-lieu*—in which opposites like interiority and exteriority, as well as subjectivity and objectivity, intersect. Underscoring the liminal status of the body, Merleau-Ponty writes: "At the same time that the body withdraws from the objective world, and forms between the pure subject and the object a third genre or gender of being, the subject loses its purity and its transparency."[24] In an effort to convey this elusive "third term," he uses a variety of figures and images. In addition to "a gaping wound" and "dehiscence," noted above, the body appears to be "a zero point of pressure between two solids," "a hinge, joint, or articulation," which forms the "pivot of the world." This pivotal joint is "a being of porosity," which "is to be compared, not to a physical object, but rather to a work of art."[25] The reason for this association between the body and the work of art becomes clear when we recall Heidegger's account of the origin of the work of art. As we have seen, Heidegger argues that, by holding apart what it draws together and drawing together what it holds apart, the *Riss* opens the spacing-timing through which form is articulated. In some contexts, Heidegger describes the work of the *Riss* as "lighting." Merleau-Ponty borrows the term "lighting" to describe the activity of the body. As *mi-lieu* in and through which subjectivity and objectivity emerge, the body is the condition of the possibility of the "lighting" (*éclairage*) necessary for perceptual experience. Like the tear of Heidegger's work of art, the body is the "dark hole" that allows lighting to emerge. By holding open "the open," the body creates the possibility of the play of differences that constitutes the spatial and temporal conditions of experience. The irreducible openness of the body implies the theatricality of its space. "Bodily space," Merleau-Ponty maintains, "can be distinguished from external space and envelop its parts instead of deploying them, because it is the obscurity necessity in the theater to light up the spectacle, the background of somnolence or the reserve of vague power against which the gesture and its aim detach themselves, the zone of non-being *in front of which* precise beings, figures, and points can come to light."[26]

While the body always remains darkly obscure, it nonetheless has a structure that Merleau-Ponty labels "the chiasmus." *Chiasmus* derives from the Greek *khiasmos,* which in turn comes from *khiazien,* meaning to mark with the letter χ. In grammar, a chiasmus is "a figure by which the order of words in one of two parallel clauses is inverted in the other." For Christians, is the sign of the cross, where crucifixion becomes resurrection. Merleau-Ponty develops his most complete analysis of the chiasmus in a chapter of *The Visible and the Invisible* entitled "L'entrelacs— le chiasme." An *entrelacs* (*entre,* betwixt, between; *lacs,* string, noose, trap) is an ornament consisting of interlacing figures. While *entrelacer* is to interlace, interweave, or intertwine, *s'entrelacer* is to entwine or twist around each other. When understood in terms of *l'entrelacs,* the chiasmus figures a complex structure of "implication" (*im-pli-cation*), "enfoldment" (*enroulement*), and "envelopment" (*enveloppement*). Merleau-Ponty chooses his words very carefully to suggest the importance of a certain *folding* in his understanding of the body. In French, *plier* (to fold) is related to words ranging from *pliable* and *plexus* to *impliquer* and *compliquer.* The same associations appear in English words deriving from the stem *plek,* which means bend, fold; braid, twist, and weave. Words that can be traced to *plek* include, inter alia, simple, complex, pleat, pliable, plight, application, comply, reply, deploy, imply, employ, complicate, duplicate, explicate, implicate, replicate, supplicate, supplement, complicity, and duplicity. It is important to hear all these resonances in what Merleau-Ponty describes as "the structure of implication."[27]

This chiasmic structure appears so complex because it interlaces differences usually held apart in such a way that everything seems to be "completely reversed or turned inside out." Through the process of *re-pli-cation,* which in this context can be translated "double enfolding," differences are interwoven in a relation of mutual implication that simultaneously reveals and conceals the "central cavity" or "hollow" in everything that appears to be solid. This *creux* incarnates the Heideggerian *Riss* and Derridean *différance* in the creases of the body. The "reversibility" of the chiasmus ensures that neither pole in differential relationships dominates the other. Like intertwined hands that almost touch each other, the chiasmus points to "a coincidence always past or always future, an experience that remembers an impossible past, anticipates an impossible future, that emerges from Being or that will incorporate itself into Being, that 'is of it' but is not it, and, therefore, is not a coincidence, a real fusion, as of two positive terms of an alloy, but a recovering or overlaying, as of a hollow and a relief that remain distinct."[28] When understood in this way, the refolding of the chiasmus results in the "invagination" of differences, through which oppositions are overcome while distinctions are maintained.

> The surface of the visible is doubled up over its whole extension with an invisible reserve, and in our flesh . . . as in the flesh of things, the actual, empirical, ontic visible, by a sort of refolding, invagination, . . . exhibits a visibility, a possibility that is not the shadow of the actual but is the principle, that is not the proper contribution of "thought" but is its condition, a style allusive, elliptical like every style, but like every style inimitable, inalienable, an interior horizon and an exterior horizon, between

which the actual visible is a pro-vision-al di-vision and which, nonetheless, open indefinitely only upon other visibles.[29]

The folds of flesh knot space and time in a way that simultaneously rends the integrity of the body and opens the doors of perception.

As the formative *mi-lieu* of subjectivity and objectivity, flesh clears the space in which objects emerge and perception occurs. Yet the body is never "here or now." Forever withdrawing in order to allow appearances to appear, the body is always already past. Time, therefore, is necessarily implied in spacing. An "original past" cuts into every present to create time for spacing. The folding of flesh is the "element" in and through which spacing-timing takes place. Serra explores this element in his most recent and intriguing work.

to torque
to complicate

The implicative structure of the body is further complicated by Serra's sculptural plications. Serra is obsessed with creating complex structures that enfold the body in a way that transfigures experience and thereby alters perception. This concern with experience, he insists, is what distinguishes art from philosophy and science and associates it with religion. Commenting on *Delineator* (1974–75) in an interview with Liza Bear, he explains:

> RS: The juxtaposition of the steel plates forming this open cross generates a volume of space which has an inside and outside, openings and directions, aboves, belows, rights, lefts—coordinates to your body that you understand when you walk through it. Now you might say that that sounds quite esoteric. Well, one of the things that you get into as you become more in tune with articulating space is that space systems are different from linguistic systems in that they're nondescriptive. The conclusion I've come to is that philosophy and science are descriptive disciplines whereas art and religion are not.
>
> LB: Well, they're experiential, aren't they?
>
> RS: Yes. What happens with *Delineator* is that the only way to understand this work is to experience the place physically, and you can't have an experience of space outside of the place and space that you're in. Any linguistic mapping or reconstruction by analogy, or any verbalization

or interpretation or explanation, even of this kind, is a linguistic de-
basement, in a sense, because it isn't true even in a parallel way. (36)

This is not to suggest that Serra is uninterested in conceptual issues. He
is, however, convinced that conceptuality and the language in which it
is articulated are epiphenomenal. Since perception, which is always
bodily, is primary, the only way to change thought is to alter perception
by transforming the conditions that make it possible. For such a transformation to occur, the subject, who, we have discovered, is no longer merely
a viewer, must be drawn into the open folds of the work of art.

Serra has long been interested in bending, curving, twisting, and folding. While many of his early works are rectilinear and display geometric
simplicity, he has always been fascinated by the complexity of curvilinear
shapes. In his 1967–68 "Verb List," he anticipates the issues to which his
most recent work is devoted: "to roll, to fold, to bend, to crumple, to
knot, to curve, to swirl, to encircle."[30] The path that has led Serra to
twisted materials and torqued spaces has been far from straight. For
nearly three decades, he has been folding (*To Lift,* 1967; *Templet,* 1967;
Slant Step Folded, 1967), rolling (*Thirty-Five Feet of Lead Rolled Up,* 1968;
Double Roll, 1968; *Slow Roll: For Philip Glass,* 1968), crumpling (*Tearing*

FIGURE 26   Richard Serra, *Delineator,* 1974–75

Lead from 1:100 to 1:47, 1968; *Scatter Piece,* 1967), bending (*La Palmera,* 1982–84; *Weitmar,* 1984; *W.W.1.,* 1984), encircling (*To Encircle Base Plate Hexagram, Right Angles Inverted,* 1970; *Spoleto Circles,* 1972), knotting (*Belts,* 1966–67; *Rosa Esman's Piece,* 1967; *White Neon Belt Piece,* 1967), and curving (*Waxing Arcs,* 1980; *Slice,* 1980; *St. John's Rotary Arc,* 1980) sculptural works. As straight lines and right angles give way to twists and turns, the object becomes more ambiguous and the subject's relationship to it grows more complex.

Consider, for example, the difference between a work like *Strike* (1969–71) and *St. John's Rotary Arc* (1980). In *Strike,* a sheet of steel measuring 8′ × 24′ × 1″ extends from the corner toward the center of an empty gallery at a 45-degree angle. This assertive work vividly calls critical attention to the conditions of its own display. By creating "ambulatory paths" within the closed space of the gallery, *Strike* can only be grasped by "peripatetic perception." *St. John's Rotary Arc,* by contrast, is a piece of steel measuring 12′ × 200′ × 2½″, which is precisely bent to form a perfectly smooth curve. Serra moves this work outside the gallery and installs it near the exit to the Holland Tunnel. The shift of site from inside to outside and the bending of the steel result in a work that is considerably less assertive and more equivocal. Though seemingly simple, the *Arc* is actually exceedingly complex. As one walks around the work, it changes from a static object to something that repeatedly alternates or oscillates between convexity and concavity. Looking back on *Arc* seventeen years after its completion, Serra reflects:

> What's important in this work is not just designating the space that's made on the edge of the volume but shaping the entire space of the volume. I think the very first curved piece I built was in the rotary. It ended up being a quarter circle about 200 feet long. One of the things that really fascinated me and made me want to build it is that, if you walk around that, even though they are not cylinders, if you walk around these curves, you can begin to sense the difference between concavity and convexity. That's something I didn't know much about and others didn't either. The two curves involve totally different physical experiences. Now it sounds like a trite thing to say, but if something is bending away from you or something is bending toward you, your awareness of it and relation to it are as different as anything can be. That's what I wanted to investigate in the curve.[31]

With the apprehension of the duplicity of even the simplest curved object, the experience of space begins to change. This transformation grows more complex in successive works.

Figure 27   Richard Serra, *Strike,* 1969–71

Even though *St. John's Rotary Arc* is free-standing, it appears to be stable. But this stability is illusory; just as Serra sees complexity in ostensible simplicity, so he discerns instability in apparent stability. Ever since *One Ton Prop (House of Cards)* (1969) and *Skullcracker Series: Stacked Steel Slabs* (1969), Serra has been creating sculptures that seem to teeter on the verge of collapse. Pushing the object to its limit by staging a play of conflicting forces, he forges sculptures that are simultaneously massive and fragile, as well as stable and unstable. In his most famous work, *Tilted Arc,* installed in the Federal Plaza in New York City in 1981 but later removed, Serra extends his investigation of the "physicality of space" by slanting the arc ever so slightly to create the trace of a cone rather than a cylinder. As the vertical axis tips, the arc balances in a way that creates a sense of interiority and exteriority in a space that nonetheless remains completely open. The curve and inclining angle combine to begin the process of folding the peripatetic subject into the sculptural work.

The duplicity of the arc is further complicated when it is doubled. During the mid-1980s, Serra completed a series of works in which symmetrical arcs are positioned in ways that create a startling range of spatial-

FIGURE 28   Richard Serra, *Tilted Arc*, 1981

temporal perceptions. In *Two Corner Curve* (1986), a steel arc measuring
10′ × 60′ × 1″ is installed inside a gallery in a way that confounds the
contrast between interiority and exteriority; in *Berlin Junction* (1987), two
curved steel plates (13′ × 42′ × 2″) are set at different angles to create
a space that opens and closes as one moves from the bottom to the top
and the top to the bottom of the work; in *Trunk* (1987), the vertical
and horizontal axes of perception are confused by two vertical plates

(323¼″ × 200¾″ × 2⅛″) that surround the body of the "viewer" like the hollow trunk of a tree; and in *Olson* (1985–86), two bent and tipped parallel concave-convex plates (10′ × 36′ × 2″) generate a remarkable sense of vertigo. The most intriguing work in this series is *Clara-Clara* (1983), commissioned for the entrance to Centre Georges Pompidou but installed in the Tuileries between the Musée du Jeu de Paume and the Orangerie. This work repeats and transforms *Circuit I* and *Circuit II* to create what is, in effect, a chiasmic structure. In contrast to the earlier works in which four rectilinear plates form a that is open in the middle, *Clara-Clara* consists of two curvilinear arcs (12′ × 120′ × 2″) tilted at angles that create a twisted χ. *Clara-Clara,* like other sculptures in this series, is cut, torn, fissured, rent. The space-time of the work of art is the opening of the gap that forms its *mi-lieu.* In the midst of this between, the static becomes mobile to open space and time for the aleatory. As the duplicity of concave-convex arcs is both doubled and inverted, the complexity of the work increases exponentially. Opposites usually held apart are folded into each other to form an invaginated space where nothing remains fixed or stable and everything becomes infinitely more twisted. As space twists, nothing remains direct, clear, or simple. The spacing-timing of these plications involves a different logic, which is as puzzling as the strange logic of MA. This new logic is the logic of complexity.

Though extending the investigation of the time and space of perception that has long preoccupied Serra, *Torqued Ellipse I* and *II* and *Double Torqued Ellipse* mark a new departure. These three works, which were fabricated at the Bethlehem Steel plant at Sparrows Point, Maryland, are closely interrelated and exhibit increasing intricacy and complexity. *Torqued Ellipse I* and *II* are made from two steel plates, each of which weighs 20–21 tons. Serra first cut symmetrical waves along the upper and lower edges of these 15′ × 40′ × 2″ plates and then bent them to form precisely calculated curves. Never having used their industrial machines for this kind of project, the workers at Sparrows Point initially encountered difficulties. On the first try, they broke a plate, and the second time, they cracked the plate. It took more than a year to make the first piece, but the second and third were built quite quickly. The basic structure of each sculpture is the same. All the works are 13′ tall and are formed by rotating parallel ellipses in such a way that the base and top are at different angles to each other. In *I,* the ellipse rotates at 55 degrees to itself, and in *II,* the ellipses at the base and the top are at right angles to each other. The variation in the rotation of the axis of the ellipse results in different angles of incline for the sides of the work. The maximum overhang for *I* is 28″ and for *II* is 5′. *Double Torqued Ellipse* repeats Serra's gesture of multiplying complexity by doubling structures. In this work, he places an ellipse within an ellipse to create a labyrinth of unprecedented complexity. While the bottom ellipses share the same major and minor axes, they do not have the same proportion to each other and actually form two separate shapes. The top ellipses rotate 70 degrees in opposite directions, thereby creating a maximum overhang of 3′ inside and 2′ outside.

The effect of these works is extraordinary. Though made of heavy industrial materials and massive, they have the delicacy of finely folded ribbon or even paper twisted to form something like a Möbius strip that never quite reaches closure. As one moves from outside to inside by passing through the gap in these works, everything shifts. Lines that appear straight on the outside bend and buckle on the inside; arcs that seem to tilt away when viewed from without bend inward to enfold subject in object when experienced from within. As twisted space surrounds or even circulates through the perceptive body, the space and time of the work of art become utterly destabilizing and disorienting.

When one enters *Double Torqued Ellipse* after having explored *I* and *II,* the effect is jarring. Instead of the open space of an empty center, one encounters a dark steel wall. By placing one ellipse within another,

Figure 29   Richard Serra, *Torqued Ellipse I,* 1996

FIGURE 30   Richard Serra, *Torqued Ellipse II,* 1996

FIGURE 31   Richard Serra, *Double Torqued Ellipse,* 1996

Serra creates an outside that is inside and an inside that is outside. Wedged between arcs that tilt in opposite directions at different angles, space constantly seems to expand and contract. This serpentine puzzle is deepened by the continual interplay of light and darkness. On the far end of the ellipse, exactly opposite the point of entry, a second cut appears. In this opening within an opening, space seems to move in opposite directions at the same time. Furthermore, the rate at which space moves is not constant but varies throughout the work. For Serra, this capacity to set space in motion is the distinguishing feature of his new work.

> Previously I was using the line to divide a field and declare it open. This placement of the line in relation to the understructure of the work had a lot to do with drawing. As the work became more open, the volume has become the issue. Whereas the line had defined the space, now it's the space that shapes the volume. I think what divides the work is the question of how to articulate space. But what has become the concern of the new body of work is the shape and volume of the space and your relation to it as the space actually moves. It sounds strange to say it, but the space *does* move. That hasn't happened before.[32]

By creating space that is in motion, Serra folds temporality into spatiality. The apprehension of these works of art not only *takes* time but also *gives* time a different twist. Time is no more linear than the space in which it is enfolded. In this convoluted intersection of space and time, Serra returns to the space-time he had discovered in Zen gardens.

There is, however, an important difference between Serra's youthful studies and these mature works. Attempting to formulate this difference, he explains: "Whereas in previous works I started with materials to create the space between, in these works I start from the void and form the object from this emptiness. In this way, the material becomes the skin of the void."[33] The distinction Serra draws between works in which materials define space and works in which space shapes volume, which is defined by materials, is as subtle as it is important. If void produces volume as much as volume produces void, then art is, in an important sense, *about* nothing. Nothing, it seems, is the generative void or creative emptiness in and through which things arise and pass away. In Serra's elliptical works, everything is in motion; shapes and space are not static but constantly morph. While often baffling, this morphing is nonetheless very precise. By twisting empty ellipses, Serra torques the space that forms the "substance" of his art.

> RS: The pieces are getting more and more complex. Now we're putting elliptical forms inside elliptical forms to create spaces where you can walk around.
>
> MT: This would seem to allow you to experience space torquing.
>
> RS: That's what it is, that's exactly what it is! . . . The space actually torques.[34]

This torquing of space has the strange effect of transforming objects into events. While *Torqued Ellipse I* and *II* and *Double Torqued Ellipse* obviously remain static, they nonetheless create a sense of motion, which reconfigures space and time. In these works, stable objects and definitive perceptions are distant memories. Serra is more interested in processes of forming, deforming, and reforming than in structures and forms as such. For this reason, the twists and turns of his recent work approximate more closely the knotted graphs with which René Thom charts morphogenesis than the rectilinear grids of Euclidean geometry and Cartesian space.[35] The domain of morphogenesis, Thom argues, is the spacing-timing that always falls *between* form and formlessness or, more precisely, order and chaos. This interstitial site is irreducibly complex.

Not only are these works, as Serra stresses, "getting more and more complex," but they are actually about complexity. According to recent theorists, complexity is not so much an attribute of objects as a characteristic of events through which ordered entities emerge.[36] Such events occur "at the edge of chaos." Along this border, the systems and structures requisite for the genesis of order are open and nonlinear. Nonlinearity is a function of the bending and rebending of intricate feedback loops to form networks of exchange and transfer. Though such structures twist back on themselves, they do not form complete circles or closed circuits. To the contrary, complex systems remain open in a way that confounds the clear oppositions definitive of fixed forms. This openness issues in what Murray Gell-Mann aptly describes as complex adaptive or coadaptive systems.[37] Since complex coadaptive systems are open, they are always in the process of becoming and hence forever incomplete.

Serra's *Torqued Ellipse I* and *II* and *Double Torqued Ellipse* display the openness and coadaptivity of complex systems. As space torques, object and subject fold into each other so as to subvert the opposition between inside and outside. Since outside envelops inside, which, in turn, enfolds outside, neither object nor subject is autonomous. Instead of a discrete thing, the work of art is a convoluted event that transpires *between* object and subject. The *issue* of the work of art, in other words, is as much a verb as it is a noun. The site of this work is an open field in which unfinished objects and incomplete subjects are constantly transformed in and through their complex implications.

Though his course has been far from straight, Serra has been moving toward the emptiness generative of form ever since he roamed the ambulatory paths of the Zen gardens in Kyoto. The pliable lines, bent planes, and twisted volumes of *Torqued Ellipse I* and *II* and *Double Torqued Ellipse* outline the learning curves that constitute Serra's career. But the lines of his inquiry extend far beyond the objects he produces. In the openness of the space-time of the work of art, Serra's learning curves become our own. As the perceptive subject enters the work of art, the work of art enters the subject to transform perception. When perception changes, thought is recast. Since Serra's torqued ellipses are shifty events rather than static objects, the complex learning curves they trace are as infinite as the space-time they define. When learning curves without ever coming full circle, it never ends.

to continue

Ten

Indifference

. . . Betrayal . . .

It began, as it always begins, with loss, lack, absence. A loss that occurred not long before I was and will continue long after I will have been. This loss was not, therefore, *my* loss, yet it is the loss that has, in no small measure, made me what I am and am not. The loss was the loss of a nameless one—a nameless one who will remain nameless or who will be named only in the absence of which "my" name has become the mark. Having always already occurred—at least for me—this loss is a strange loss of what I have never possessed or ever will possess. A loss that occurs as never-having-occurred cannot be lost but must be borne by being born again and again and again—as if eternally. Since loss is interminable, every recovery is an impossible and unavoidable re(-)covery. In the wake of unrecoverable loss, giving is taking and taking is giving. The endless play of give-and-take marks all giving with the trace of giving not. To give not is not not to give but is to give the not that is life as much as death and death as much as life.

Have I betrayed her by telling only this much? Perhaps. But how can I not betray? How can I betray not? Haunted by the specter of betrayal, I shall say no more—at least for now. But, of course, this not-saying remains a saying, which *might* be saying-not. It is as impossible not to say as it is to say not. I am always unavoidably thinking about, talking about, teaching about, writing about what I am not saying. This not, which is almost nothing, is—but how can not be?—the not I cannot (not) think, speak, teach, or write.

. . . In(-)difference . . .

The conversation, which is not precisely ours, has been going on so long that it is beginning to seem infinite. It began by beginning again a few miles down the road from Middletown, in New Haven on what was, if memory can be trusted, an ordinary evening. No longer day but not yet night, evening is a time of lingering, which gives pause to (be) thought. So much time has passed that it is difficult to recall the names of the speakers. Let us call one Professor Eucalyptus—a name that obviously is not proper. Like a purloined letter deliberately placed on the mantel, "eucalyptus" reveals its concealment by showing it.

New Latin *EU* + Greek *kaluptos,* covered (from the flower, which is covered before it opens), from *kuluptein,* to cover, hide.

What is this word—what is any word hiding? Even when clearly defined, words are not always revealing. Sometimes, it seems, the best way to keep a secret is to tell it.

Professor Eucalyptus does not seem to know the secret he names. To hear what the professor says without saying, we must listen to the doubtful words of an other he has never met. This other, who (or which) is no one yet is not precisely two or more than two, remains nameless. As the infinite conversation in which we are hopelessly caught unfolds by becoming ever more convoluted, the ordinary begins to seem both less and more than ordinary.

On the one hand:

> The dry eucalyptus seeks god in the rainy cloud.
> Professor Eucalyptus of New Haven seeks him
> In New Haven with an eye that does not look
>
> Beyond the object. He sits in his room, beside
> The window, close to the ramshackle spout in which
> The rain falls with a ramshackle sound. He seeks
>
> God in the object itself, without much choice.
> It is a choice of the commodious adjective
> For what he sees, it comes in the end to that:
>
> The description that makes it divinity, still speech
> As it touches the point of reverberation—not grim
> Reality but reality grimly seen
>
> And spoken in paradisal parlance new
> And in any case never grim, the human grim
> That is part of the indifference of the eye
>
> Indifferent to what it sees . . .[1]

And on the other:

> There is a moment in the life of a man—consequently, in the life of men—when everything is completed, the books written, the universe silent, beings at rest. There is left only the task of announcing it: this is easy. But as this supplementary word threatens to upset the equilibrium— and where to find the force to say it? where to find another place for it?—it is not pronounced and the task remains unfinished. One writes only what I have just written, finally that is not written either.

> He remembers their conversation: he was questioning him in a weary manner; he seemed attentive, discreet, indifferent—he understood everything right away, this was visible; but on his face there was an expression of incuriosity, an inexpressive expression that was turning the words aside.[2]

Two eyes; two I's:

> ... an eye that does not look
> Beyond the object. ...
> ... part of the indifference of the eye
> Indifferent to what it sees. ...

> ... when everything is completed, the books written, the universe silent, beings at rest ... on his face there was an expression of incuriosity, an inexpressive expression ... attentive, discreet, indifferent ...

Two eyes, which neither meet nor cross, yet are not exactly indifferent. Two I's who, in thinking not beyond the object, think not differently by thinking different beyonds. Two eyes/I's whose difference is their indifference. Two indifferences: one says "Yes" but too often only "Yes"; one says "No" but too often only "No." "Yesyes," "Nono" but never "Yesnonoyes." Is such a word sayable?

What is critical in this conversation, which, we must remember, has not taken place, is not what is said but what is unsaid, not what is thought but what is unthought, not what is asked but what remains unasked: Might there be a different indifference? What would it mean to live (with) indifference?

It is easy—all too easy—to be indifferent to indifference. Its time seems to have passed; and, in a certain sense, it *has* (always) passed. Yet, precisely because its time has always passed, indifference is always still to come. To think this inescapable coming, it is necessary to think indifference differently. In the past, indifference has been thought to be the lack of difference. This lack, whose other name is identity, is supposed to constitute the essential, which always has been, is, and will be. But things are not quite so simple. This essential indifference or indifferent essence is always slipping away and, thus, is never present. Even when it seems near, indifference remains impossible. Strangely, the impossibility of indifference does not engender indifference; rather, its impossibility is what makes indifference so alluring.

The attraction of indifference, however, is not always the same; sometimes its draw is difference rather than identity. Contrary to received wisdom, indifference is not necessarily the lack of difference, which constitutes identity, but can be the lack of identity, which articulates differences. Far from mere privation, indifference implies the difference in every difference. From this point of view, indifference is never itself but is (though, of course, it is not) in-difference.

. . . Abandonment . . .

In the beginning there is life; before the beginning there is death. Not my death but the death of the other who (or which) gives me life. The abiding trace of death in life is what renders birth traumatic. The catastrophe with which life begins leaves an irreparable wound. Without this wound *I* am not; with this wound I *am* not. Since wounding is the unavoidable condition of my being, recovery is impossible. Though this wound is unfathomably deep, there is another that is deeper still. This is the wound inflicted by a cut that never occurs. Sometimes the ties that bind cannot be severed.

The birth had been a long time coming. Far too long. At times the waiting must have been unbearable. Or so I surmised, but none of this was ever discussed. There had been doctors and more doctors, consultations and more consultations. But nothing worked. As procedure led to procedure and indignity was heaped upon indignity, hope gave way to a despair whose intensity was measured by its silence. They stopped talking about it—and of much else. What must those quiet breakfasts and dinners have been like? What must those ordinary mornings and evenings have been like? What must those endless nights of waiting have been like?

And then, just when all seemed lost, the impossible occurred. "You are going to have a child," he announced. She could say nothing but only weep tears more eloquent than words. In the days, weeks, and months that followed, she lost the melancholy that had always been her mien. It was as if she grew lighter as her weight increased. Or so I surmised, but none of this was ever discussed.

But as the date approached, she grew more anxious. "I don't care what the tests indicate, something is not right," she insisted.

"Nothing is wrong," he said. But the words hung empty in the air and did not quell her dread.

"Perhaps, perhaps nothing *is* wrong." She waited and waited.

When she awoke, the news was not good. "I'm sorry, we did everything we could. These things happen."

. . .

"No, no, nothing was wrong. The baby was healthy; a beautiful little girl. It was the cord, it got wrapped around her neck."

. . .

"No, no, it happened before she was born. We don't know exactly when. It doesn't really matter now."

Cause and effect of death: indifference. The indifference of a cut that never occurred. The trauma of an event that never took place. Indifference: lack of difference. Indifference: absence of concern. But whose indifference? The doctor's indifference? The nurse's indifference? His indifference? Her indifference? Or, perhaps, a more menacing, a more horrifying indifference?

As the reality of loss sank in, she realized that the name they had so lovingly chosen would never be bestowed. Though not alone, she felt abandoned—utterly and absolutely abandoned. Then she began to cry, and she cried long into the melancholy night from which she would never awake. The night so absorbed her that she forever carried it within her. Or so I surmised, but none of this was ever discussed.

To live with something that does not concern him.

> This is a sentence easily received, but in time it weighs upon him. He tries to test it. "To live"—is it really life that is involved? And "with"? Would not "with" introduce an articulation that precisely here is excluded? And "something"? Neither something nor someone. Finally, "this does not concern him" distinguishes him still too much, as though we were appropriating to himself the capacity to be discerned by this very thing that does not concern him. After that what remains of the sentence? The same, immobile.
>
> To live (with) what does not concern.

There are various ways of responding to this situation. Some say: we must live as though living did not concern us. Others say: since this does not concern, we must live without changing anything about life. But then others: you are changing, you are living non-change as the trace and the mark of that which, not concerning, could not change you.[3]

Concerning not: living . . . the trace and the mark of . . . not concerning. To live the trace and mark of not concerning is to live carelessly. Carelessness issues in abandonment, which issues in carelessness, which . . . But what does it mean to live (with) abandon(ment)? Who abandons? What abandons? Who is abandoned? What is abandoned?

We are born in an abandonment of which we have no memory. We can, therefore, never be sure that it occurred, where it occurred, whether it occurred. Nonetheless, we always "know"—or so it seems—that we have been abandoned. More ancient than time, abandonment occurs as the occurrence or time itself. Though abandonment occurs, no one, nothing abandons.

This strange (non)event of abandonment can only be suffered—suffered as infinite indifference. To live (with) indifference is to live (with) what does not concern us because it has always already turned away. Such living with is, of course, not living with, or is living (with) the impossibility of living with.

Since abandonment turns away even when it turns toward, living with abandon is always a diversion even when it seems hopelessly serious. But not all diversions are the same. The diversions that seem most frivolous are serious and those that seem most serious are frivolous. Or worse. The most frivolous diversions are those that turn away from the turning away that leaves us abandoned. The duplicity of this turning involves a re-turning designed to undo what a-band-onment has done by re-binding immemorial wounds. The name, or one of the names, of this rebinding is *religion*. Religion: *re* + *ligare*—to bind back. The dream of binding back is to bind together—to bind together the self by binding self to God. Bound to God we are supposed to be able to dispel the nightmare of indifference—menacing, horrifying, cosmic indifference—by turning away from the turning away that leaves us abandoned.

But what if God is indifferent? Or, more precisely, what if God is Indifference? What if binding back does not bind together but binds us to abandonment? What if there is no turning away from that which turns away and turns itself away? As we ponder such questions, it becomes clear that indifference cannot be thought religiously. To think indifference, we must unthink religion by turning away from the turning away from that which turns away. This turning away is, of course, a turning toward turning away. To live (with) indifference is to live an infinite detour with abandon.

Though nameless, her name would have been Noel. Or was it Noelle? No El . . . No Elle. Male or female? English or French? Jewish or Christian? I am not sure; none of this was ever discussed. It would have been her father's name, and so would have been my father's name. An unnamed sister who nonetheless bore the name of our father. Is my dead sister my father? Is my dead sister my mother? Is s/he both? Noel. No El. No, El.

. . . Disappointment . . .

It was one of those long, lazy afternoons that were so common near the end. We sat together and occasionally spoke. Her time and mine were out of sync. Though she had little, her time seemed endless; though I had much, my time was never enough. Her infinite patience provoked my endless impatience. I thought I had more important things to do; she knew enough to realize we do not.

She spoke about disappointment. About times of disappointment and about the disappointments time inevitably brings. There was no bitterness in her voice, nor any disappointment. It was as if she were able to speak of disappointment because she had passed beyond it. She now realized that disappointment disappears when we become indifferent. I knew there was wisdom in her words, but I was not ready to listen to it.

> Everything began for him, when everything seemed to have come to an end, with an event from which he could not free himself; not that he was obliged to think of it constantly or remember it, but because it did not concern him. He only perceived, and no doubt well after it had come about—so long a time that he preferred to place it, and perhaps with reason, in the present—that something had happened—something apart from the glowing history, rich with meaning yet motionless in which everyone was taking part—by noting, among the innumerable facts and great thoughts that were soliciting him, the possibility that this had occurred, not without his knowledge—of necessity, he knew—but without his being interested.[4]

Since thought is always timely, not every thought can be thought at any time. Thoughts unthinkable at one time become unavoidable at another time. Morning thoughts differ from thoughts of noon as much as evening thoughts differ from thoughts of night. Morning can no more be thought in evening than evening can be thought in morning. Thinking evening thoughts casts mourning in a different light.

When everything seems to have come to an end, the books written, the universe silent, what remains but indifference? In the light of evening, indifference reflects and provokes disappointment. The book was to have made a difference—but it did not. It never does. The career was to have made a difference—but it did not. It never does. Nothing ever makes a difference. Nothing. When nothing makes a difference, everything becomes pointless, and this pointlessness, this loss of the point is what is so terribly disappointing. At least for a while.

We dream of making a difference; that is what makes it all worthwhile. Or so we are told and so we tell others as well as ourselves. But what we eventually discover is indifference to the difference we thought we had made. Such indifference is not simply indifferent but is carefully calculated to make a difference. Indifference to the difference I make is the way others attempt to make a difference. But their strategy is no more successful than mine; indifference begets indifference until everything becomes infinitely disappointing.

Disappointment is what begins when everything seems to have come to an end. As evening approaches, disappointment appears in a different light. Things that once made a difference no longer make any difference. Through a reversal that cannot be anticipated, the acceptance of not-making-a-difference makes disappointment far less disappointing. Gradually we are led to conclude that things disappoint only when we expect them to be otherwise. Disappointment is a way of saying no to what is for the sake of what might be or should have been. But such a no does not have to be disappointment's final word. Sometimes disappointment turns back on itself by becoming disappointed with disappointment. With this re-turning, disappointment frees us to live indifferently—to "live as though living did not concern us." To live (with) indifference— and what other way is there for us to live if we do not turn away from what turns away?—is to give up the dream of making a difference. Freed from the compulsion to make *our* point, we can overcome indifference to others. Paradoxically, it is the cultivation of indifference that opens us to difference. In this way, disappointment enables us to live in(-)differently.

. . . Timing . . .

Following in the wake of abandonment, indifference gives time. Gives the time we are given by giving time's give-and-take. Time is never simple, for it constantly wavers between differences it joins but cannot unite. Bestowing what it withdraws and withdrawing what it bestows, time is in(-)different. Though compelled to search for reasons, we are eventually forced to admit that time gives and takes indifferently. The indifference *of* time breeds indifference *to* time. If time gives and takes indifferently, what's the difference?

Yet time does make a difference, or, more precisely, timing is a matter of differences. The differing of time is a question of rhythms. Time is always the same but inevitably passes differently. The hour can be fast or slow, long or short. The rhythms of time are not at our disposal; they arrive and depart as if they had wills of their own. We cannot make the bad times pass more quickly any more than we can make the good times last. Good or bad, time comes and goes indifferently.

Indifference gives time. Gives time in other ways by giving and taking differently. When the indifference of time is met with indifference, time changes. One of the many paradoxes of time is that the more we have, the less we seem to have, and the less we have, the more we seem to have. When time stretches before us like a seemingly infinite horizon, we never seem to have enough of it. This lack of time reflects the lack of indifference. Still convinced that we can make a difference, we never have enough time to leave our mark. Always on the move, the rush of rushing becomes addictive; the quick, we are told, inherit the earth. But the story time repeatedly tells to those who slow down to listen is that the fix of speed fixes nothing. The point once made is unavoidably disappointing. And so, turning a deaf ear to the tolling of time, we try to make a new point, a different point, a point that has never before been made. But, of course, no point has been made more often than the point that has never before been made. Point by point, the new becomes old, terrifyingly old until, having seen it all before, we become indifferent.

Indifference gives time. When it is a matter of time, it often seems that the less we have, the more we have. As the dream of making a difference fades, the rhythm of time alters. Everything slows down; rushing gives way to lingering. Lingering indifferently. At this point, we have time enough to realize that we never have time because time always has us. In this moment, we become free to confess that it doesn't matter if it gets done today even if tomorrow never comes.

Confession transforms by the power of the word. Suddenly days that once seemed far too short grow longer and longer until, near the end, they become too long, far too long. Then the vacancy of pointless days, which once had been exhilarating, seems horrifying. Time becomes an emptiness that no longer can be filled by running from it. Distractions do not distract, diversions do not divert. But between too short and too long, between too little and too much, there are many ordinary evenings that can be quite extraordinary.

. . . Letting-Go . . .

Over a thousand miles from home, the family—or what was left of it— gathered around the grave. The inconspicuous marker bore nothing— no name, no number, no trace. The attendant had trouble finding the plot. The burial had taken place during the war and records were not always accurate. As he departed, he assured us that this was in fact the place. With heads bowed, we lingered for what seemed like a very long time. But nothing was said. Nothing. She could not speak because she had not let go and her silence echoed in ours.

The most difficult lesson time teaches is the necessity of letting-go. This lesson begins before we begin, for we find ourselves always already having been let go. This letting-go is a release that gives by abandoning. Abandonment, in turn, releases indifferently. Since to be is to have been released, being is inevitably a letting. The letting that lets us be is a leasing that renders all being renting. We always live on borrowed time, yet we know not to whom the rent is due. Perhaps, though we can never be certain, we owe no one; perhaps, though we can never be certain, we own nothing.

Torn by a rent that can never be repaired or repaid, we do not own what we seem to possess. All having is a not-having, which is a having-not. To have-not is to be dispossessed of everything—even ourselves. To live the dispossession of being, having must become a not-having, which is impossible apart from letting-go.

To have-not is to let go of what we never possess. Possessed by posses-sion(s), we struggle to deny our not-having, but the harder we cling, the less we have. When we finally discover the courage to be not, disposses-sion comes as a great release. This re-lease repeats and extends the release that is not ours. Having been abandoned, we now abandon by letting go of everything and everybody once held dear. This letting-go is a letting-be. There can be no letting-go without letting-be and no letting-be without letting-go.

This letting-go that is a letting-be and letting-be that is a letting-go must be done with indifference. Indifference releases while expecting nothing in return. Absolutely nothing. To let go indifferently is to give unconditionally. Since recognition perpetuates the cycle of debt, an unconditional gift can never be acknowledged as such. A giving, which is not a taking, lets go of the struggle for recognition by neither creating debt nor accepting credit.

Release becomes unconditional when we accept abandonment by letting ourselves be abandoned. We never really let go until we allow others to let go of us. If we expect anything other than the other's indifference, we have not yet let go. Letting-go only occurs when we live (with) indifference by becoming indifferent to indifference.

. . . Loving . . .

"I love you no matter what."
"No matter what?"
"No matter what."
"No matter what I do?"
"No matter what."
"No matter what I don't do?"
"No matter what."

We have heard the words so often that they no longer seem extraordinary. "No matter what? . . . No matter what." How can such familiar words be made strange?

Love, it appears, is a matter of indifference. For love to be love, it must be unconditional: I love the other no matter what. What the beloved does makes no difference to the lover, for love's only law is to be without return. This law is, of course, unlawful, for it breaks (with) every legal economy. Love is beyond the law—it is a matter of grace, amazing grace.

Grace is indifferent. It is given, if at all, freely—without regard for what has been done or left undone. As such, grace is undeniably careless. Though it seems impossible, I care most deeply when I care not. The carelessness of "No matter what" is aweful—truly awful. If it doesn't matter, who cares? If no one cares, nothing seems to matter. And, in a certain sense, nothing *does* matter. In the profitless economy of grace, no one can afford (to) care. Care remains bound to and by the law; not just any law but the law of laws, which is the law of return.

"It doesn't matter."
"But."
"No, really, it doesn't matter. It was nothing."

To give as if giving nothing is to give everything by giving not. Always unlawful, the indifference of grace involves boundless generosity. The generous deed is senseless: it is offered without reason and with no expectation of return. Generosity, in other words, must always be given freely. Absolute generosity, if such were possible, would not only give freely but would give nothing less than freedom. To give freely by giving freedom is to let go by letting-be and to let be by letting-go.

Love is indifferent. Indifferent to what the other does or does not do. I can only love the other by letting-go, withdrawing, a-band-oning. Love does not re-bind but releases; releases absolutely and unconditionally. The words of love—and no words are more important or more difficult—are always a matter of indifference.

"No matter what?"
"No matter what. I don't care. Really, I don't care."

. . . Lightness . . .

The miracle: barely having after having had not. The indifference to indifference harbors duplicity. In a world where nothing matters, nothing is ever what it seems. Having is having-not and not-having is, perhaps, the only way of having. Nothing seems more grave than indifference. The burden of "Nothing matters" can plunge one into a fathomless abyss of despair. After all, what weight could be greater than the weight of nothing? Yet "No matter" is light—terribly light. The recognition of the insubstantiality of it all prepares the way for overcoming gravity. In the new physics, which is no longer a metaphysics, equations must be rewritten and calculations refigured:

$$\text{Gravity} = \text{Everything matters}$$
$$\text{Levity} = \text{Nothing matters}$$

With the loss of gravity, nothing remains serious. When nothing weighs us down, we lose our moorings and are left to float freely. The levity that allows us to float freely is not measured by our distance from the ground but by the way we walk the earth. Paradoxically, the loss of gravity allows us to remain earthbound.

The lightness of touch signals—albeit indirectly—a serious grasp of nothing. To walk the earth with indifference, we must hold on by letting-go. If we are not to sink under the weight of responsibility for making a difference, our holding must be a releasing. Having is a miracle because our having is always a having-not. When we have by having-not, we are able to hold on by letting go. If levity is what allows us to remain earthbound, then nothing is more serious than the lack of gravity, which renders everything bearably light. Far from insignificant, this levity is nothing more and nothing less than the bearable lightness of being not.

. . . Ordinariness . . .

Our last conversation was nothing special. I had always thought it would end with an exclamation point or at least a period. But it did not. I had always thought we would discuss what all the while we had not been discussing. But we did not. Rather than a period, the three points of an ellipsis marked what we had always left out. We did not talk about anything out of the ordinary. To the contrary. Would it have been different had we known it was the last? I doubt it. As I have pondered what was said and left unsaid, what has come to seem so extraordinary is the ordinariness of the last time.

This ordinary evening in New Jersey recalled the lessons of "An Ordinary Evening in New Haven."

> It is fatal in the moon and empty there.
> But, here, allons. The enigmatical
> Beauty of each beautiful enigma
>
> Becomes amassed in a total double-thing.
> We do not know what is real and what is not.
> We say of the moon, it is haunted by the man

Of bronze whose mind was made up and who, there-
    fore, died.
We are not men of bronze and we are not dead.
His spirit is imprisoned in constant change.

But ours is not imprisoned. It resides
In a permanence composed of impermanence,
In a faithfulness as against the lunar light,

So that morning and evening are like promises kept,
So that the approaching sun and its arrival,
Its evening feast and the following festival,

This faithfulness of reality, its mode,
This tendence and venerable holding-in
Make gay the hallucinations in surfaces.[5]

But how? How can we "make gay the hallucinations in surfaces" when "we do not know what is real and what is not"? How can we "make gay the hallucinations in surfaces" when "permanence [is] composed of impermanence"?

The ordinariness of evening is an even-ing that levels everything and everyone. As time draws to a close, differences that once seemed to make such a difference no longer matter. Being-toward-death does not individ-uate but depersonalizes until everyone finally becomes indifferent. The even-ing of differences, which indifference brings, creates an equanimity that is both dreadful and wonderful. At the end of the day, when we finally realize that we do not know what is real and what is not, we discover that the ordinary is quite extraordinary. Though this point might seem obvious—even superficial—it implies a gay wisdom that changes everything not once, not twice, but constantly. "Constant change" only imprisons "men of bronze" who, with minds made up, do not know how to let go. Those who have learned the lessons of indiffer-ence by embracing a world in which "permanence [is] composed of im-permanence" are released from the unbearable weight of depth. Indiffer-ence harbors a disillusion with disillusion that creates the possibility of overcoming "unhappy consciousness." The gay hallucination in surfaces is nothing more and nothing less than an endless "bacchanalian revel in which no member remains sober." The wisdom of this revel involves a superficiality that is profound. Paradoxically, this profundity can appear only when the dream of depth disappears. In the absence of depth, there is nothing beyond. This nothingness transforms the ordinary into the extraordinary. This insight is nothing special; indeed, we should have known it all along. But to see it, we need the eyes of gods who seem to have vanished long ago. Such vision occurs, if at all, only near the end when day gives way to night—on long, lazy evenings that are nothing if not ordinary.

There had been a diary . . . a secret diary. I had stumbled on it a few years before her death while looking for some writing paper in a drawer in her desk. It was obvious that she had concealed her thoughts carefully. A small daybook with a light blue cover and lined pages bordered with light green designs. For each day there was a biblical quotation. The writing was unmistakably hers; the grace of the letters bore the trace of a hand I knew all too well.

She had kept the diary during the year of the birth that had been a death. I had just begun to read it when the sound of her footsteps forced me to return the diary to its hiding place. The page my eyes fell upon as if by chance described the room they had prepared for the baby. The vivid words and carefully wrought phrases were those of the literature teacher she had been and would once again become. The scene she described was bright with expectation: the crib, the curtains, the freshly painted walls, the clothes, the quilt she had so lovingly crafted. Though she gave no hint, it was clear that birth was near.

I never finished reading the diary. When we faced the melancholy task of emptying the house after he died, the drawer of her desk was where I went first. But the diary was gone. In all the drawers, all the boxes, all the closets, it never turned up. Had he found it when going through her things? Did she have second thoughts about writing what she had never said? Did she consider (her) writing a betrayal? Did she show him the book before she died? Or did he discover it accidentally as I had done? Did they discuss it? Did they decide together to burn the book? Did they think they could take their secret to their graves? Were they afraid to betray their secret? Did they fear I would betray their secret? Didn't they see that the secret was not theirs to betray or betray not? Didn't they understand that they had always been betraying the secret by not betraying it? Didn't they know that their not-telling was telling? Did they realize, long before I, that the writing I believed was my own betrayed a secret I did not know by rewriting a diary I had never read?

Chapter One

Reprinted from *JAAR* 62 (1994): 603–23.

1. Herman Melville, *The Confidence-Man: His Masquerade,* ed. Hershel Parker (New York: Norton, 1971), p. 1. Hereafter references to this work are given in the text.

2. Karl Marx, *Capital,* trans. Samuel Moore and Edward Aveling (New York: International Publishers, 1972), 1:126.

3. Friedrich Nietzsche, "On Truth and Lie in an Extra-moral Sense," in *The Portable Nietzsche,* ed. Walter Kaufmann (New York: Penguin Books, 1980), pp. 46–47.

4. Edgar Allan Poe, "The Gold-Bug," in *Poetry and Tales* (New York: Library of America, 1984), p. 653. Hereafter references to this work are given in the text.

5. More of a "punster" than the characters he so describes, Melville plays with almost all the names in his tale in a way that turns them from proper to the improper. "Frank Goodman" suggests both the cosmopolitan's forthrightness and his belief in the fundamental goodness of human nature. But, as John Irwin notes, Melville also indicated that "Goodman" was "the Puritan title of address" as well as "a cant term for a thief . . . and a Scottish title for the Devil" (*American Hieroglyphics: The Symbol of the Egyptian Hieroglyphics in the American Renaissance* [Baltimore: Johns Hopkins University Press, 1983], p. 336). The barber's name, William Cream, calls attention to the veneer applied to strip away the masks or to create the disguises people wear. Cream objects to Goodman's confidence in his fellow human beings: "What, sir, to say nothing more, can one be forever dealing in macassar oil, hair dyes, cosmetics, false moustaches, wigs, and toupees, and still believe that men are wholly what they look to be? What think you, sir, are a thoughtful barber's reflections, when, behind a careful curtain, he shaves the thin, dead stubble off a head, and then dismisses it to the world, radiant in curling auburn?" (199).

6. For an elaboration of this point, see chapter 7.

7. Jean Baudrillard, *Simulations* (New York: Semiotext(e), 1983), p. 2.

8. Ibid., p. 8.

Chapter Two

Reprinted from *Critical Inquiry* 20 (summer 1994): 594–610.

1. This essay is written in the margins of the texts of G. W. F. Hegel, Søren Kierkegaard, Thomas J. J. Altizer, Jacques Derrida, Georges Bataille, Maurice Blanchot, Martin Heidegger, Jean-Luc Nancy, and unnamed others.

Chapter Three

Reprinted from *JAAR* 59 (1991): 1–38.

1. Leo Steinberg, "The Philosophical Brothel," *Art News,* October 1972, p. 40.

2. Rita Ransohoff, *Berggasse 19: Sigmund Freud's Home and Offices, Vienna, 1938,* ed. Edmund Engleman (New York: Basic Books, 1976), p. 58.

3. Ibid., p. 19.

4. Pierre Girmal, *The Dictionary of Classical Mythology,* trans. A. R. Maxwell-Hyslop (New York: Blackwell, 1986), p. 341.

5. Friedrich Nietzsche, *The Birth of Tragedy,* trans. Francis Golffing (New York: Doubleday and Co., 1956), p. 52. Hereafter references to this work are given in the text.

6. *Oxford English Dictionary.*

7. For a consideration of some of the issues at stake in this debate, see *Against Theory: Literary Studies and the New Pragmatism,* ed. W. J. T. Mitchell (Chicago: University of Chicago Press, 1985).

8. Modernism is, of course, a notoriously vague term whose meaning changes from context to context and field to field. While modern philosophy is generally thought to have started with Descartes's work in the middle of the seventeenth century, the beginning of modern theology is usually dated from Schleiermacher's *Speeches on Religion* (1799). In this context, I use the term "modernism" to refer to the radical innovations in the visual arts that emerged during the last decades of the nineteenth century and the first decade of the twentieth century. Though anticipated by Manet and Cézanne, Picasso's *Les Demoiselles d'Avignon* (1907) is frequently identified as the painting in which modernism decisively appears.

9. The word *primitivism* is itself a modern invention. William Rubin points out that "the word was first used in France in the nineteenth century, and formally entered French as a strictly art-historical term in the seven-volume *Nouveau Larousse illustré* published between 1897 and 1904: *'n.m. B-arts. Imitation des primitifs.'* Though the Larousse reference to 'imitation' was both too extreme and too narrow, the sense of this definition as describing painting and sculpture influenced by earlier artists called 'primitives' has since been accepted by art history; only the identity of the 'primitives' has changed. The Larousse definition reflected a mid–nineteenth century use of the term insofar as the 'primitives' in question were primarily fourteenth- and fifteenth-century Italians and Flemings. But even before the appearance of the *Nouveau Larousse illustré,* artists had expanded the connotations of 'primitive' to include not only Romanesque and Byzantine, but a host of non-Western arts ranging from the Peruvian to the Javanese—with the sense of 'primitivism' altering accordingly" (*"Primitivism" in Twentieth-Century Art: Affinity of the Tribal and the Modern* [New York: Museum of Modern Art, 1984], 2:2).

10. The primary examples that Durkheim uses are Australian Aborigines and Native Americans.

11. This passage is particularly revealing for several reasons. First, it underscores important similarities between Durkheim's argument and Lévy-Bruhl's position. Durkheim actually borrows the term "société inférieure" from Lévy-Bruhl's work entitled *Les Fonctions mentales dans les sociétés inférieures,* which was published two years before *Elementary Forms* (trans. Ward Swain [New York: Free Press, 1965]). Second, the binary inferior/advanced explicitly underscores the evaluative presuppositions of the primitive/modern contrast. And finally, in his later work, *La Mentalité primitive* (1922), Lévy-Bruhl identifies the definitive characteristic of primitive mentality as a "participation mystique" in which self and world are not yet clearly differentiated.

12. In another context, Durkheim stresses the pathological nature of religious activity: "It is certainly true that religious life cannot attain a certain degree of intensity without implying a psychical exaltation not far removed from delirium. That is why the prophets, the founders of religion, the great saints, in a word, the men whose religious consciousness is excessively sensitive, very frequently give signs of an excessive nervousness that is even pathological" (*Elementary Forms,* 258).

13. Sigmund Freud, *Civilization and Its Discontents,* trans. James Strachey (New York: Norton, 1961), pp. 15–17.

14. As will become clear in what follows, Freud associates the primitive not only with the child but also with the neurotic and psychotic and thus repeats the common triad of primitive, child, and mad.

15. Sigmund Freud, *Totem and Taboo,* trans. James Strachey (New York: Norton, 1950), p. 161. Elsewhere Freud writes: "For our purpose it is enough to draw attention to the great care which is devoted by the Australians, as well as by other savage peoples, to the prevention of incest. It must be admitted that these savages are even more sensitive on the subject of incest than we are. They are probably liable to a greater temptation to it and for that reason stand in need of fuller protection" (p. 9).

16. Sigmund Freud, *Beyond the Pleasure Principle,* trans. James Strachey (New York: Norton, 1961), p. 30.

17. Ibid., p. 32.

18. Ibid., p. 48.

19. Freud's data are considerably more limited than Durkheim's. Most of Freud's information is gleaned from the writings of Frazer, though at crucial points he also draws on the work of Robertson Smith. While aware of Durkheim's work, he dismisses it in a single sentence.

20. Freud's argument requires the matrilineal descent of the totem. He asserts but does not demonstrate that "descent through the female line is older than through the male line" (*Totem and Taboo,* p. 5 n).

21. Sigmund Freud, "The Uncanny," in *The Standard Edition of the Complete Psychological Works of Sigmund Freud,* ed. James Strachey (London: Hogarth Press, 1964), p. 244.

22. Friedrich Nietzsche, *The Will to Power,* trans. Walter Kaufmann (New York: Vintage Books, 1968), p. 550. It is somewhat misleading to claim that *The Will to Power* concludes with this passage. The aphorisms that make up this text were not intended for publication but were gathered from Nietzsche's notebooks of the years 1883–88 and published by his sister, Elisabeth Förster-Nietzsche. *The Will to Power* has had a checkered history. Elisabeth married Bernhard Förster, who was an outspoken anti-Semite. Thus she was not adverse to allowing her brother's work to be appropriated by the Nazis. In addition to this, *The Will to Power* became widely known in a one-volume edition put together by Alfred Bäumler, who was also a Nazi. This editorial history has decisively influenced the reception of *The Will to Power* as well as Nietzsche's other writings.

23. Denis Hollier has collected a selection of the College's proceedings in a volume entitled *The College of Sociology, 1937–39,* ed. Denis Hollier, trans. Betsy Wing (Minneapolis: University of Minnesota Press, 1988).

24. Georges Bataille, *Theory of Religion,* trans. Robert Hurley (New York: Zone Books, 1989), pp. 56–57. Hereafter references to this work are given in the text.

25. *Violence and the Sacred* is, of course, the title of René Girard's much discussed book. When compared to the richness of Bataille's analysis, Girard's argument appears both limited and superficial. The limitation of Girard's work is, at least in part, a function of the Christian apologetic interests that inform his reading of myth and ritual.

26. Georges Bataille, *Death and Sensuality: A Study of Eroticism and the Taboo* (New York: Arno Press, 1977), p. 129. Again following Freud, Bataille associates the site of this coincidence with the body of woman, or, more precisely, with the body of the mother. In his works of fiction, he graphically depicts the uncanny abjection of woman as disgusting yet strangely attractive. Consider the following typical passage from a work entitled *My Mother:* " 'You have turned out to be nice,' she said. 'I deserved something else. I should have found myself with some buck who would have abused me. I'd have preferred that. The gutter, the dungheap, that's where your mother feels at home. You shall never know what horrors I am capable of. I'd like you to know, though. I like my filth. Today I'll end up being sick, I have had too much to drink, I'd feel better if I vomit' " (trans. A. Wainhouse [London: Jonathan Cape, 1976], p. 18).

27. Georges Bataille, *Visions of Excess: Selected Writings, 1927–1939,* trans. Alan Stoekl (Minneapolis: University of Minnesota Press, 1985), pp. 138, 142–43.

28. As we shall see in chapter 7, the *Gesamtkunstwerk* and the tendencies surrounding it can be read very differently. The developments we are considering in this chapter have led to remarkably diverse social, political, artistic, and religious tendencies in the course of this century.

29. Philippe Lacoue-Labarthe, *Heidegger, Art, and Politics,* trans. Chris Turner (New York: Blackwell, 1990), p. 64.

30. Ibid.

31. Martin Heidegger, *Poetry, Language, Thought,* trans. Albert Hofstadter (New York: Harper and Row, 1071), p. 123.

32. Ibid., p. 94.

33. Ibid., p. 93.

34. Josef Chytry, *The Aesthetic State: A Quest in Modern German Thought* (Berkeley: University of California Press, 1989), p. 154. It is important to note that Hölderlin's use of "organic" to refer to egoistic impulses is contrary to the more common romantic practice of characterizing harmonious social relations as organic.

35. Bataille uses the term *l'expérience intérieure* to describe an experience that is virtually identical to Hölderlin's *Innigkeit.*

36. Lacoue-Labarthe, *Heidegger, Art, and Politics,* p. 70. Lacoue-Labarthe's preoccupation with establishing a direct link between fascism and the aestheticization of politics leads him to overlook other ways in which art and politics have intersected in this century. For a consideration of alternatives Lacoue-Labarthe ignores, see chapter 7.

37. Jacques Derrida, *Dissemination,* trans. Barbara Johnson (Chicago: University of Chicago Press, 1981), pp. 92–93.

Chapter Four

1. See, for example, Michael I. Posner and Marcus E. Raichle, *Images of Mind* (New York: Scientific American Library, 1994).

2. Jonathan Z. Smith, *The Map Is Not the Territory: Studies in the History of Religions* (Leiden: E. J. Brill, 1978), p. 290.

3. Sherry B. Ortner, "Theory in Anthropology since the Sixties," *Comparative Studies in Society and History* 26 (1984): 126–27.

4. Pascal Boyer, *The Naturalness of Religious Ideas: A Cognitive Theory of Religion* (Berkeley: University of California Press, 1994), p. 1.

5. Ortner, "Theory in Anthropology since the Sixties," pp. 128–29.

6. Clifford Geertz, "Religion as a Cultural System," in *The Religious Situation* (Boston: Beacon Press, 1968), p. 641. Hereafter page numbers to this work are given in the text.

7. *American Heritage Dictionary.*

8. Richard Dawkins, *River out of Eden: A Darwinian View of Life* (New York: Basic Books, 1995), p. 19.

9. Steven Levy, *Artificial Life: A Report from the Frontier Where Computers Meet Biology* (New York: Random House, 1992), pp. 113, 117, 118.

10. Richard Dawkins, *The Selfish Gene* (New York: Oxford University Press, 1976), p. v.

11. Sigmund Freud, "One of the Difficulties of Psycho-Analysis," in *Collected Papers,* ed. Joan Riviere (New York: Basic Books, 1924–50), 4:351, 355.

12. Dawkins, *River out of Eden,* p. 19.

13. Richard Dawkins, *The Extended Phenotype: The Gene as the Unit of Selection* (San Francisco: W. H. Freeman and Co., 1982), p. 290.

14. Dawkins, *Selfish Gene,* p. 192.

15. Ibid.

16. Dawkins, *Extended Phenotype,* p. 286.

17. Michael Schrage, "Revolutionary Evolutionist," *Wired* 3 (July 1995): 172.

18. Dawkins, *Selfish Gene,* p. 192.

19. Boyer, *Naturalness of Religious Ideas,* p. 278. Hereafter page numbers to this work are given in the text.

20. Ortner, "Theory in Anthropology since the Sixties," p. 135.

21. Ibid.

22. Claude Lévi-Strauss, "The Effectiveness of Symbols," in *Structural Anthropology,* trans. Claire Jacobson and Brooke Schoepf (New York: Basic Books), p. 203.

23. Ibid., p. 201.

24. Rodolphe Gasché, *The Tain of the Mirror: Derrida and the Philosophy of Reflection* (Cambridge: Harvard University Press, 1986), p. 240.

25. Ernest Nagel and James R. Newman, *Gödel's Proof* (New York: New York University Press, 1958), p. 6.

26. Derrida, *Dissemination,* pp. 220, 219.

27. Roger Penrose, *Shadows of the Mind: A Search for the Missing Science of Consciousness* (New York: Oxford University Press, 1994), p. 12. Hereafter page numbers to this work are given in the text.

28. Daniel Dennett, *Consciousness Explained* (New York: Little, Brown and Co., 1991), pp. 253–54.

29. It is important to note that this extension of the principles of quantum mechanics to neurophysiological processes has provoked considerable criticism and resistance among many biologists and biochemists. Neurotransmission, critics argue, involves macroprocesses to which microprocesses of quantum mechanics do not directly apply.

Chapter Five

Reprinted from *Religion, Modernity, and Postmodernity,* ed. Paul Heelas, David Martin, and Paul Morris (Oxford: Blackwell, 1998), pp. 36–54.

1. Quoted in Caroline Tisdall and Angelo Bozzolla, *Futurism* (New York: Oxford University Press, 1978), p. 123.

2. Filippo Marinetti, "The Founding Manifesto of Futurism," in *Marinetti: Selected Writings,* ed. R. W. Flint (New York: Farrar, Strauss and Giroux), p. 41.

3. Filippo Marinetti, "The Birth of a Futurist Aesthetic," in *Marinetti,* p. 81.

4. Quoted in Robert Hughes, *The Shock of the New* (New York: Knopf, 1991), p. 11.

5. Ibid., pp. 37–38.

6. See Paul Virilio, *Speed and Politics: An Essay on Dromology,* trans. Mark Polizzotti (New York: Semiotext(e), 1986).

7. Marinetti, "Founding Manifesto of Futurism," p. 42.

8. Quoted in Howard Rheingold, *Virtual Reality* (New York: Summit Books, 1991), p. 323.

9. Mircea Eliade develops a survey of the historical background of alchemy in *The Forge and the Crucible: The Origins and Structures of Alchemy* (Chicago: University of Chicago Press, 1978; hereafter page numbers to this work are given in the text). I have drawn on Eliade's insights throughout my account of alchemy.

10. Joseph Shipley, *The Origins of English Words* (Baltimore: Johns Hopkins University Press, 1984), p. 7.

11. Allison Coudert, "Elixir," in *The Encyclopedia of Religion,* ed. Mircea Eliade (New York: Macmillan Publishing Co., 1987), 5:96.

12. Eliade, *The Forge and the Crucible,* p. 19.

13. Ibid., pp. 174–75.

14. Gershom Scholem, *On the Kabbalah and Its Symbolism,* trans. Ralph Manheim (New York: Schocken Books, 1965), p. 159. See also pp. 158–204. Two other works on the golem are particularly instructive: Moshe Idel, *Golem: Jewish Magical and Mystical Traditions on the Artificial Anthropoid* (New York: State University of New York Press, 1990); Emily Bilski, *Golem! Danger, Deliverance, and Art* (New York: Jewish Museum, 1988).

15. H. A. M. Snelders, "Romanticism and Naturphilosophie and the Inorganic Natural Sciences, 1797–1840: An Introductory Survey," *Studies in Romanticism* 9 (1970): 194.

16. F. W. J. Schelling, *Ideas for a Philosophy of Nature,* trans. Errol Harris and Peter Heath (New York: Cambridge University Press, 1988), pp. 99–100.

17. G. W. F. Hegel, *Philosophy of Nature,* trans. Michael Petry (New York: Humanities Press, 1970), 2:170.

18. Ibid., p. 174.

19. G. W. F. Hegel, *Phenomenology of Spirit,* trans. A. V. Miller (New York: Oxford University Press, 1977), p. 493.

20. Marshall McLuhan, *Understanding Media: The Extensions of Man* (New York: McGraw-Hill, 1964), p. 4.

21. Ibid., p. 25.

22. Quoted in Theodore Roszak, *The Cult of Information: The Folklore of Computers and the True Art of Thinking* (New York: Pantheon Books, 1986), p. 150. Roszak, whose book *The Making of the Counter-Culture* remains the most insightful analysis of the social trends of the '60s, also stresses the importance of the electronic music and light shows for the mind-expanding rituals of the youth culture.

23. Queen Mu and R. U. Sirius, editorial, *Mondo 2000,* no. 7 (fall 1989). Quoted in Andrew Ross, *Strange Weather: Culture, Science and Technology in the Age of Limits* (New York: Verso, 1991), p. 163. Ross's chapters entitled "New Age: A Kinder, Gentler Science?" and "Cyberpunk in Boystown" are particularly informative discussions of the social and cultural tendencies that I am examining in this essay.

24. Rheingold, *Virtual Reality,* p. 234.

25. Quoted in Isabella Sharp, "Virtual Reality: The Uses of Techno-Utopia," *1-800* (spring–summer 1991): 25.

26. Ibid.

27. Freud, *Civilization and Its Discontents,* p. 11. Hereafter page numbers to this work are given in the text.

28. Rheingold, *Virtual Reality,* p. 256.

29. Paul Virilio, *L'écran du désert: Chroniques de guerre* (Paris: Galilée, 1991), p. 70.

Chapter Six

1. Joel Kurtzman, *The Death of Money* (New York: Simon and Schuster, 1993), p. 51. In reconstructing the details of these financial developments, I have drawn on Kurtzman's lucid summary.

2. Fredric Jameson, *Postmodernism, or The Cultural Logic of Late Capitalism* (Durham: Duke University Press, 1991), p. 35.

3. Fredric Jameson, "Postmodernism and Consumer Society," in *The Anti-Aesthetic: Essays on Postmodern Culture,* ed. Hal Foster (Port Townsend, WA: Bay Press, 1983), pp. 124–25.

4. Fredric Jameson, "Surrealism without the Unconscious," in *Postmodernism,* p. 94.

5. David Harvey, *The Condition of Postmodernity* (Cambridge, MA: Basil Blackwell, 1989), p. 350.

6. Shakespeare, *Timon of Athens,* act 4, scene 3, lines 377–92. Marx cites these lines in *Grundrisse,* trans. Martin Nicolaus (New York: Penguin Books, 1973), p. 163.

7. David Carpenter, "Money," in *The Encyclopedia of Religion,* ed. Mircea Eliade (New York: Macmillan, 1987), 10:51. "This paper money," Carpenter points out, "is still in use in Taiwan, where four principal types are found: 'gold' paper money, offered to the gods; 'silver' money, offered to ghosts and ancestors; 'treasure money' for repaying the 'debt of life'; and 'money for the resolving of crisis,' used primarily in rites of exorcism."

8. Shipley, *Origins of English Words,* p. 248; William H. Desmond, *Magic, Myth, and Money: The Origin of Money in Religious Ritual* (New York: Free Press, 1962), p. 124.

9. Horst Kurnitsky, "Das liebe Geld: Die wahre Liebe," in *Museum des Geldes: Über die seltsame Natur des Geldes in Kunst, Wissenschaft, und Leben* (Düsseldorf: Städtische Kunsthalle, n.d.), p. 39.

10. Henry Wolfson, *The Philosophy of the Church Fathers: Faith, Trinity, Incarnation* (Cambridge: Harvard University Press, 1956), p. 387.

11. Glyn Davies, *A History of Money: From Ancient Times to the Present Day* (Cardiff: University of Wales Press, 1994), pp. 61–62.

12. Anselm, *Cur Deus Homo? A Scholastic Miscellany: Anselm to Ockham,* ed. Eugen Fairweather (Philadelphia: Westminster Press, 1956), p. 177.

13. Marc Shell, *Art and Money* (Chicago: University of Chicago Press, 1995), p. 15.

14. Ibid., pp. 13, 19.

15. G. W. F. Hegel, *The Philosophy of History,* trans. J. Sibree (New York: Dover Publications, 1956), p. 319.

16. G. W. F. Hegel, *Science of Logic,* trans. A. V. Miller (New York: Humanities Press, 1969), p. 441.

17. G. W. F. Hegel, *Lectures on the Philosophy of Religion,* trans. E. B. Speirs and J. Burdon Sanderson (New York: Humanities Press, 1962), 3:18.

18. Hegel, *Science of Logic,* p. 412. Hereafter page numbers to this work are given in the text.

19. Marx, *Grundrisse,* pp. 221, 225.

20. Marx, *Capital,* p. 104.

21. Marx, *Grundrisse,* p. 163.

22. Ibid., p. 231.

23. Ibid., pp. 270, 263.

24. Ibid., p. 266.

25. Ibid., p. 516.

26. Hegel, *Science of Logic,* p. 842.

27. Marx, *Grundrisse,* pp. 790, 80.

28. Marx, *Capital,* p. 126.

29. Ibid., p. 125.

30. Georg Simmel, *The Philosophy of Money,* trans. Tom Bottomore and David Frisby (New York: Routledge, 1978), p. 56. Hereafter page numbers to this work are given in the text.

31. In chapter 7, I present a more detailed analysis of the relation between Kant and Hegel on this complex issue. At that point, further social and political implications of the process of aestheticization of the token of exchange will become clear.

32. Jean Baudrillard, *Symbolic Exchange and Death* (London: Sage Publications, 1993), pp. 21–22.

Chapter Seven

1. Thomas Moore, "Bets Are Riding on Bible Theme Park in Gambling Capital," Reuters, Nando.net, August 9, 1997. The names of both Carl God-frey and Thomas Moore are suggestive enough to raise suspicions whether the report about this remarkable venture is a fabrication.

2. M. H. Abrams, *Natural Supernaturalism: Tradition and Revolution in Romantic Literature* (New York: Norton, 1971), p. 334.

3. Immanuel Kant, *Critique of Judgment,* trans. James Meredith (New York: Oxford University Press, 1973), p. 22.

4. Ibid., pp. 22, 24, 21. This description of the organism represents a remarkable anticipation of what today's complexity theorists describe as "emergent self-organizing systems." While Kant insists that organisms are natural, recent developments in information technology suggests that emergent self-organizing systems are also cultural. Supporting his claim, Kant argues: "Hence one wheel in the watch does not produce the other, and, still less, does one watch produce other watches, by utilizing, or organizing, foreign material; hence it does not of itself replace parts of which it has been deprived, nor, if these are absent in the original construction, does it make good the deficiency by the subvention of the rest; nor does it, so to speak, repair its own causal disorders" (22). As research in the new field known as artificial life is making clear, it now is possible to create "machines" that can both repair themselves and reproduce. Self-correcting computer programs have been developed, which can write programs their creators have not imagined and could not produce.

5. Friedrich Schiller, *On the Aesthetic Education of Man: In a Series of Letters,* trans. Elizabeth Wilkinson and L. A. Willoughby (New York: Oxford University Press, 1967), p. 35. Hereafter page numbers to this work are given in the text.

6. Chytry, *Aesthetic State,* p. 19.

7. While Schiller is, to my knowledge, the first to describe the responsibility of the avant-garde in these terms, he does not actually use this term. Victor Margolin points out that Olinde Rodrigues, a close friend of Saint-Simon, was "the first to use the term avant-garde for artistic practice rather than military purposes" (*The Struggle for Utopia: Rodchenko, Lissitzky, Moholy-Nagy, 1917–1946* [Chicago: University of Chicago Press, 1997], p. 2).

8. Quoted in Chytry, *Aesthetic State,* p. 80.

9. Hegel, *Science of Logic,* p. 736.

10. Hegel, *Phenomenology of Spirit,* p. 14.

11. Clement Greenberg, "Modernist Painting," in *Modernism with a Vengeance, 1957– 1969,* ed. John O'Brian (Chicago: University of Chicago Press, 1993), 4:85.

12. Clement Greenberg, "Avant-Garde and Kitsch," in *Perceptions and Judgments, 1939–1944,* ed. John O'Brian (Chicago: University of Chicago Press, 1986), 1:12.

13. Ibid., p. 13.

14. As the unspeakable terrors of this century mounted, Greenberg's vision grew ever darker. Robert Storr points out that "[d]espite his condemnation in 'The Plight of Culture,' of Eliot's Spenglerian excesses, in fact, Greenberg has shown a long-standing affinity for Spengler's epochal fatalism and has recently owned up to it. 'Cultures and civilizations do run their "biological courses,"' he told a 1981 conference on modernism, 'evidence says that and the evidence forces me to accept Spengler's scheme in largest part.' This scheme, however, precludes anything like a dialectical relation between society and culture—and more particularly between avant-garde and kitsch—insofar as an eventual and definitive failure of creative will presents itself as a foregone conclusion" ("No Joy in Mudville: Greenberg's Modernism Then and Now," in *Modern Art and Popular Culture: Readings in High and Low,* ed. Kirk Varnedoe and Adam Gopnik [New York: Henry Abrams, 1990], p. 170).

15. Greenberg, "Avant-Garde and Kitsch," p. 14.

16. I will consider relevant aspects of pop art in the next section.

17. Walter Gropius, *The Bauhaus* (Cambridge: MIT Press, 1986), p. 36.

18. As we have seen in chapter 3, there have also been dark chapters in the history of this idea.

19. Gropius, *Bauhaus,* p. 106.

20. Oskar Schlemmer, in ibid., pp. 65–66.

21. For an elaboration of this point, see chapter 6.

22. Christina Lodder, *Russian Constructivism* (New Haven: Yale University Press, 1987), p. 1.

23. Margolin, *Struggle for Utopia,* p. 81.

24. Quoted in Camilla Gray, *The Russian Experiment in Art, 1863–1922* (New York: Henry Abrams, 1962), p. 249.

25. Lodder, *Russian Constructivism,* p. 1.

26. Hubertus Gassner, "The Constructivists: Modernism on the Way to Modernization," in *The Great Utopia: The Russian and Soviet Avant-Garde, 1915–1932* (New York: Solomon R. Guggenheim Foundation, 1992), p. 299. This volume, which accompanied the Guggenheim's exhibition in 1992, is an invaluable resource for understanding the art of this period.

27. Andy Warhol, "What Is Pop Art? Answers from 8 Painters," *Artnews* 62 (November 1963): 26.

28. As I have noted, there are precedents for subverting the high/low distinction in the work of some of the very artists Greenberg uses to make his case for formalism and

abstraction. As Robert Rosenblum points out in an article entitled "Cubism as Pop Art," Parisian cubists "beginning in 1911 were determined to absorb into their art as into their daily lives the fullest impact of a teeming world of popular culture that by convention would have been censored out of the purer domain of high art" (in *Modern Art and Popular Culture,* p. 128).

29. Andy Warhol, *The Philosophy of Andy Warhol* (New York: Harcourt Brace, 1975), p. 92. Hereafter page numbers to this work are given in the text.

Chapter Eight

1. Wassily Kandinsky, *Point and Line to Plane,* trans. Howard Dearstyne and Hilla Rebay (New York: Dover Publications, 1979), p. 57.

2. Fred Sandback, "Remarks on My Sculpture, 1966–1986," in *Fred Sandback Sculpture, 1966–1986* (Mannheim: Kunsthalle, 1986), p. 12.

3. Rosalind E. Krauss, *Passages in Modern Sculpture* (Cambridge: MIT Press, 1993), p. 254.

4. Ibid., p. 262.

5. Fred Sandback, *The Art of Fred Sandback: A Survey* (Krannert, IL: Krannert Art Museum, 1985).

6. Ibid.

7. Fred Sandback, *Katalog zur Ausstellung: Fred Sandback, Vertical Constructions* (Münster: Westfälischer Kunstverein, 1987), p. 14.

8. Lynne Cooke, *Fred Sandback* (New York: DIA Center for the Arts, 1996).

9. Martin Heidegger, "The Thing," in *Poetry, Language, Thought,* pp. 168–69.

10. Jacques Derrida, *The Truth in Painting,* trans. Geoff Bennington and Ian McLeod (Chicago: University of Chicago Press, 1987), pp. 63, 9, 81.

11. Nietzsche, *Birth of Tragedy,* pp. 42, 9.

12. Wallace Stevens, *Opus Posthumous: Poems, Plays, Prose,* ed. Samuel French Morse (New York: Knopf, 1957), p. 178.

13. Nietzsche, *Birth of Tragedy,* pp. 22, 34, 35, 56, 145.

14. Ibid., p. 145.

15. Torataro Shimomura, "Nishida Kitaro and Some Aspects of His Philosophical Thought," in Nishida Kitaro, *A Study of the Good,* trans. V. H. Viglielmo (Tokyo: Japanese Government Printing Bureau, 1960), pp. 216–17.

16. Yoshinori Takeuchi, "The Philosophy of Nishida," *Japanese Religions* 3, no. 4 (1963): 3–4.

17. Nishida Kitaro, *Last Writings, Nothingness, and the Religious Worldview,* trans. David Dilworth (Honolulu: University of Hawaii Press, 1987), p. 82.

18. Ibid., p. 61.

19. Shin'ichi Hisamatsu, *Zen and the Fine Arts,* trans. Gishhin Tokiwa (Tokyo: Kodansha International, 1982), pp. 50–51.

20. Keiji Nishitani, *Religion and Nothingness,* trans. Jan Van Bragt (Berkeley: University of California Press, 1982), p. 98.

21. Nietzsche, *Birth of Tragedy,* p. 41.

22. Derrida, *Truth in Painting,* p. 140. The word *taille* is particularly suggestive in the context of a consideration of sculpture. *Sculpture* derives from the Latin *sculpere* (to carve), which, in turn, can be traced to the stem *(s)kel,* which means cut or sharp. In addition to edge, *taille* can mean cutting or cut. *Tailler* means to cut, to cut out; to carve;

to cut up; to hew; to prune, to trim; to sharpen; to frame, to shape; or to cut for the stone. The multiple nuances of *taille* and *tailler* expose sculpture as double-edged. The limits of the work of art are inevitably de-limiting.

23. Jean-Luc Nancy, "The Sublime Offering," in *Of the Sublime: Presence in Question,* trans. Jeffrey S. Librett (Albany: State University of New York Press, 1993), p. 29.

24. Ibid., pp. 30, 29.

25. Immanuel Kant, *Critique of Pure Reason,* trans. Norman Kemp Smith (New York: St. Martin's Press, 1965), p. 112.

26. Derrida, *Truth in Painting,* p. 126.

27. This nonpresence, which nonetheless is not an absence, points to a subtle but important difference between Nishida and Nishitani, on the one hand, and, on the other, Kant as read through Derrida and Nancy. Nishida clings to the dream of a "theology of the absolute present," which is "neither theistic nor deistic" (*Nothingness and the Religious Worldview,* p. 76). Nishitani perpetuates this dream by inscribing the notion of emptiness in a speculative dialectic designed to establish the identity of opposites. "Sunyata [i.e., emptiness] represents the endpoint of an orientation to negation. It can be termed *absolute negativity,* inasmuch as it is a standpoint that has negated and thereby transcended nihility, which was itself the transcendence-through-negation of all being. It can also be termed an *absolute transcendence of being,* as it absolutely denies and distances itself from any standpoint shackled in any way whatsoever to being. In this sense, emptiness can well be described as 'outside' of and absolutely 'other' than the standpoint shackled to being, provided we avoid the misconception that emptiness is some 'thing' distinct from being and subsisting 'outside it.' . . . Hence talk of transcendence does not entail the withdrawing off of some transcendent 'thing' called emptiness or nothingness. Emptiness lies absolutely on the near side, more so than what we normally regard as our own self. Emptiness, or nothingness, is not something we can turn to. It is not something 'out there' in front of us. It defies objective representation; no sooner do we assume such an attitude toward it than emptiness withdraws into hiding" (*Religion and Nothingness,* p. 97). As we shall see, however, this withdrawal is not the same as the hiding of the imagination's neither/nor through which the event of presentation repeatedly occurs.

28. Nancy, "Sublime Offering," p. 37. The French word *ça* is the French translation of Freud's term *es,* which rendered in English as *id.* Lacan constantly plays on the multiple nuances of *ça.* The unrepresentability of the Lacanian Real refigures the nonpresentability of the Kantian sublime. In addition to this, he suggests but does not develop an important relation between *la chose freudienne* and the Heideggerian thing. See Jacques Lacan, "The Freudian Thing," in *Écrits,* trans Alan Sheridan (New York: Norton, 1977), pp. 114–45; Jacques Lacan, *The Four Fundamental Concepts of Psychoanalysis,* trans. Alan Sheridan (New York: Norton, 1978).

29. Kant, *Critique of Judgment,* p. 107.

30. Søren Kierkegaard, *The Concept of Anxiety,* trans. Reidar Thomte (Princeton: Princeton University Press, 1980), pp. 42, 41.

31. Wallace Stevens, "The Snow Man," in *The Collected Poems of Wallace Stevens* (New York: Knopf, 1981), p. 10.

Chapter Nine

Reprinted from *Richard Serra: Torqued Ellipses* (New York: Dia Foundation, 1997), pp. 33–59.

1. Conversation, April 1, 1997.

2. In Richard Serra, *Writings, Interviews* (Chicago: University of Chicago Press, 1994), pp. 257–58.

3. Teiji Itoh develops helpful accounts of the history and significance of different kinds of gardens in the following books: *The Japanese Garden: An Approach to Nature* (New Haven: Yale University Press, 1972); *The Gardens of Japan* (New York: Kodansha International, 1984); and *Space and Illusion in the Japanese Garden* (New York: Weatherhill/Tankosha, 1983).

4. Conversation, April 1, 1997.

5. Serra, *Writings, Interviews,* p. 29.

6. Arata Isozaki, *MA: Space-Time in Japan* (New York: Cooper-Hewitt Museum, n.d.), p. 13.

7. Ibid., p. 12.

8. Jacques Derrida, *Margins of Philosophy,* ed. Alan Bass (Chicago: University of Chicago Press, 1982), p. 8.

9. Heidegger, *Poetry, Language, Thought,* pp. 17, 72, 47–48, 63.

10. Ibid., p. 204.

11. Serra, *Writings, Interviews,* p. 28. Hereafter page numbers to this work are given in the text.

12. Conversation, April 1, 1997.

13. Rosalind Krauss, "Richard Serra Sculpture," in *Richard Serra: Sculpture,* ed. Laura Rosenstock (New York: Museum of Modern Art, 1986), p. 27.

14. Yves-Alain Bois, "A Picturesque Stroll around *Clara-Clara,*" in *Richard Serra,* ed. Ernst-Gerhard Güse (New York: Rizzoli, 1988), p. 52.

15. Michael Fried, "Art and Objecthood," in *Minimal Art: A Critical Anthology,* ed. Gregory Battcock (Berkeley: University of California Press, 1995), p. 140.

16. Ibid., p. 144.

17. Ibid., p. 146.

18. Serra, *Writings, Interviews,* p. 255.

19. Conversation, April 1, 1997.

20. Maurice Merleau-Ponty, *Phenomenology of Perception,* trans. Colin Smith (London: Routledge and Kegan Paul, 1978), p. 242.

21. Ibid., p. 254.

22. Maurice Merleau-Ponty, *The Visible and the Invisible,* trans. Alphonso Lingis (Evanston: Northwestern University Press, 1968), pp. 147, 146.

23. Merleau-Ponty, *Phenomenology of Perception,* pp. 198, 212, 80.

24. Ibid., p. 350.

25. Ibid., pp. 148, 82, 150.

26. Ibid., pp. 100–101.

27. Ibid., p. 149. For an insightful and influential analysis of the fold, see Gilles Deleuze, *The Fold: Leibniz and the Baroque,* trans. Tom Conley (Minneapolis: University of Minnesota Press, 1993). Deleuze's work has had a significant impact on recent architecture. See *Folding in Architecture, Architectural Design* (1993).

28. Merleau-Ponty, *The Visible and the Invisible,* pp. 143, 149, 123, 122–23.

29. Ibid., p. 152.

30. In Serra, *Writings, Interviews.*

31. Conversation, April 1, 1997.

32. Ibid.

33. Conversation, June 23, 1997.

34. Conversation, April 1, 1997.

35. René Thom, *Structural Stability and Morphology: An Outline of a General Theory of Models,* trans. D. H. Fowler (New York: Addison-Wesley, 1989).

36. See, inter alia, John L. Casti, *Complexification: Explaining a Paradoxical World through the Science of Surprise* (New York: Harper and Row, 1994); Ilya Prigogine and Isabelle Stengers, *Order out of Chaos: Man's New Dialogue with Nature* (New York: Bantam Books, 1984); M. Mitchell Waldrop, *Complexity: The Emerging Science at the Edge of Order and Chaos* (New York: Simon and Schuster, 1992); John Holland, *Hidden Order: How Adaptation Builds Complexity* (New York: Addison-Wesley, 1995).

37. Murray Gell-Mann, *The Quark and the Jaguar: Adventures in the Simple and the Complex* (New York: W. H. Freeman, 1994).

Chapter Ten

1. Wallace Stevens, "An Ordinary Evening in New Haven," in *Collected Poems of Wallace Stevens,* p. 475.

2. Maurice Blanchot, *The Infinite Conversation,* trans. Susan Hanson (Minneapolis: University of Minnesota Press, 1993), p. xv.

3. Ibid., p. xxi.

4. Ibid., p. xviii.

5. Stevens, "An Ordinary Evening in New Haven," p. 472.

References for Illustrations

FIGURE 1   Pablo Picasso, *Les Demoiselles d'Avignon,* Paris, (June–July 1907). Oil on canvas, 8′ × 7′8″ (243.9 × 233.7 cm). The Museum of Modern Art, New York. Acquired through the Lillie P. Bliss Bequest.
© 1998 Estate of Pablo Picasso/Artist Rights Society (ARS), New York. Photograph © 1998 The Museum of Modern Art, New York.

FIGURE 2   Theodore A. L. DuMoncel, *The Telephone, the Microphone, and the Phonograph.*

FIGURE 3   Theodore A. L. DuMoncel, *The Telephone, the Microphone, and the Phonograph.*

FIGURE 4   Theodore A. L. DuMoncel, *The Telephone, the Microphone, and the Phonograph.*

FIGURE 5   Theodore A. L. DuMoncel, *The Telephone, the Microphone, and the Phonograph.*

FIGURE 6   José Márquez, Las Vegas.
Permission of the photographer.

FIGURE 7   José Márquez, Las Vegas.
Permission of the photographer.

FIGURE 8   New York, New York, Las Vegas.
Permission of New York, New York.

FIGURE 9   Pablo Picasso, *Still Life with Chair Caning,* 1912.
© ARS, New York. Musée Picasso, Paris. Giraudon/Art Resource, New York.

FIGURE 10   Jasper Johns, *Painted Bronze II,* 1960.
© Jasper Johns/Licensed by VAGA, New York, NY.

FIGURE 11   Aleksandr Rodchenko, *Shouldn't We Produce Pencils We Can Use?* 1923.
© Estate of Aleksandr Rodchenko/Licensed by VAGA, New York, NY.

FIGURE 12   Aleksandr Rodchenko, *Film Poster for Dziga Vertov,* Cine-Eye, 1924.
© Estate of Aleksandr Rodchenko/Licensed by VAGA, New York, NY.

FIGURE 13   Andy Warhol, *Window Display, Bonwit Teller,* 1961.
© 1998 Andy Warhol Foundation for the Visual Arts/ARS, New York, NY.

FIGURE 14   Andy Warhol, *À la Recherche du Shoe Perdu,* 1951.
             © 1998 The Andy Warhol Foundation for the Visual Arts/ARS, New
             York, NY.

FIGURE 15   Andy Warhol, *Telephone,* 1961.
             © 1998 The Andy Warhol Foundation for the Visual Arts/ARS, New
             York, NY.

FIGURE 16   Andy Warhol, *Front and Back Dollar Bills,* 1962.
             © 1998 The Andy Warhol Foundation for the Visual Arts/ARS, New
             York, NY.

FIGURE 17   Andy Warhol, *Self-Portrait,* 1979.
             © 1998 The Andy Warhol Foundation for the Visual Arts/ARS, New
             York, NY.

FIGURE 18   New York, New York, Las Vegas.
             Permission of New York, New York.

FIGURE 19   New York, New York, Las Vegas.
             Permission of New York, New York.

FIGURE 20   José Márquez, Las Vegas.
             Permission of the photographer.

FIGURE 21   José Márquez, Las Vegas.
             Permission of the photographer.

FIGURE 22   Fred Sandback, *Sculpture,* Dia Center for the Arts, September 12, 1996–
             September 25, 1998.
             Permission of the artist.

FIGURE 23   Fred Sandback, untitled, 1977.
             Permission of the artist.

FIGURE 24   Richard Serra, *One Ton Prop* (*House of Cards*), 1969.
             Permission of the artist.
             Photo: Peter Moore.

FIGURE 25   Richard Serra, *Shift,* 1971–72.
             Permission of the artist.

FIGURE 26   Richard Serra, *Delineator,* 1974–75.
             Permission of the artist.
             Photo: Gordon Matta-Clark.

FIGURE 27   Richard Serra, *Strike,* 1969–71.
             Permission of the artist.
             Photo: Peter Moore.

FIGURE 28   Richard Serra, *Tilted Arc,* 1981.
             Permission of the artist.
             Photo: Dith Prahn.

FIGURE 29   Richard Serra, *Torqued Ellipse I,* 1996. Weatherproof steel. 12′ × 29′ ×
             20′5″ (plate thickness: 2″). Collection Dia Center for the Arts (gift of
             Leonard and Louise Riggio).
             Permission of the artist.
             Photo: Dirk Reinartz, Buxtehude, Germany.

FIGURE 30   Richard Serra, *Torqued Ellipse II,* 1996. Weatherproof steel. 13′1″ ×
29′11″ × 20′7″ (plate thickness: 2″). Collection Dia Center for the Arts
(gift of Leonard and Louise Riggio).
Permission of the artist.
Photo: Dirk Reinartz, Buxtehude, Germany.

FIGURE 31   Richard Serra, *Double Torqued Ellipse,* 1996.
Permission of the artist.